D1732059

Die Reihe „Weltwirtschaft und internationale
Zusammenarbeit"

edited by

Prof. Dr. Hartmut Sangmeister, Hochschule für Wirtschaft,
    Technik und Kultur (HWTK), Berlin
Prof. Dr. Aurel Croissant, Universität Heidelberg
Prof. Dr. Detlef Nolte, GIGA Institut für
    Lateinamerika-Studien Hamburg

Volume 15

Erika Günther

Food and Nutrition (In-)Security in the Caribbean

The Double Burden of Food Import Dependency and Health Risks

 Nomos

Funded by the „Hochschule für Wirtschaft, Technik und Kultur" (HWTK)

Die Deutsche Nationalbibliothek lists this publication in the
Deutsche Nationalbibliografie; detailed bibliographic data
is available in the Internet at http://dnb.d-nb.de

a.t.: Heidelberg, Univ., Diss., 2014

ISBN   978-3-8487-1553-4 (Print)
         978-3-8452-5722-8 (ePDF)

British Library Cataloguing-in-Publication Data
A catalogue record for this book is available from the British Library.

ISBN   978-3-8487-1553-4 (Print)
         978-3-8452-5722-8 (ePDF)

Library of Congress Cataloging-in-Publication Data
Günther, Erika
Food and Nutrition (In-)Security in the Caribbean
The Double Burden of Food Import Dependency and Health Risks
Erika Günther
290 p.
Includes bibliographic references.

ISBN   978-3-8487-1553-4 (Print)
         978-3-8452-5722-8 (ePDF)

1. Edition 2014
© Nomos Verlagsgesellschaft, Baden-Baden, Germany 2014. Printed and bound in Germany.

Acknowledgements

This thesis was developed as teaching and research assistant at the Working Group of Development Politcs at the Department of Economics.

First and foremost, I would like to express my gratitude to my supervisor Prof. Dr. *Hartmut Sangmeister* for making this project possible. I am grateful for his guidance and the scientific freedom he gave me, which enabled me to learn and develop professionally as well as personally. I also want to thank Prof. Dr. *Hans Diefenbacher*, who kindly agreed to be my second supervisor, for his constructive comments and helpful feedback.

The infinite support in all imaginable and unimaginable manners from my dear *'colegas' Katja Hilser, Bernd Lämmlin, Junhong Meng, Julia Rückert*, and *Alexa Schönstedt-Maschke* will be unforgettable. Your advice and constructive comments were invaluable.

Special thanks to Dr. *Florian Neuhann* for giving me an insightful look into a field I was not familiar with, and for introducing me to his team of the Public Health Institute of the University of Heidelberg. I would like to express my sincere thanks to Dr. *Claudia Baiersmann* for sharing her knowledge and time with me.

I would like to offer my special thanks to *Lisa Martinez* and *Robert Best* from the UN FAO Trinidad and Tobago office for their interest in my work and their time. Your insightful comments, information, and suggestions were an enormous help to me. In addition, I want to thank *Sylvan Roberts* from the UN ECLAC Caribbean headquarters and *Reginald Andall* from CARDI Grenada who gave me the opportunity to get to know their work on the ground.

I am deeply grateful to my dear friends for their immeasurable support and encouragement. My special thanks go to *Rawya Mari* for her continuous, patient and thoroughly proofreading. Special thanks also to S*ila Sahverdi* for her constructive comments and amendments.

I owe my deepest appreciation to *Maria Alles*, who always gave me the greatest strength and love throughout this journey. I am deeply grateful to my brother for his great support and encouragement. My deepest heartfelt appreciation goes to my parents, to whom I dedicate this thesis.

Heidelberg, August 2014   Erika Günther

Editor's preface

The international development cooperation is being confronted by a new challenge: the "double burden". This term describes the coexistence of under-nutrition and over-nutrition. Under-nutrition is the result of insufficient intake of food that does not meet the minimum dietary energy requirements, poor absorption and/or poor biological use of nutrients consumed, leading to loss of body weight. Over-nutrition refers to the excessive intake of food above average dietary energy requirements, resulting in overweight and/or obesity. A "double burden" exists when under-nutrition and over-nutrition are simultaneously prevalent in a society.

Over several decades, under-nutrition accounted as the most urgent nutrition problem in developing countries. Subsequently, the international community declared the eradication of hunger as a primary goal of the Millennium Development Goals (MDGs), in 2001. However, the target-setting for MDG 1 – to halve, between 1990 and 2015, the proportion of people who suffer from hunger – will not be met by all developing countries. According to the World Health Organization (WHO), world-wide about 170 million children are underweight and 3 million thereof die each year as a result of being underweight.

Meanwhile, in many emerging countries and countries with rapidly growing economies a quite different nutrition problem became apparent: malnutrition that leads to over-nutrition, resulting in severe health problems.

According to WHO statistics, today, two out of three overweight people live in developing countries. In 2012, worldwide more than 40 million children under five were overweight, 30 million thereof in developing countries. Overweight and obesity cause health problems such as diabetes type II, cancer, heart disease or stroke. More people die as a result of being overweight and obese than of being underweight – many of them in developing countries, but still most of them in middle and high income countries.

Social and economic progress has led to a greater consumption of meat, oils and sugar in the form of cheap processed foods. At the same time, the consumption of fruits, vegetables and cereals decreased.

Overweight and obesity are, inter alia, the result of changing lifestyles and nutritional habits, especially of the urban population. The consumption of energy-dense and nutrient poor foods increased, while simultaneously the physical activity decreased. The urban population spends less time preparing food at home than the rural population; prefering meals that are rapidly and easily prepared or readily available. These meals are mostly cheap and consist mostly of processed food that contains fewer nutrients and vitamins, and more fat, sugar and salt.

For a better understanding of the "double burden", numerous scientific studies have been conducted, predominantly focusing on emerging countries or low income countries. So far, the Caribbean has been largely disregarded. In this regards, with her thesis, *Erika Günther* fills this research gap. For Caribbean countries, she demonstrates how the "double burden" of malnutrition fits into the concept of Food and Nutrition Security (FNS).

The main research question of her analysis is: "What are the main implications of food and nutrition insecurity in the Caribbean?" To answer this question, the author has divided her study into three parts. After a short introduction, in part I, she presents and discusses the theoretical concept of FNS and its four dimensions as well as the problems relating to its empirical examination. In part II, the author provides a methodically sophisticated, empirically solid and scientifically sound classification of the Caribbean countries in accordance to their FNS status. Part III of the study entails a detailed presentation of the structural causes of food imports and their consequences in the Caribbean economies. It concludes with a presentation of the economic and social costs of nutrition related diseases.

With her study, the author provides a very detailed and multi-faceted analysis of complex relationships between socio-economic structures, food and nutrition (in-)security and resulting health risks in the Caribbean countries. In addition, the study also provides an insightful look into the Caribbean history, economy, and society, which clearly reveals the heterogeneity and diversity within the region. This reading provides a comprehensive knowledge about the distinctive features of the specific "double burden" problem in the Caribbean region, even to those readers that are not familiar with the particular socio-economic details of this region.

Berlin, July 2014   Hartmut Sangmeister

Table of Contents

Abbreviations

ADER	Average Dietary Energy Requirement
AIDS	Acquired Immune Deficiency Syndrome
ATT	Annual Totals Table
BMI	Body Mass Index
BNR	Barbados National Registry
BoP	Balance of Payments
CAP	Community Agricultural Policy
CARDI	Caribbean Agricultural Research and Development Institute
CARICOM	Caribbean Community
CARIFTA	Caribbean Free Trade Association
CARPHA	Caribbean Public Health Agency
CCHD	Caribbean Commission on Health and Development
CDB	Caribbean Development Bank
CEPALSTAT	Comisión Económica para América Latina y el Caribe Statistics
CET	Common External Tariff
CFNI	Caribbean Food and Nutrition Institute
CFS	Committee on World Food Security
CHD	Coronary Heart Disease
COMTRADE	Commodity Trade Statistics Database
COI	Cost-of-Illness
COPD	Chronic Obstructive Pulmonary Disease
CPA	Country Poverty Assessment
CPI	Consumer Price Index
CPFI	Consumer Price Food Index
CRD	Chronic Respiratory Diseases
CSME	Caricom Single Market and Economy
CSO	Central Statistical Office
CVD	Cardiovascular Disease
DALY	Disability-Adjusted Life Year
DES	Dietary Energy Supply
DFID	Department for International Development
ECLAC	Economic Commission for Latin America and the Caribbean
ED	Euclidean Distance
EIU	Economist Intelligent Unit

EM-DAT	Emergency Events Database
EPA	European Partnership Agreement
EU	European Union
EVI	Economic Vulnerability Index
FAO	Food and Agriculture Organization
FAOSTAT	Food and Agriculture Organization Statistics
FBDG	Food-Based Dietary Guidelines
FBS	Food Balance Sheets
FERDI	Fondation pour les Études et Recherches sur les Développement International
FIB	Food Import Bill
FPI	Food Price Index
FNS	Food and Nutrition Security
GBD	Global Burden of Disease
GDP	Gross Domestic Product
GFSI	Global Food Security Index
GGHE	General Government Health Expenditure
GHI	Global Hunger Index
GNI	Gross National Income
GNS	Gross National Savings
GIZ	Gesellschaft für Internationale Zusammenarbeit
HDI	Human Development Index
HECORA	Health Care Organizers and Advisors
HFLAC	Hunger Free Latin America and the Caribbean Initiative
HIPC	Heavily Indebted Poor Countries
HIV	Human Immunodeficiency Virus
IAASTD	International Assessment of Agricultural knowledge, Science and Technology for Development
IADB	Inter-American Development Bank
IBRD	International Bank of Reconstruction and Development
ICI	Import Capacity Index
ICN	International Conference on Nutrition
IDA	Iron Deficiency Anaemia
IDD	Iodine Deficiency Disorders
IDF	International Diabetes Federation
IDR	Import Dependency Ratio
IFPRI	International Food Policy Research Institute
IHME	Institute for Health Metrics and Evaluation
IICA	Inter-American Institute for Cooperation on Agriculture

ILO	International Labour Organization
IMF	International Monetary Fund
Int$	International Dollar
KBCs	Key Binding Constraints
LAC	Latin America and the Caribbean
MDER	Minimum Dietary Energy Requirement
MDG	Millennium Development Goal
MI	Myocardial Infarction
MoA	Ministry of Agriculture
MoH	Ministry of Health
MUAC	Mid-Upper Arm Circumference
NAEX	Net Agricultural Exporters
NAIM	Net Agricultural Importers
NCDs	Non-communicable Diseases
NFEX	Net Food Exporting Countries
NFIM	Net Food Importing Countries
NHI	National Health Insurance
NYU	New York University
ODI	Overseas Development Institute
OECS	Organization of Eastern Caribbean States
OOP	Out-of-Pocket
PAHO	Pan American Health Organization
PIOJ	Planning Institute of Jamaica
PPP	Purchasing Power Parity
PoU	Prevalence of Undernourishment
PvtHE	Private Health Expenditure
RFNSP	Regional Food and Nutrition Security Policy
RFNSAP	Regional Food and Nutrition Security Action Plan
SAP	Structural Adjustment Program
SIDS	Small Island Developing States
SITC	Standard International Trade Classification
SLA	Sustainable Livelihoods Approach
SPSS	Statistical Package for the Social Sciences
SSR	Self-Sufficiency Ratio
THE	Total Health Expenditure
ToT	Terms of Trade
UDHR	Universal Declaration on Human Rights
UK	United Kingdom
UN	United Nations

UNAIDS	United Nations Programme on HIV/AIDS
UNCED	United Nations Conference on Environment and Development
UNCSD	United Nations Commission on Sustainable Development
UNCTAD	United Nations Conference on Trade and Development
UN DESA	United Nations Department of Economic and Social Affairs
UNDP	United Nations Development Program
UNGASS	United Nations General Assembly Special Session
UNICEF	United Nations Children's Fund
UNSCN	United Nations Standing Committee on Nutrition
US(A)	United States (of America)
USAID	United States Agency for International Development
USDA	United States Department of Agriculture
US$	US-Dollar
UWI	University of The West Indies
VAD	Vitamin A Deficiency
VAT	Value Added Tax
VoFP	Value of Food Production
WDI	World Development Indicators
WFP	World Food Programme
WHO	World Health Organization
WIF	West Indian Federation
WTO	World Trade Organization
WTTC	World Travel and Tourism Council
YLD	Years Lived with Disability
YLL	Years of Life Lost
cf.	confere
e.g	exempli gratia
i.a.	inter alia
Kca	kilocalories
Kg	kilogramme
km²	square kilometre
m²	square metre
n.a.	not available
n.e.s.	not elsewhere specified
n.r.	no results
n.s.	not specified
p.c.	per capita

List of Figures

List of Tables

List of Boxes

1. Introduction

In the year 2000, a number of world leaders adopted the *Millennium Declaration* and agreed to eradicate global hunger and poverty under the first Millennium Development Goal (MDG). The year 2015, the deadline set to reach this goal, is approaching fast. Today, the first MDG is still one of the highest priorities on global political agendas, but its realization seems to be far out of reach. From a global standpoint, hunger is one consequence of an array of problems, mainly related to poverty and political impotence. Food and hunger crises can be triggered by factors such as soaring world food prices, extreme weather events, and social and civil conflicts. Limited fertile land and the growing demand for cereals, soy, meat, and dairy products mobilise countries searching for new land, in order to secure food and energy production. These foreign land acquisitions consequently, rush investors to bet on increasing food prices. Within a changing geopolitical context, hunger or undernourishment became more complex issues. Highly subsidised food is flooding global markets, while changing consumption patterns increase the hazardous implications of nutrition related health risks. As a consequence, and in order to achieve Food and Nutrition Security (FNS) in a sustainable manner, the discussion on the narrow concept of hunger has to extend its focus on issues that directly or indirectly interrelate to it.

FNS exists within the framework of a social environment, a cultural and historical background, and economic, political and financial stability. Moreover, FNS depends on agriculture, ecosystems, and healthy environments, and, therefore, includes different purviews of life and interdisciplinary sciences. Insecurity of food and nutrition refers not only to a range of problems related to undernourishment but includes other forms of malnutrition, such as micronutrient deficiencies and overnutrition. This is an important fact, since overnutrition and associated health risks such as overweight and obesity are rapidly increasing in many countries – not only in high income countries, but also in economic, social and environmental deprived low income countries. These rapid changes have far-reaching and serious effects on human development and most probably impact economic productivity, as well.

In small and remote or isolated countries, in the Caribbean, these problems are more complex and more severe, because these countries have fewer resources to cope with external shocks or with the consequences of food and nutrition insecurity. In 2012, Jamaica and Trinidad and Tobago celebrated their 50th year of independence. In these past five decades, the independent Caribbean countries were able to integrate into global markets, while experiencing rapid economic growth and an overall positive socio-economic development. However, environmental and economic shocks such as the 2008/09 world economic, financial and food crises showed that the countries' socio-economic structures were still vulnerable. Import dependency, decreasing exports, changing consumption patterns, and the epidemic of Non-communicable Diseases are the most severe consequences, resulting from the developments of the past decades. Confronted with these problems, several Caribbean countries have realised the urgent need to address them and put FNS at the forefront of their agenda.

1.1   Current state of research

Food and nutrition insecurity is commonly referred to undernutrition and measured by FAO's indicator 'prevalence of undernourishment'. This one-sided perspective of food and nutrition insecurity draws the attention to the hunger and poverty-stricken countries and regions. In a global economy, where food systems are becoming increasingly powerful, and unhealthy consumption patterns lead to an epidemic of Non-communicable Diseases (NCDs), it is increasingly important to examine FNS as a holistic concept, in order to design relevant policies and strategies addressing these complex issues. This also draws the attention to countries, such as the Caribbean countries, where hunger and undernutrition are not commonly and widely spread as in other parts of the world. In these economically and environmentally vulnerable countries, the current issues of food and nutrition insecurity are becoming more complex. Moreover, it puts emphasise on the relevant issues by means of appropriate policies and strategies, and examining the direct and indirect impacts and underlying causes of food and nutrition insecurity in the Caribbean.

The research on food and nutrition insecurity in the Caribbean to date has been focussing on the agricultural food production capacity or deficiency. Caribbean agriculture and trade is often discussed in reference to agriculture exports as a traditional strategy for economic growth. Far too little attention has been paid on high food import dependency and its consequences for the economies as a whole and for the consuming population.

More recent studies from regional or national institutions focus on the increasing health problems linked to poor nutrition in the Caribbean. However, there has been little discussion about the causes and consequences of the rising incidence and mortality rates due to NCDs. This leads to a significant research gap in the Caribbean countries, which is due to the considerable lack of data on the issue of health and NCD risk factors. Even on a global level, such data is scarcely available and scientific evidence – on the rise of incidence and mortality due to NCDs – is mainly given through few but comprehensive studies. Evidence in this field of research lacks the proof through adequate data collection and surveillance, not only in the Caribbean.

1.2   Research objectives and scope of the study

The Caribbean region faces severe problems in the context of FNS, such as persisting undernourishment, poverty, a dramatic increase in food imports, soaring food prices, and a rapid increase of the incidence of NCDs. In addition, the past food crises have revived the discussion about food self-sufficiency, food import dependency and agricultural development. Particularly, small island states are characterized by vulnerable environments, geographical remoteness and physical constraints, lacking the capacity to grow an adequate amount of food to meet national demand. Under these conditions, countries are highly vulnerable to external shocks and struggle to respond adequately by the means of limited available resources. The Caribbean countries used as a sample in this thesis, face a variety of common socio-economic problems: high financial debt levels, low diversified economies, heavy dependence on international markets for imports of food and exports of services or commodities, poverty and inequality, migration, economic and environmental vulnerability, and high prevalence of nutrition related diseases.

This directly leads to the main research question of this thesis: What are the main implications of food and nutrition insecurity in the Caribbean? The aim of this thesis is to address this question by assessing the current situation of food and nutrition security or insecurity in the selected set of Caribbean countries, based on a multidimensional and holistic understanding of the FNS concept. For this purpose, it is important to keep the legacy of former imperialistic structures in mind, for it contributed to the current economic and social constraints in the Caribbean countries. The FNS assessment in this thesis is guided by three leading research questions:

1.	*Problem identification*: What is food and nutrition security, and why is the Caribbean considered to be food and nutrition insecure?
2.	*Problem analysis*: Which countries of the sample are most affected by food and nutrition insecurity, and what are the main issues of food and nutrition insecurity in the Caribbean?
3.	*Results*: What are the most severe consequences of food and nutrition insecurity for the selected Caribbean countries, and which countries are the most affected?

In particular, the scope of this thesis comprises a detailed analysis on the two main identified problems in the context of FNS in the selected Caribbean countries:

1. The burden of high food import dependency and a subsequent high food import bill.
2. The burden of increasing nutrition related health risks and the high prevalence of Non-communicable Diseases.

Food and nutrition insecurity is not only about undernourishment. In the particular case of the Caribbean it is about the double burden of high food imports and health risks, which have far-reaching effects on the economic, social and human development.

This precise focus on the main identified problems in the Caribbean excludes an analysis – but does not ignore it – of FNS related issues such as undernourishment, communicable or infectious diseases and an in-depth study on general trade theory and practice.

1.3   Methodology and data availability

The approach to research adopted for this thesis was one of quantitative methods completed by qualitative assessments. A variety of methods and indicators can be used to assess a certain state of FNS. Most common and prevalent indicators aim to reflect the overall global situation of FNS and to make results comparable across countries and time. The Food and

Agriculture Organization (FAO) of the United Nations (UN) provides a set of food security indicators based on data availability for all regions and countries and for a period of time from 1990 until recently.

In order to assess the FNS situation in the Caribbean and to detect important differences and commonalities between countries, data and indicators have been selected from the set of FAO's food security indicators based on suitability and relevance for this study. Data is retrieved for a certain period of time, which serves to reflect the present state of FNS in each country and to avoid variations between different years. For this purpose, a quantitative cluster analysis serves to group the 13 selected Caribbean countries into meaningful clusters. These clusters make a further quantitative analysis and thus meaningful interpretations of the comprehensive study on the double burden of food imports and health risks feasible. Ultimately, the clusters can serve to investigate possible implementations of common policies or strategies.

Data collection in the Caribbean is challenging, because of institutional and financial obstacles. Reliable and adequate data availability for the investigative period of time is limited. This lack of data limits the detailed and significant analysis on certain issues, at some points of this thesis. In order to overcome these constraints of a quantitative analysis, data has been drawn from multiple sources and databases. The research data in this thesis is drawn from five main sources: the Caribbean Community (CARICOM) Secretariat Regional Statistics database, the Economic Commission of Latin America and the Caribbean (ECLAC) statistical database CEPALSTAT, the FAO Statistics Division FAOSTAT database, the World Development Indicators (WDI) of The World Bank, and the UN Commodity Trade Statistics Database (COMTRADE).

In order to avoid insignificance in the interpretation and comparison of results, a data-mix, from different sources in quantitative calculation procedures has been avoided as far as possible.

1.4   Structure of thesis

The overall structure of this thesis takes the form of seven chapters, including this introductory chapter, and is divided into three parts. **Part I** comprises **Chapter 2** and begins by introducing the theoretical ground, on which the concept of FNS evolved. A theoretical conceptualization derives from the relevant review of common literature on the issue and from the attempt to define food security and nutrition security separately. From the multidimensional characteristic of the concept results the question of the possibility and feasibility of different quantitative measurement methods of FNS.

The **Part II** of this thesis is concerned with the setting and background of the selected research sample of countries and the methodology used for this study. In **Chapter 3**, the historical background of the Caribbean countries is displayed, for it plays an important role in explaining the causes and driving factors, which led to the current socio-economic structures of the countries. Based on this information, **Chapter 4** examines the current FNS situation for the selected countries in the context of vulnerability, which proves to be a prevailing and strong feature, particularly in the investigative countries. By means of a cluster analysis, relevant common or different features of FNS are revealed in each group of countries.

Part III analyses the particular problems of food and nutrition insecurity and vulnerability in the selected countries and for the computed clusters of countries. **Chapter 5,** therefore, examines the causes and consequences of high food imports for the sample countries and investigates the degree of food import dependency and implications to different purviews of the economy. The burden of food imports is identified by analysing the macroeconomic costs and structures of food imports. **Chapter 6** presents and analyses the current and alarming health risks factors and the prevalence of Non-communicable Diseases in the Caribbean countries. It focuses on the risk factors and the current state of health and disease within and across these sample countries. The burden of the identified health risks comprises the public health situation and the burden represented by high mortality rates and the loss of a healthy and productive life among the affected population.

Continuously throughout this thesis, every chapter closes with a conclusion including a short discussion on the respective foregoing analysis. Therefore, **Chapter 7** draws upon the entire thesis and gives a final conclusion by reviewing the study results. It includes a discussion of the findings and implications for FNS policies and strategies that can possibly be drawn for the Caribbean. Ultimately, a suggestion for the need for action completes this thesis and emphasizes the necessity for future research in this area.

Part I: Theory and Concept

The Food and Nutrition Security (FNS) concept is based on different theoretical approaches and has been influenced by various scientific purviews. This chapter aims to review the most fundamental theoretical approaches, to outline the development of the FNS concept, which contributed to the understanding of this multidimensional concept and its dimensions. On a global and national level, the concept is used to detect the causes and consequences of food and nutrition insecurity, measure their magnitude, and thus to formulate corresponding policies and strategies. This first part serves to define the concept of FNS, which further will be used to assess the state of FNS in the Caribbean.

Key questions:

1. In which context did the discussion on Food and Nutrition Security emerge and how has it evolved?
2. What is the difference between Food Security and Nutrition Security?
3. What defines the Food and Nutrition Security concept's multidimensional nature?

2.   Food and nutrition security – theoretical conceptualization

The essential meaning of 'security' derives from the Latin notion '*securitas*', meaning 'carefree' or 'freedom from care', is the freedom of danger or risk, thereby creating a feeling of safety. Beyond political discussions, 'security' adapts various definitions and concepts and is being interpreted according to the contextual framework. In the context of development economic studies, Food and Nutrition Security (FNS) evolved as a concept, which is primary used to examine underlying and interlinked causes of hunger on a global, regional, national or household level, and has been identified as a practical concept to implement relevant policies and strategies on the respective levels. Various studies on hunger and poverty have shown that both are cause and consequence of one another, which can result in a vicious circle. From past and current experiences of hunger crises and extreme poverty derives the attempt to understand the reasons and to estimate the consequences of these precarious situations. Because reasons and consequences differ from region to region and from country to country, the FNS concept provides a basis for a coherent examination on different levels and in different contexts. This first chapter provides a basis for the qualitative investigation of FNS.

The first subchapter 2.1 discusses some fundamental theories from social and economic development studies, which essentially contributed to the formation and the development of the FNS concept. Based on these approaches, subchapter 2.2 defines the two elements of the concept, 'food' and 'nutrition' security. A short history on the development of the FNS concept in the context of global food crises highlights the importance of this issue. This leads to the question, how the FNS are actually conceptualized. The last subchapter 2.3, therefore, examines the different dimensions of the concept and its practical application on global and national policies. Depending on the investigated dimension or interpretation of FNS, usually a defined state of Food and Nutrition Insecurity is being measured. A variety of indicators and methods can be used to assess FNS in different contexts and levels. Selected methods and indicators are presented in this last subchapter.

2.1   Food and Nutrition Security: Theoretical foundations

The discussion of FNS has been circulating even before the notion emerged in the 1970s albeit it has not been labelled as such. There is no single basic theory, from which the concept of FNS emerged, but rather economic and social development theories and related approaches built the foundation, on which the dynamic and multidimensional concept grounds. Most of these fundamental theories were translated into poverty and hunger reduction policies and strategies. The greatest impact of these practical translations derived from the concept of human development, which provides a holistic understanding of the relationship between food, nutrition, health and human development. The following sections review the main theories, which influenced the conceptualisation of FNS and may provide a foundation to further analyse the FNS concept.

2.1.1   Fundamental theoretical approaches to Food and Nutrition Security

This section provides an overview of the fundamental approaches, which originate in the social and economic development theories, and build the basis of the FNS concept. Most of these approaches emerged within the context of food crises, attempting to provide an explanation to persistent poverty and hunger. The interrelationship between poverty and hunger will be discussed in chapter 2.2.2, whereas the following approaches focus merely on the aspect of food, i.a. the absence of it.

The Malthusian approach, Neo-Malthusian and Techno-ecological perspectives

The first global discussion on the relationship between the growth of the world population and global food supply has been an early and incisive thought of Thomas Robert Malthus (1766-1834) in the 18th century. In his work *Essays on the Principle of Population* (1798) he predicted that an 'uncontrolled' population would grow faster than domestic food production. The growth of the population in a country is determined by overall economic living and health conditions. Malthus pointed out that, if the living conditions of the poor improved, and mortality rates decreased, the population would rise uncontrolled. His examination was based on historical observation and shows that "population [...] increases in a geometrical ratio", whereas "subsistence increases [...] in an arithmetical ratio" (Malthus, 1798: 4). By "subsistence" Malthus refereed to food production, what he also used as "production of the earth" (Malthus, 1798: 8). This would leave an ever-growing number of the population with less food, whereas domestic food production would not be able to adjust to this unrestrained demographic development. Consequently, food supply and food availability per capita would constantly decline. The only effective solution to this problem would be a rigid population control. According to Malthus' observations, an adjusted and sufficient increase of domestic food production would be impossible with the cultivation practices at that time. Although he was aware of the possibilities to increase the output of agricultural production through an enlargement of cultivation of land, he ignored the possibility of technological progress in cultivation practices that certainly could outpace population growth, and ensure a sufficient supply of food (cf. Malthus, 1798).

Based on Malthus' theory, the *Neo-Malthusian* perspective uses its essence to argue that overpopulation and expanding food production causes environmental degradation of the earth's resources (cf. Bongaarts, 1996). Although, nowadays there are possibilities to extent food production through the extensive use of land and technologies, the Neo-Malthusian perspective emphasises that an extensive use of them would threaten food supply for future generations (cf. Scanlan, 2001). Sustainability in the sense of food, means to meet current demand of food, without threatening the possibility to maintain food security for the future human population (cf. Scanlan, 2003). Thus, population pressure and limited natural resources such as land, water and energy may impede the ability to produce sufficient food and to meet the demand for food of the current and future generations.

The more optimistic *techno-ecological* approach suggests that food and nutrition insecurity is not a problem of scarcity, because new agricultural production methods can be adapted through technological achievements and extent food production. Population growth was no longer seen as the main problem but could be overcome with an increase in food supply through agricultural production. This approach became the basis for the *Green Revolution* (cf. Scanlan, 2001, 2003). The key problem with this view is that the implementation of technological practices in food production may threaten natural resources, causing environmental destruction, which in turn threatens sustainable production for the future generations.

Sen's entitlement approach

A detailed analysis on the reasons of hunger and food crises was made by Amartya Sen, Nobel laureate in economics. His studies on Indian and African famines sought to identify the underlying causes of poverty and famines, others than the limits of food production and population growth. In his book *Poverty and Famines* (1981) he showed that even if food on national, household or even individual level is sufficiently available, people starve from hunger and are affected by poverty. He recognized that hunger is not necessarily a consequence of scarcity, but an issue of insufficient demand (cf. Sen, 1981). Malthus' failed to consider that each individual is endowed with tangible and intangible resources, which both directly and indirectly influence the demand of food.

> "What we can eat depends on what food we are able to acquire. The mere presence of food in the economy, or in the market, does not entitle a person to consume it." (Drèze and Sen, 1989: 9).

Tangible resources such as land, seeds, animals, equipment, and monetary and non-monetary transfers have a direct impact on the availability of food, whereas intangible resources, such as knowledge, skills and labour, indirectly influence the access to food. A person's endowment set is determined by a combination of both, tangible and intangible resources, giving each individual the possibility to use or exchange their own resources for other necessities. The resources a person can claim her or his own, tangible or intangible, are what Sen calls 'entitlements'. Entitlements enable individuals to purchase goods in exchange of her or his entitlements or set of entitlements (endowment) (cf. Sen, 1981). As a result, an individual's entitlement to food depends on her or his exchange entitlements and possibilities, and on its endowments. These entitlements vary across individuals. Although, availability of food does not determine directly hunger or starvation, it is more likely that a decline of food per head leads to starvation (cf. Sen, 1981). Starvation, therefore, is the result of an 'entitlement failure', which can be due to a decline of a person's endowments, for instance because of the loss of land or due to "an unfavourable shift in her exchange entitlement", e.g. increasing food prices or the loss of employment (Drèze and Sen, 1989: 23). Sen further distinguishes between 'direct entitlement failures' and 'indirect entitlement failures'. The former refers to food producers, whose production has declined due to external causes that reduce the output of food production (e.g. natural hazards) or factors that reduce the demand of the produce. 'Indirect entitlement failures' refer to food consumers who have to trade their commodities for food, as their exchange value or the availability of food declines (cf. Sen, 1981).

Sen's capability approach

The *capability approach* has mainly emerged in the book *Hunger and Public Action* (1989) by Jean Drèze and Armatya Sen and is based on Sen's earlier book *Commodities and Capabilities* (1985). Capability according to Drèze and Sen (1989) means that a person pursuits to be valuable and influential. It is, therefore, a much broader approach than the entitlement approach, including the concepts of *well-being, desire, happiness,* and *achievements*.

> "[…] with more specification on the quality of life, the object of public action can be seen to be the enhancement of the capability of people to undertake valuable and valued 'doings and beings'" (Drèze and Sen, 1989: 12).

The authors thereby change the perspective from the entitlement approach to the capability of a person "to avoid undernourishment and to escape deprivations associated with hunger" (Drèze and Sen, 1989: 13). The focus of this approach lies not merely on wealth and commodities, but on the human life and the capabilities of humans to fulfil certain achievements and values. The capability to be free from undernourishment and ill health, under prevalent conditions is determined by "a person's access to health care, medical facilities, elementary education, drinking water, and sanitary facilities", and count as such achievements (Drèze and Sen, 1989: 13). Nutritional achievements, however, vary across individuals depending on their age, sex, health conditions and metabolism. By including *nutritional capabilities* of individuals, this approach focuses not only on the ability to access food or the sufficient supply of food, but focuses on other factors, which also determine a person's nutritional and health status.

The basic needs approach

The discourse of the *basic needs approach* not only influenced the concept of poverty, but also the debate on FNS. The approach was emphasised in the 1970s, when economic growth orientated development strategies failed to eliminate persistent poverty and hunger in the developing countries (cf. ODI, 1978). Followed by several reports that challenged the predominant paradigm of economic growth, such as the famous report *The Limits to Growth* compiled by the *Club of Rome*, the International Labour Organization (ILO) promoted the basic needs approach as a new development paradigm, in 1976 (cf. Meadows, 1972; ILO, 1976).

There is no single definition or even a detailed list of the basic needs; the meaning of these needs derives from Abraham Maslow's (1943) *Hierarchy of Needs Pyramid,* which defines five basic needs: physiological needs, safety-security, love and belongingness, self-esteem, and self-actualization. Based on behavioural science, the pyramid of basic needs is led by the assumption that humans are led by their motivation of a wish or desire (cf. Goble, 2004). According to Maslow, a human being is motivated by two different hierarchical needs, the basic needs or *deficiency needs* and *growth needs* or *being values*. The former needs, comprise the first two steps of the pyramid: physiological needs (air, water, food, shelter, and sleep), and safety and security. By fulfilling these needs, humans are motivated by growth needs, such as love and belongingness, and self-esteem. Maslow describes all these needs as steps on the way to fulfil the last step, self-actualization (cf. Goble, 2004). According to Maslow's assumption, food is one of the most basic needs of a person, which first has to be satisfied before being able to climb further steps of fulfilling growth needs. Consequently, the lack of food and other basic needs, to some extent impedes human development and self-actualization. Although food is a basic commodity to survive, it does not guarantee good health and human development *per se*. It is important to consider further conditions and factors which influence the FNS status of a person.

The Sustainable Livelihoods Approach

The concept of Sustainable Livelihoods Approach (SLA) has been commonly used for poverty reduction strategies and to improve food insecurity. Chambers and Conway (1991) provide the following definition for livelihood:

> "A livelihood comprises people, their capabilities and their means of living, including food, income and assets. [...] A livelihood is environmentally sustainable when it maintains or enhances the local and global assets on which livelihoods depend [...]. A livelihood is socially sustainable which can cope with and recover from stress and shocks, and provide for future generations" (Chambers and Conway, 1991: 1).

First and foremost, the approach comprises three key elements: capabilities, equity and sustainability, and puts people who suffer from poverty in the centre of observation, whose "livelihoods [...] are based on multiple activities and sources of food and their resources" (Chambers, 1995: 174). According to Chamber (1991), these elements are both, ends and means in the SLA (cf. Chambers, 1988; Chambers and Conway, 1991). It focuses on the lives of humans and on their assets, which are similar to endowments in the entitlement approach, and considered to be indispensable for a living (cf. Chambers and Conway, 1991; Burchi and De Muro, 2012). Assets comprise five different elements: stores (e.g. food stocks), resources (e.g. land, water, and livestock), claims for support and access (e.g. gifts, loans, and work), and access (e.g. services, information, and employment) (cf. Chambers and Conway, 1991).

For food security and poverty analysis an array of development agencies and organizations have been using the SLA in development cooperation practice. In the 1990s, the British Department for International Development (DFID) has, therefore, designed a *Sustainable Livelihood Framework*. This framework represents the relationship between governmental and sectoral factors and structures that influence a person's living. People's objectives in life translate into *livelihood strategies* to achieve certain *livelihood outcomes* (e.g. income, well-being, and food security). Additionally, the framework is also concerned with vulnerability, since human beings are constantly exposed to uncontrollable shocks, stress and risks, which may affect their assets, thereby their food security, as well as their livelihood decisions (cf. DFID, 1999). Further discussion on FNS and vulnerability follows in chapter 4.1.1. The livelihood approach substantially changed the perspective of development and guided the development policies and practices, particularly in addressing rural poverty (cf. Solesbury, 2003).

2.1.2   Relationship between food, nutrition and human development

The most common concept of *human development* emerged with the first *Human Development Report* published by the United Nations Development Program (UNDP) in 1990. This widely accepted understanding of human development comprises three main elements: a long and healthy life, knowledge (education), and access to resources for a decent standard of living. Based on this understanding "human development is a process of enlarging people's choices" (UNDP, 1990: 10). Thus, the three elements of human development are necessary preconditions to gain freedom of choice. This includes various individual choices, which can create political, economic and social freedom. Although income is considered to be a factor that can increase choices, it is "not the sum total of human life" and, therefore, only indirectly incorporated into the concept (UNDP, 1990: 9). The perception of this concept emphasizes a different way of understanding the human being itself as an end not as a mean, and the factors that influence a person's development are the centre view of this fundamental approach (cf. UNDP, 1990). It recognizes that

> "People are the real wealth of a nation. The basic objective of development is to create an enabling environment for people to enjoy long, healthy and creative lives" (UNDP, 1990: 9).

Moreover, this approach indicates that there is a strong relationship between health and human development. Meaning that being healthy gives humans abilities and choices for their lives. In this regard, a considerable amount of literature has been published on the relationship between nutrition, health, and human development associated with education and productivity.

According to Weingärtner (2009), nutrition is a function of food intake and health status (cf. Weingärtner, 2009). This means that the nutritional and health status of an individual derives from the outcome of food intake and nutrition. Depending on a person's physical precondition he or she can achieve a certain status of health through adequate nutrition. Burchi and De Muro (2012) describe the undeniable relationship between health and FNS as 'bilateral'. On the one hand, diseases can cause malnutrition or undernutrition by reducing the ability to absorb food and its nutrients or by simply reducing one's appetite, which can lead, vice versa, to malnutrition and poor health. On the other hand, maintaining a poor and monotonic diet makes a person more susceptible to diseases (cf. Burchi and De Muro, 2012). Health is, therefore, an essential component of human development, and good health is a precondition to develop physical well-being and cognitive abilities. Malnutrition in form of undernutrition, particularly in early life is linked to chronic health problems in adulthood, such as adult size, intellectual ability, economic productivity, reproductive performance, and metabolic and cardiovascular disease. A person's nutritional status in childhood consequently influences his or her health status in future and can be transmitted inter-generational (cf. Currie, 2009). In order to demonstrate this far-reaching relationship between health and human development outcomes, scientist have conducted several studies to examine the existence of relationships between health, educational attainment, labour market outcomes in form of productivity, wages, and income (cf. Bloom et al., 2004; Strauss and Thomas, 1998). Figure 1 illustrates the simplified relationship between nutrition, health, and productivity.

Figure 1:   Relationship between food, nutrition, health and productivity

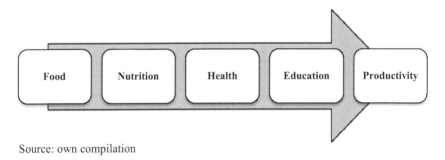

Source: own compilation

The complex inter-relationship between health, education and economic development

The relationship between education and health has been studied from different purviews of sciences such as social sciences, health, economics and medical science. The most well-established findings of these studies suggest, that there is a positive correlation between health and education, in a way that good health leads to improvement in schooling or higher educational attainment (cf. Currie, 2009; Grossman, 1973; Victora et al., 2008). Currie (2009) analysed the reverse effect and found that poor health leads to lower educational attainment (cf. Currie, 2009). An earlier major study by Grossman (1980) of the relationship between health and schooling, demonstrated that low birth weight has negative effects on achievements in schooling (cf. Edward and Grossman, 1980). These findings are supported by Victora (2008) who founds an inverse relationship between undernutrition and early childhood (<2 years) leading to lower attainment in schooling. Adverse health conditions which may be caused by undernutrition can have negative effects on the brain, causing damage and impeding the physical development of a child; which can obstruct cognitive development (cf. Victora et al., 2008). Cognitive abilities, in turn, are essential for success in education and vital for the future economic and social life of adults.

The correlation between health and educational success does not necessarily indicate causality and can be weaker than the studies suggest. Behrman (1996) argues that evidence of the recurrent correlation between health and education is not necessarily given, since direct or indirect variables such as unobservable characteristics, innate abilities, motivation and behaviour are ignored in these studies (cf. Behrman, 1996). However, based on these findings, nutrition is directly linked to health, and health, in turn, is connected to physical well-being, which is a precondition to further achievements in schooling, whether these are influenced by strong cognitive abilities or unobservable variables.

Moreover, there can be a reverse effect of education on health. Grossman (1973) shows that higher education can increase the current health status, and health has a positive effect on productivity and hourly wage rates (cf. Grossman, 1973). Evidence from different country studies correspondingly shows, that better nutrition and good health are associated with higher productivity (cf. Strauss and Thomas, 1998). Workers that are physically and mentally healthy are more productive and do not miss as many work days or hours because of ill health. In lower income countries, where the primary and secondary sector of the economy predominates and a higher proportion of workers are engaged in manual labour, reduced hourly wages and lower productivity have significant effects on economic growth and development (cf. Bloom et al., 2004). The correlation between health and labour market outcomes such as higher wages or income has also been noted by Currie and Madrian (1999). Figure 2 presents this important relationship. Evidence from further socio-economic studies on health and productivity proves that success in schooling leads to greater outcomes on the labour market, which emphasizes the following conclusion. Merging all these findings, health in childhood is positively correlated to future outcomes on the labour market such as higher incomes, directly or due the relationship between adult health and productivity and the effect of education on productivity. Poor health in childhood leads to poor future health and, therefore, to lower productivity (cf. Currie and Madrian, 1999). These results jointly demonstrate the complex inter-relation between nutrition, health and education, which are essential to a person's well-being and to human development and the key to social and economic development. In conclusion, FNS and human development are closely inter-related and affect the capability of a person's life giving her or him, the ability to live a healthy and productive life.

Figure 2:   Relationship between health and education and labour market outcome

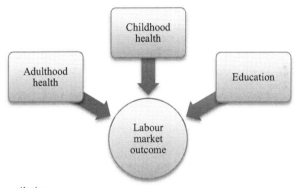

Source: own compilation

2.2   Food and Nutrition Security definition(s)

The rationale behind the attempts to explain the causes of hunger and poverty, by means of theoretical approaches, was to lay the foundation for formulating hunger-reduction strategies and policies. The defined concept of FNS is based on these approaches and has evolved out of the on-going discussions in the development circle on the world's problem of hunger and poverty. This subchapter presents the different definitions separately for food security and nutrition security. Each definition is a subject to different assumptions, but closely linked to one another. A short overview of the history and the current global discussion on the FNS concept is given at the end of this chapter.

2.2.1   Food security and nutrition security – definitions and concepts

The most widely adopted FNS definition resulted from the FAO's 1996 *World Food Summit* (WFS) in Rome:

> „Food Security exists when all people, at all times, have physical, social and economic access to sufficient, safe and nutritious food that meets their dietary needs and food preferences for an active and healthy life" (FAO, 1996).

This definition includes the previously described theoretical components of the concept. Access to food derives from the entitlement approach, whereas the availability is assumed to be the premise of sufficiency. The emphasize of nutritious food for health refers to the capability and the human development approach, which make an inclusion of public services, education and further influencing factors to nutrition and health necessary. Therefore, this definition recognizes the multidimensional nature of the concept.

Food Security

Food security should not merely be defined as a static state of being or an outcome of certain conditions or interventions, but rather as a dynamic concept. The FAO recognizes that food insecurity can be classified into two types by adding a time dimension. Thereby, *chronic food insecurity* is a long-term or persistent problem, deriving from extended periods of poverty, the lack of assets and inadequate access to productive or financial resources. *Transitory food insecurity* is being understood as a short-term and temporary problem, which derives from short-term shocks, affecting availability of and access to food. It is mainly caused by natural hazards, extreme environmental disasters, economic and financial crises or political conflicts, and a cyclical or regular pattern depending on seasonal factors (cf. FAO, 2008; Weingärtner, 2009).

In the context of the persistent problems of hunger and poverty, food insecurity has been viewed solely as a supply problem. In this perspective, hunger and undernourishment were the outcome of food shortages. It was not until the entitlement approach and the comprehensive study *Food First* by Lappé and Collins (1977) that the perspective on food security changed. Lappé and Collins discovered that there was actually no shortage but an abundance of food, since the agricultural sector was producing a steady surplus on global level (cf. Lappé and Collins, 1977). Alongside with this surplus, *food poverty* and, therefore, the access to food, because of entitlement failures has been identified as an actual problem that led to hunger and deprivation (cf. Scanlan, 2003). Thus, the perception of food insecurity as being a problem on the macro-economic level widened the focus to the micro-economic level focussing on individuals and households.

In the context of food security on a macro level to provide an adequate supply of food, the discussion can be extended to a widely discussed and crucial strategy of *food self-sufficiency,* which aims to achieve food security through agriculture and trade policies. Although, there is no definition given to what is 'enough' or 'sufficient' food, it is a part of the overall definition of FNS (cf. Maxwell and Smith, 1992). Food self-sufficiency on a macro-economic level can be interpreted in terms of growing domestically sufficient food to meet the population's need of adequate nutrition. If total domestic food supply derives from domestic food production, a country is food self-sufficient, meaning it can secure the availability of food on a national level (cf. Drèze and Sen, 1989; Sen, 1989). Conversely, if a country is not able to meet sufficiency of food through domestic production, it has to rely on trade for food imports or on food aid – in case of transitory food insecurity. Food self-sufficiency, however, does not imply an adequacy of food supply; people could still suffer from hunger or undernutrition. *Food adequacy* is neither an immediate result of food self-sufficiency, nor a result from the reliance of food imports for a sufficient food supply in the absence of self-sufficiency (cf. Drèze and Sen, 1989). Food self-sufficiency puts the role of the agricultural sector as the only source of food supply in the focus. This strategy may not be applicable in all regions and countries, particularly where food production depends on limited inputs and resources such as land, water, employment or seeds. In addition, in regions and countries where food production is constrained by difficult production conditions, creating vulnerability to climatic variations, food self-sufficiency, may not be an ideal solution (cf. Thomson and Metz, 1998).

Nevertheless, countries not only rely on food imports, in order to secure their national supply, but to extend the variations of domestic food supply. This leads to the argument for countries aiming to benefit from liberal agricultural trade by shifting their efficiency of production from one sector to the other non-food sector, based on comparative advantages and the endowments of a country. However, trade benefits from this strategy of *food self-reliance* depend on the capacity of a country to generate foreign

45

exchange for purchasing food imports. Many small island economies and developing countries with a narrow export structure and high demands for food may not be able to be self-reliant. For such countries, it may be advantageous to focus on the efficiency of their agricultural sector (cf. FAO, 2003).

In times of the *Green Revolution*, which most countries in Asia aggressively adopted as panacea to their problems of hunger, starvation and poverty in the 1960s-1970s, this strategy also aimed to achieve food self-sufficiency. Particularly India and China achieved to reduce hunger by means of this approach (cf. Drèze and Sen, 1989). However, the rapid population growth, urbanization, changing consumption patterns, and the employment shift from the agriculture to the manufactured sector, increased the demand of food and of different foodstuff, which also may have caused an increase for imported food in a large extent. Self-sufficiency is not merely a question of production or import capacity, but one of price efficiency in the domestic food production sector.

One concept that opened the discourse about agricultural independence goes even beyond the thought of the possibilities to be independent of food imports through food self-sufficiency. Enhancing domestic agricultural production and demands on the enforcement of the Human Right to Food, and the right of a nation to protect its food and agricultural sector from food imports and adverse effects from international trade was initiated and globally spread in the 1990s. *Food sovereignty* emanated as a small farmers social movement, called *La Via Campensina,* in 1993 (cf. La Via Campensina, 2013). In order to protect local small farmers and to achieve agricultural sustainability, people and countries have the right to define their own food and agricultural policies. People who participate in local food production should be given access to inputs to enable food production and use these inputs sustainably; people, therefore, should be entitled to land, water, seeds and credit. An important principal in the view of La Via Campensina to achieve food sovereignty is the perception of food as a basic human right (cf. Windfuhr and Jonsén, 2005).

Nutrition Security

While Food Security focuses on the physical availability, on sufficient food and the access to it, *Nutrition Security* focuses on the nutritional aspects of food security. According to the capability approach, it is important to include determining health factors and to define nutritional capabilities of individuals.

> "Nutrition is not just the availability of food, but embodies concepts such as the quality of food, dietary diversity, food safety, cultural acceptability, healthy eating habits, preparation, as well as feeding patterns, such as breastfeeding. Nutrition is therefore the result of the combination of food, health and care that a person receives" (Stuart, 2006: 21).

According to this definition, Nutrition Security refers to the adequacy of nutritional intake and focuses on the nutritional outcome. Oshaug (1994) points out that three necessary, but not sufficient conditions have to be realised, in order to achieve nutrition security: "food security, adequate care and adequate prevention and control of disease" (Oshaug et al., 1994: 498). With this understanding of nutrition and nutrition security, it is important not to focus merely on the problems resulting from insufficiency of food, but on the use of food and the outcomes of nutrition. The nutritional status of an individual depends on crucial factors, such as health and healthy living conditions, as well as the adequate intake of macronutrients and micronutrients. It further depends on education and the knowledge about adequate diets in the particular cultural context to achieve nutritional well-being (cf. FAO, 1992). Ultimately, nutrition is determined by the household income or the incomes of individuals. While increasing incomes may improve entitlements and, therefore, the access to food, it does not necessarily or directly improve nutritional well-being of the household members. Since households may spend their additional income on less nutritious food, the income-effect may only indirectly improve the nutritional status through higher expenditure on better care or living conditions, for instance (cf. Braun et al., 1992). In the 1990s, when the term Nutrition Security emerged, the focus lied on the adequate intake of macro- and micronutrients, whereas later with the elaboration of the concept, the FAO adopted the following definition:

> "Nutrition security is achieved when secure access to an appropriately nutritious diet is coupled with a sanitary environment, adequate health services and care, to ensure a healthy and active life for all household members" (FAO, 2011a).

Opposed to Nutrition Security, nutrition insecurity is manifested as condition of *malnutrition*, which results from a combination of basic, underlying and immediate causes. In the 1990s, the United Nations Children's Fund (UNICEF) has recognized the severe problem of nutritional problems in the most vulnerable groups of the population, children and (pregnant) mothers, and has, therefore, drawn a concept of malnutrition. Most commonly UNICEF uses the notion of malnutrition synonymously with undernutrition (cf. UNICEF, 1990, 2013a). However, further definitions of malnutrition identify two or three different forms of nutritional problems covered by this notion. Earlier in 1985, Payne defines malnutrition as "state in which the physical function of an individual is impaired, where she or he can no longer maintain an adequate level of performance" (Payne, 1985: 1). There is no universally accepted definition of malnutrition, whether in literature nor on the international discourse level of FNS. Malnutrition can be referred to as energy or protein-energy inadequacy or as micronutrient deficiency (cf. Svedberg, 2000). According to FAO's perception, malnutrition is a broader term, including three forms of malnutrition "caused by inadequate, unbalanced or excessive consumption of macronutrients and/or micronutrients":

- Undernutrition
- Overnutrition, and
- Micronutrient deficiency (cf. FAO, 2014b).

Undernutrition refers to insufficient intake of dietary energy. The United Nations (UN) *Standing Committee on Nutrition* (SCN) (2004) defines undernutrition as "the result of undernourishment, poor absorption or poor biological use of nutrients consumed" (UN SCN, 2004: 146). Undernourishment is a coinciding notion, which can be described as an "unsatisfactory state of being", in which a person's nutritional/food intake does not reach the minimum dietary energy requirements (FAO, 2013c; Drèze and Sen, 1989: 14). The FAO determines the minimum intake of energy in calories according to different population and country specific characteristic of age and sex (cf. FAO, 2013d). Nevertheless, the calculation and determination of a minimum cut-off level for an average person is as controversial as difficult. This procedure requires comprehensive information about a person's physical conditions and activities, depending on a person's body mass, age, level of physical activity and physiological health conditions (such as illness, infection, pregnancy and lactation), metabolic rate, nutrition absorption, and climatic conditions (cf. Drèze and Sen, 1989; FAO, 2012c). Undernourishment is also used exchangeable to the notion 'hunger'[1], which is an emotive term to describing the feeling of discomfort from not eating (cf. Welthungerhilfe, 2013). Nevertheless, the state of undernourishment increases the short-term risk of disability, morbidity and mortality (cf. chapter 6.2); while the long-term consequences could affect intellectual ability, economic productivity, reproductive performance, metabolic and cardiovascular diseases. These severe consequences can even lead to an "intergenerational transmission of poverty" and ill health (cf. Black et al., 2008; Grantham-McGregor et al., 2007: 60). Undernutrition is usually measured by the weight of a person. In order to measure undernutrition in children (<5 years), three anthropometrical methods are used to assess their nutrition condition: *underweight* by measuring weight for age; *stunting* is measured by the height for age, and *wasting* is measured by the weight for height (cf. UNICEF, 2013b). Undernutrition in adults is less common, but can be measured by the Body Mass Index (BMI)[2].

Overnutrition refers to a permanent excess intake or over-consumption of dietary energy in relation to the average dietary energy requirements, resulting in excess body mass (overweight or obesity) (cf. CFS, 2012). "Overweight and obesity are defined as abnormal or excessive fat accumulation that may impair health", measured by the BMI (WHO, 2013h). Overweight and obesity are risk factors related to various health problems and Non-communicable Diseases (NCDs) (cf. WHO, 2013h). Overweight and obesity can coexist with undernutrition both at high prevalence levels within a country. This phenomenon appears in countries and regions, where poverty, undernourishment and low-incomes are widely spread. Overnutrition as a special form of malnutrition is the major subject of chapter 4, and subsequently will be further discussed in the context of the selected research object.

Micronutrient deficiencies also referred to as *hidden hunger* derives from inadequate dietary patterns, disease, or from a deficient intake of micronutrients such as vitamins and minerals, which are essential for the health of individuals. Micronutrient deficiency is "technically a form of undernutrition", but can also co-exist with overnutrition (Bouis et al.,

---

1   For the purpose of this thesis the terms undernutrition or undernourishment and hunger will be used interchangeably.

2   The BMI is calculated as a person's weight in kilograms divided by the square of his height in meters (kg/m2) (WHO, 2013c).

2013: 4). Most commonly assessed nutritional health consequences include i.a. Vitamin A Deficiency (VAD), Iron Deficiency Anaemia (IDA), and Iodine Deficiency Disorders (IDD) (cf. WHO, 2013g). Other micronutrients such as zinc, selenium, and Vitamin B12 are also essential to human health, but lack sufficient data for appropriate measurements (cf. Bouis et al., 2013).

In conclusion, malnutrition is the generic term for any condition, in which the nutrition intake is insufficient, inadequate or unbalanced (including the poor absorption of food consumed) for the body to function properly, and thereby hindering good health. Figure 3 presents an overview of the discussed forms of malnutrition, their definitions and specific health consequences. Individuals affected by undernutrition, overnutrition, or micronutrient deficiency increase the susceptibility to diseases and the reduction of mental and physical capacities.

Figure 3:   **Three forms of Malnutrition and health consequences**

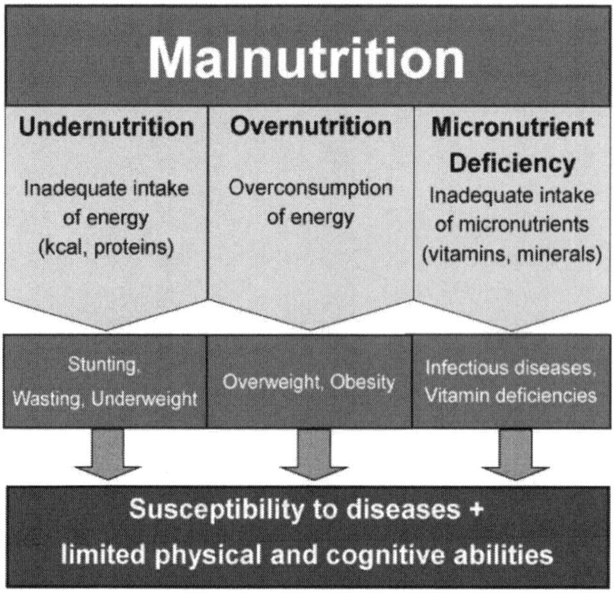

Source: own compilation

The causes of malnutrition are multiple, ranging from social, economic and physical factors. The economically and socially deprived groups of the population are more susceptible to malnutrition, because they lack access to resources like income and health services, as well as the sufficient and adequate intake of food and essential nutrients. The framework of malnutrition helps to overview the main causes of malnutrition and to understand the multi-facetted nature of the problem. It has been designed to identify the main causes of malnutrition and to address them through appropriate policies and strategies. The main causes are presented in Figure 4, based on the concept of malnutrition, which was developed by UNICEF in 1990.

Inadequate dietary intake and disease most significantly and directly cause malnutrition. A human body suffering from a disease may affect dietary intake and appropriate absorption of nutrients, whereas inadequate dietary intake may lead to the body's susceptibility to disease. Disease may be caused by inadequate care, prevention and control of disease, and insufficient health care service in combination or solely by living in an unhealthy environment, where unclean and non-potable water, inadequate sanitary facilities and pollution increase the likelihood of becoming ill. Inadequate dietary intake can also be caused by inadequate access to food or supply of food. Underlying causes are mostly interrelated, and the particular cause of inadequate dietary intake or disease can only be determined in the respective context of examination. On a national level, a society is endowed with potential resources that determine the production of food. The capacity of food production is a function of environmental, technological, economic, social and political factors. Consequently, basic causes of malnutrition root in socio-cultural, economic and political environments, which influence the food supply and access to food (cf. UNICEF, 1990). These structures most significantly influence the distribution of resources and the control and management over these resources within a society. Thereby, they determine how resources, including human, economic and organizational resources, are used to provide healthy environments, health services and adequate access to food for the population (cf. FAO, 2004b).

Figure 4:   The causes of malnutrition

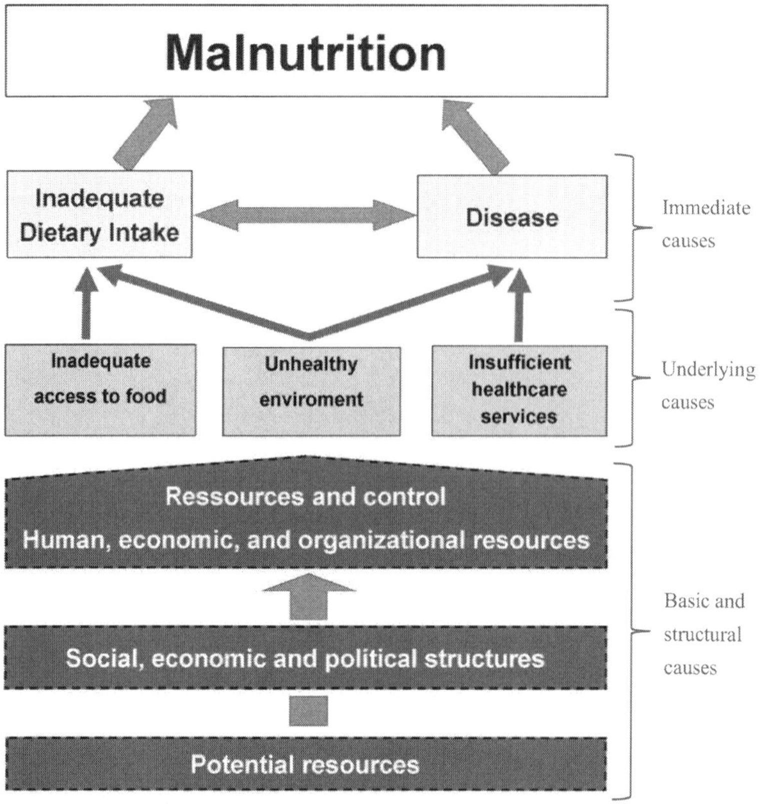

Source: own compilation based on UNICEF (1990)

The 2006 World Bank *Repositioning Nutrition as Central to Development Report* recognizes that investing in nutrition, and thereby reducing malnutrition, can result in high benefits of economic growth and poverty reduction for the individuals and the economy as a whole (cf. The World Bank, 2006). Poverty is one of the major causes of malnutrition, particular for undernutrition. Both concepts are strongly interrelated through a vicious cycle. Undernutrition and ill health impair a person's physical and cognitive development, which in turn limit his or her ability to actively participate in a productive social, economic and political life. This limitation subsequently impedes the individuals to generate income, and thereby does not allow securing their basic needs; leading again to poverty and malnutrition (cf. The World Bank, 2006).

2.2.2   Food and Nutrition Security in a global context

The origins of the international debate about hunger began during the World-War-II era, from the United Nations *Conference on Food and Agriculture* in 1943, where 44 governments met and set the foundations for the Food and Agriculture Organization (FAO) (cf. Shaw, 2007). Since the first session of the FAO in 1945, its mandate was to improve the nutrition situation of the people, increase agricultural productivity, increase the standards of living of the population, and contribute to economic growth (cf. FAO, 2014c; Shaw, 2007). The persistent situation of widespread poverty and hunger called for an immediate intervention of FAO, which back then estimated that one billion people worldwide were suffering from hunger – estimations were based on little reliable and barely available data (cf. Shaw, 2007). In 1948, in the aftermath of the Second World War, the Universal Declaration of Human Rights (UDHR) in Article 25 declared that every person "has the right to a standard of living adequate for the health and well-being of himself and of his family, including food" (UN, 1948). With rising technological achievements, mechanisation in the agricultural sector, in some parts of this world, countries achieved to increase productivity in the agricultural sector. Particularly North America rapidly managed to produce a surplus of food of mainly grain, which became a large exporter of grain and supplier of food aid (cf. Headey and Fan, 2010; Shaw, 2007). The discussion on food surplus absorption, initiated through the Seventh Session of FAO Conference in 1953, led to new ideas of utilizing surpluses as food aid for developing countries, where agriculture and industry could not provide sufficient food for the people living there (cf. FAO, 2005b). Later in 1966, the *Human Right to Food* was again emphasized and conserved in Article 11 of the *International Covenant on Economic, Social and Cultural Rights*, which entered into force in 1976 (cf. UN, 1966). Currently, 161 parties and 70 signatures agreed to "recognize the right of everyone to [...] adequate food" and to "the fundamental right of everyone to be free from hunger", in order to realise these rights through a range of measures specified in Article 11 (2) (UN, 1966). Although, the supply of food has increased in the past decades, in the early 1970s many world regions were affected by a food crisis, triggered by a huge price increases in staples such as maize, rice and wheat (cf. Headey and Fan, 2010). In 1974, when food prices peaked, the first *World Food Conference* was held in Rome, reaffirming the Human Right to Food through the *Universal Declaration on the Eradication of Hunger and*

Malnutrition. The international community committed to increase development aid for developing countries and eliminate hunger and malnutrition through "higher food production and a more equitable and efficient distribution of food" to reasonable prices (UN, 1974). FAO then in its Council Resolution 1/64 reaffirmed:

> "[…] the urgent need for effective international action aimed at ensuring the availability at all times of adequate world supplies of basic foodstuffs […] to sustain a steady expansion of consumption in countries with low levels of per caput intake, and offset fluctuations in production and prices […]" (FAO, 1974).

The *International Conference on Nutrition* (ICN) by FAO and WHO followed in 1992, where a range of organizations and representatives from 159 countries discussed the persistent problem of undernutrition and hunger. Four years later, the *World Food Summit* in Rome was marked as a historical event in 1996, when 185 international representatives committed to the *Rome Declaration on World Food Security,* and thereby recognized food insecurity to be not only a problem of insufficient production, but also one of inadequate access. Consequently, poverty has been identified as the main cause of food insecurity. Food security has to be achieved on the individual, household, national, regional and global level. The most significant outcome of the Summit's *Plan of Action* has been the target to half the number of undernourished people – at that present time estimated at 800 million people – until 2015. The eradication of poverty, reducing inequitable distribution of food, and beneficial trade policies are main challenges to achieve food security. The *World Declaration on Nutrition,* which emanated from the preceding ICN laid the ground for the commitment to ensure food safety and adequacy to meet energy and nutrient requirements of the population, and governments to provide health care. The FAO Committee on World Food Security (CFS) has declared responsibility to monitor the implementation of the Plan of Action (cf. FAO, 1996). The target set in 1996, was repeated in the *Millennium Declaration* of the United Nations, which has been adopted by 152 heads of states, promising to halve the number of people suffering from hunger by 2015. The FAO has the mandate to monitor the progress towards the achievement of this target (cf. FAO, 2014a). From the Millennium Declaration, eight Millennium Development Goals (MDGs) and different 20 targets were formulated which should be achieved by the year 2015.

Since the progress towards reducing hunger by 2015 has been noticed to be slow, the international community searched for answers on the most recent 2009 World Food Summit in Rome. World leaders recognized that poverty could only be eradicated, and food security could only be achieved through investments in the agricultural sector and boosting production and productivity (cf. FAO, 2009). The World Bank's *World Development Report* 2008 emphasized that the agricultural sector is key to poverty eradication. It recognized that the poor mainly live in rural areas and heavily depend on this sector for their livelihood. The report also found that different income groups within a population disproportionately benefit from investments into the agricultural sector. An investment into the sector significantly benefits the poor by reducing poverty levels (cf. The World Bank, 2008).

These legions of events shaped the evolution of the FNS concept and its impact on international strategies and policies to improve the life of the people suffering from the consequences of food and nutrition insecurity. The theoretical foundations from chapter 2.2.1 in combination of the existing definitions of FNS and its evolution presented in this subchapter, do not reveal the complexity of the concept itself but provides an understanding of the different elements of the concept.

2.3   The conceptual framework of Food and Nutrition Security

The FNS concept is based on fundamental approaches and theories from different scientific purviews, ranging from economic and political to natural sciences. As such, there is no universal definition of FNS; it rather adopts various denotations and interpretations, depending on the perspective point or level of observation. It would be constrained to think of FNS as an objective and a static state of being. This subchapter argues that FNS is a complex, but also a multidimensional and dynamic concept, which bases on theoretical foundations and includes a variety of important elements on different dimensions.

Subchapter 2.3.1 describes the four dimensions of the concept of FNS, expressing its complexity and holistic understanding. Based on these dimensions, the FNS concept does not only serve for theoretical analyses of special issues to food and nutrition insecurity, but also for practical purposes of FNS policies and strategies. Therefore, chapter 2.3.2 presents a framework for analysing the impact of policies on different socio-organizational levels of the FNS concept. The operationalization of the concept further requires the possibility to measure FNS. Consequently, the last subchapter 2.3.3 explains different measurement methods and indicators of FNS.

2.3.1 The four dimensions of Food and Nutrition Security

Given the definition of FNS, it can be assumed that it is a multidimensional and complex concept influenced by economic, political and social factors. A commonly used definition of FNS has derived from the international discussion on food security and nutrition and the decisive 1996 *Rome Declaration on World Food Security*. The U.S. Agency for International Development (USAID) additionally contributed to the amplification of this definition and the elaboration of the concept of FNS, which on the policy level fulfils its operational purposes. The basis of the definition and understanding of food security as a broad concept consists mainly of four dimensions: availability, access, utilization, and stability (cf. Figure 5). These are indispensable to analyse the particular issues of food and nutrition insecurity in a country- or region-specific context (cf. USAID, 1992).

Figure 5:   **The four dimensions of Food and Nutrition Security**

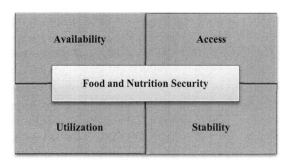

Source: own compilation

Availability

Availability of food refers commonly to *physical availability* and is determined by the amount of domestic food production, food imports, international food aid or domestic food stocks dispersion (cf. Weingärtner,

2009). The most important or principal source of food supply is the domestic food production sector, originating in the agricultural sector. This perception centres the agricultural sector in the focus of FNS policies. The increase in agricultural production and productivity was and still is a development paradigm for different reasons, which can be ascertained merely in a country or region specific context. Nevertheless, the importance of the agriculture sector goes beyond its sole function of producing food and inputs for production. A country's society, economy and its environment depend significantly on agriculture and the mode of production (cf. IAASTD, 2009). If domestic production does not meet domestic demand – for different reasons of population growth or consumption patterns, which underlie rapid changes – this insufficiency of food supplies can result in a 'food gap', when demand exceeds the supply of food. In such a situation of food shortages or a food gap, food has to be purchased on the international markets, through imports or donations of food in form of food aid. International food aid, at its beginnings in the 1950s has been considered as an ideal relief for countries, suffering from food shortages, and a useful tool to dispose food surpluses, serving donor countries (cf. Mousseau, 2005). Later, it has become a highly debated issue, since it can provoke unintended and adverse effects on local markets (cf. Barrett, 2006). Over the years, food aid or food assistance, has adopted different forms and donors can deliver food assistance through different tools (cf. Barrett et al., 2011; Harvey et al., 2010).[3] In case of food shortages, the dispersion of food stocks does not only serve to increase domestic food availability, but more importantly it is used for reasons of price regulations (cf. GIZ, 2013).

Moreover, availability of food is determined by seasonality and uncertainty. Seasonal fluctuations are predictable and can be foreseen by certain measures or systems. Due to the fact that food and agricultural production capacities, natural conditions, financial capacities, trade and economic structure vary significantly across countries, food availability can only be reasonably analysed within a country specific context.

---

3   The World Food Programme (WFP) recognizes three types of food aid: emergency, project and program food aid (cf. WFP, 2012).

Access

As past experiences show, increasing solely the supply of food through augmented domestic food production does not necessarily implicate an equal distribution of food among the population or individuals and households. The basic approaches that underlie this FNS dimension are the basic needs, entitlement and the sustainable livelihood approach. FAO's definition of FNS refers to physically, socially and economically accessible food.

Overall access to food is mainly determined by an individual's or household's endowment with resources, which they can use for own food production or trade in exchange for food (cf. Maxwell and Smith, 1992; Sen, 1981). Income is one of these necessary resources to purchase food, if food production itself is not an option. The lack of resources, income differentials or so-called entitlement failures lead to an insufficient *economic access* to food (cf. Sen, 1981). General access to food certainly requires physical and sufficient availability of food (cf. Riely et al., 1999). Albeit availability of food is sufficient, individuals can lack necessary entitlements to secure access to food (cf. Braun et al., 1992). Each individual requires a certain amount and variation of nutrients to achieve a healthy and productive life. Despite sufficient food availability and adequate access to food, individuals might not be able to achieve nutritional requirements and healthy diets. This may occur when household decisions overrule the preference of expenditure on food by the acquisition of other goods, or because of an unequal distribution of food among household members or an inadequate utilization of food (cf. Braun et al., 1992; Ecker and Breisinger, 2012).

Further factors, such as food prices, determine the economic access to food. This requires that prices for food are stable and predictable, for producers as well as consumers, which usually base their income or expenditure decisions on current and future prices respectively. In addition, the share of income-expenditure on food depends on the prices for food items. Thus, for food to be accessible it has also to be affordable. Access to food is not only determined by income, but also by markets and prices.

Physical access to food is given through infrastructure, which enables consumers as well as producers to access local and regional markets. This access can be deterred by civil conflict and war, poor or fragile infrastructure, ineffective logistics for food distribution and ineffective markets (cf. Sharma, 1992). Countries of vulnerable and fragile social, political, economic and environmental structures are even more susceptible to such problems.

> "Food access [...] is a function of the physical environment, social environment, and policy environment which determine how effectively households are able to utilize their resources to meet their food security objectives" (Weingärtner, 2009: 26).

Although *social access* to food is not specified in literature or by FAO, based on the entitlement approach, social access may refer to social and public security systems that support households and individuals, if entitlements to food fail (cf. Drèze and Sen, 1989; Sen, 1981). Hence, individuals or households vulnerable to food and nutrition insecurity are also more susceptible to malnutrition and rely on support from their families, the community, and on social security systems. In conclusion, physical, social and economic access to food is restricted by entitlements, food prices, infrastructure, as well as availability of food.

Utilization and Consumption

The third dimension of FNS refers to the adequate daily food and nutrient intake, which depends on individual habits, cultural and religious factors, on food safety and quality, on access to safe drinking water, as well as on health supporting environments and health care services. The 'nutritional capabilities' as part of the capabilities approach (cf. chapter 2.1.1), has a significant influence on the dimension of food utilization and consumption, considering the 'biological utilization' of food (cf. Weingärtner, 2009).

> "The relationship between food intake and nutritional achievement can vary greatly depending not only on sex, age, pregnancy, metabolic rates, climatic conditions, and activities, but also on access to complementary inputs such as health care, drinking water, etc." (Drèze and Sen, 1989: 13).

How and what foods are used or consumed by households and individuals can be analysed on the household level, and in a broader sense depends on socio-economic and cultural factors. If food is sufficiently available and accessible, ultimately utilization and consumption decisions of households and individuals, on the one hand, depend on preferences, cultural habits and lifestyles, and on the other hand it depends on the knowledge and information of consumers about adequate nutrition and healthy consumption (cf. Weingärtner, 2009). "Food security and nutritional well-being are connected through the actual use of food by individuals" (Braun et al., 1992: 10). Empirical evidence shows that even if there is sufficient and nutritious food available and accessible, distribution of food within households and among its members may be unequal – particularly children, pregnant and lactating women are affected by these inequalities (cf. Haddad, 1994; Maxwell and Smith, 1992). Nevertheless, this evidence is partly inconsistent, because food utilization depends on cultural differences across regions and nations. Individuals or households may suffer from poor nutritional and health status, when the consumed food quantity, quality, diversity or nutrient absorption is low because of ill health, or if access to fresh and clean water and sanitation is limited (cf. The World Bank, 2012a). Utilization is further determined by the variety of food available on national and household level, and indirectly by prices for food, since prices may also narrow the variety of food consumption choices. With price increases, individuals will try to substitute costly food items with cheaper ones. Thereby, they may choose more affordable but less nutritious and low quality foodstuff. Further increasing prices may even lead to a lower caloric intake, which does not meet daily energy requirements and, therefore, increasing the risk of becoming malnourished (cf. The World Bank, 2012a).

Stability

This fourth dimension, which completes the FNS concept, refers to the partial phrase of the FNS definition "at all times" (FAO, 1996). Stability is a supporting and temporal element, of the other three dimensions: availability, access and utilization (cf. Weingärtner, 2009). Preferably, availability and access are not only a short-term phenomenon, but a stable situation of FNS. Stability is also interchangeably used with sustainability, which can mean sustainable utilization and consumption of food, sustainable environments, financial and economic structures, and sustainable food production practices which will ensure FNS for current and future generations. Stability, therefore, depends on ecological factors such as climate and environmental endowments of a country, on economic factors such as trade and food prices, and on political and social factors such as governance and security. FNS, therefore, is not a static state, but it can be disturbed by several external and structural factors.

Food stocks play also a crucial role to FNS stability, since they can mitigate the negative effects of transitory food security, which might be present due to adverse weather events, or because of external economic shocks such as price shocks and economic crises. Hence, FNS stability and a country's resilience and capacity to cope with external shocks, highly depends on the environmental, social and economic structure of a country. Further discussion on vulnerability and external shocks regarding FNS follows exemplarily for the case study in chapter 4.1.

The examination on the four pillars of the FNS concept shows that the four dimensions are closely interrelated and also mutually dependent. Issues or determining factors on one dimension influence FNS outcomes on the other. A range of cross-cutting factors play a crucial role to FNS and have to be considered in country or regional specific contexts. Ultimately, the examination of all four dimensions emphasizes the need to consider the complexity of one problem on one dimension and requires a food system-based approach to address these complex issues in the context of FNS.

2.3.2 Food and Nutrition Security on socio-organizational levels

In order to address specific issues on each dimension, the multidimensional concept of FNS has to be examined in more detail and on different socio-organizational levels in a socio-economic context. The four dimensions of FNS differ and interact with each other on different levels – on the macro and micro level. Analyses of FNS may focus either on the micro, household or individual level, or the macro, national or regional level. Therefrom relevant policies ideally induce changes on one level with the intent of a positive effect on both levels. Nevertheless, factors or policies on both levels can mutually influence FNS.

Figure 6 represents three relevant levels and a framework for analysing the impact of policies on different socio-organizational levels. All three levels are connected by their relationship and different features. On the **macro level**, various policies in different sectors of the economy can influence household FNS on the micro level. Economic and social policies on the macro level can enhance availability of food on a national level but may also influence the accessibility of food to households through certain policies. The existing social, political and economic framework further determines the household's endowment and its possibilities to use its income, employment, and assets in exchange for food. A household's possibilities may be limited by its health status and education, and ultimately by its cognitive and physical capabilities to make use of them for productivity purposes (cf. Bokeloh, 2009).

Macro policies also determine the function and structure of markets and a country's infrastructure. The link between the macro and micro level is represented through the **meso level**, at which households meet to purchase food on markets, which they physically can reach through infrastructure. Food itself becomes available for consumers on markets, where producers can also purchase production inputs. Both, consumers and producer can access credits and offer labour to increase their income. Most certainly, macroeconomic policies can influence the supply, demand and prices for food, inputs, credits, and labour on these markets, channelling policy effects on the household level through the meso level (cf. Bokeloh, 2009).

Social infrastructure, for instance, refers to health care, education and other social security services, which should be accessible and adequately available for households and individuals; whereas *institutional infrastructure* refers to organizations and institutions providing services for the population. Relevant policies that change or influence markets or infrastructure ultimately also influence a household's income and its assets and, therefore, its access to food (cf. Bokeloh, 2009). For instance, improvement of physical infrastructure through investment policies in remote areas, improves access for farmers to local markets, concomitantly improving their access to food through higher incomes; while increasing the availability of food on this local market. Health policies, which strengthen the national health system, may also have a positive influence on the nutritional status of individuals.

Entitlements and assets of households determine the aggregate demand for food, which in turn and ideally influences the supply of food, under the assumption that markets are efficient. The supply of food is the sum of three elements: domestic food production, subsistence production, and food imports (cf. Bokeloh, 2009). The availability of food depends on the domestic food supply determined by domestic food production and ultimately by world food prices and foreign exchange availability to import food. The lack of effective demand leads to the assumption that there might be large income differentials or 'entitlement failures'. However, it is possible that countries are food-deficient because they command only limited resources deterring access to world market or because of domestic production constraints.

Figure 6:   The relationship between different levels of Food and Nutrition Security

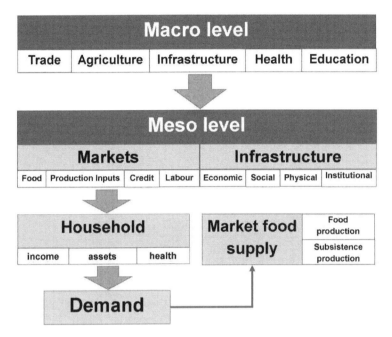

Source: own compilation based on Bokeloh (2009)

Given this model of different determination factors and policies and the socio-economic framework in which they interrelate, reveals and re-emphasizes the importance to include natural, social and economic sciences into the FNS analysis. Moreover, it serves to draw adequate policies and strategies in order to ensure or improve FNS on all possible levels. This holistic view of FNS allows a detailed examination of drivers, determinants and factors of underlying causes, which subsequently requires measuring the outcomes of these policies.

2.3.3 Measuring Food and Nutrition Security: A review of indicators and indices

The purpose of measuring FNS is to reveal at least one dimension or one aspect of it. The questions that arise, however, are whether the adopted measurement method is appropriate, and what kind of conclusion can be drawn from the results? This is important since the conclusions might be translated into relevant policies and strategies, and it is possible to monitor the progress of operative goals as in the case of the Millennium Development Goals (MDGs).

The challenge of measuring FNS lies in its complexity and multi-faceted nature. The extended focus on FNS, from 'hunger' to a broader concept of four dimensions, led to the necessity to measure FNS by dint of various indicators and indices which are developed to assess the FNS situation in specific contexts. Hence, the choice of a suitable indicator or the set of indicators depends on the concept of FNS and its underlying interpretation. The same indicators can be used on micro and macro level, but require different interpretations since the underlying causes might differ between the levels. A review of the widely common used indicators and indices in this section serves as a short overview of the current and dominant measurements and reveals possible advantages and deficiencies of each method.

If the intention is to reflect a preferably broad concept of FNS, a bundle of indicators have to be identified and included into the method of measurement. In addition, the selection of indicators depends on the level, on which the FNS situation will be assessed. For example, measuring hunger and under-nutrition on the household level requires a set of social, economic and health indicators which can give a roughly coherent understanding of the FNS situation of the individuals and households.

However, the use of a single indicator is acceptable; for instance, if there is one specific aspect that influences FNS significantly, and then rapid response to it is necessary. As for instance in a crisis situation of malnutrition where the severity of the situation is assessed through anthropometric methods, such as the Mid-Upper Arm Circumference (MUAC) measuring tape indicating the state of a one- to five-year old child's level of undernutrition[4].

The most accepted and adapted indicators by international experts and development agencies for measuring FNS on the macro level are: The Global Hunger Index (GHI) created by the International Food Policy Research Institute (IFPRI) and the German *Welthungerhilfe*, the Global Food

---

4   Severe acute malnutrition corresponds with a MUAC of less than 115 millimeters (mm) and moderate acute malnutrition with a value between 115 and 125 mm (cf. UNICEF, 2013b).

Security Index (GFSI) constructed by the Economist Intelligent Unit (EIU), and the FAO Prevalence of Undernourishment (PoU) indicator. Apart from the mentioned indicators and indices there are further methods to measure, such as the *Food Security Assessment Model* created by the United States Department of Agriculture (USDA) or the FAO's *Global Information and Early Warning System* constructed to monitor, and predict food emergencies to support governments. The review of further indicators such as the *Hunger Reduction Commitment Index*, *Anthropometric Indicators*, the *Dietary Diversity Scores*, the *Household Hunger Scale*, the *Medical and Biomaker Indicators*, while numerous others are not introduced in this section because they are either used in combination of household surveys or aimed to assess the current implementation of certain FNS strategies, which would exceed the scope of this study. The focus, therefore, lies on indicators and indices which comprise a broad array of FNS issues on the global and macro level.

The multidimensional concept of the **Global Hunger Index (GHI)** comprises three equally weighted indicators: Undernourishment[5], child underweight[6] and child mortality[7]. Since 2006, the GHI is being calculated and released in the GHI Report by IFPRI. The newest report of 2013 reflects the hunger situation of 120 countries, mostly low- and middle-income countries, which have been selected due to sufficient data availability of the indicators and due to relevance (cf. IFPRI, 2013). The countries are ranked according to the magnitude of hunger on a scale from 0 to 100. Zero is the best score indicating that the population does not suffer from hunger at all, whereas 100, the worst score, indicating that there is an extreme situation of hunger. According to this, the severity of hunger reaches five stages: "low", "moderate", "serious", "alarming" and "extremely alarming" (IFPRI, 2013: 8-9). The GHI is an outcome indicator responsible for tracking the progress, or the failure of the reduction of hunger. It discloses information about the direct and indirect health consequences of hunger among the affected population. Immediate actions should address these consequences, according to their stage of severity.

---

5   The proportion of undernourished as a percentage of the population (data provided by the FAO).

6   The proportion of children younger than the age of five who are underweight (data provided by the WHO).

7   The mortality rate of children younger than the age of five (data provided by the UNICEF).

Although it considers three important aspects of hunger, double counting due to correlations among these aspects cannot be shunned and, therefore, attracts criticism (cf. Masset, 2011). For this index and other indices in general, there is a drawback of interpreting scores or a weighted set of indicators compiled into one index. Countries belonging to the same interval, for which also the same conclusion is drawn, the values of the used indicators can still differ widely from one another depending on the scores they hit. Results have to be interpreted with carefulness.

In 2012, the **Global Food Security Index (GFSI)** was developed and currently uses 27 indicators of three food security dimensions: Affordability[8], availability[9], quality and safety[10], (cf. EIU, 2013). The weight of the dimensions and indicators can be changed depending on their relevance. Data was either obtained from international organizations, or – If not available – constructed by internal country and economic experts. This establishes the first food security index comprising the most important and wide-range aspects of food security. A set of 107 countries from developing as well as developed world regions, have been selected, based on subjective criteria such as "regional diversity, economic importance, and size of population" (EIU, 2013: 30). Besides its comprehensive measurement, it is adjusted to the fluctuating food prices and, therefore, updated quarterly (cf. EIU, 2013). However, it is not clear on what basis FNS indicators are selected. Further, different policy actions and strategies require strategies to tackle the problem of food insecurity, and this will be difficult without a clear understanding of the factors that led to a certain state of food insecurity (cf. Pangaribowo, 2013).

The FAO uses, inter alia, the **Prevalence of Undernourishment (PoU)** indicator to estimate the extent of 'hunger' and monitor food security in the world. Undernourishment describes the circumstances under which individuals lack the ability to meet a sufficient dietary energy requirement, and consequently suffer from permanent insufficient food intake followed

---

8   "Measures the ability of consumers to purchase food, their vulnerability to price shocks, and the presence of programs and policies to support consumers when shocks occur" (EIU, 2012).

9   "Measures the sufficiency of the national food supply, the risk of supply disruption, national capacity to disseminate food, and research efforts to expand agricultural output" (EIU, 2012).

10   "Measures the variety and nutritional quality of average diets, as well as the safety of food" (EIU, 2012).

by chronic undernutrition. The energy requirement of a person depends on its body size, the level of physical activity and its current, and long-term health status (cf. FAO et al., 1985). Individuals are chronically undernourished when their *daily energy consumption* is lower than the threshold level: the Minimum Dietary Energy Requirement (MDER) (cf. FAO, 2013c). The PoU indicator comprises three assumptions, and the parameter estimates, which are necessary for the model based estimation of undernourishment, namely the individual dietary energy consumption, the distribution of energy consumption and the caloric threshold (cf. FAO, 2012c). The concept of the PoU indicator is not only based on observations but also on estimations due to the lack of reliable data. There are further elementary obstacles to determine a person's energy requirements by only observing the intake of calories. First of all, the dietary energy intake of a person is basically unobservable. Secondly, the individual metabolic absorption of food cannot be precisely assessed due to the interpersonal variations of nutritional requirements (cf. FAO, 2012c). Moreover, it is questionable to use calorie availability as a predictor for human development, nutrition satisfaction and productivity. Critics on this measuring method of food security derive from the essence of the nutrition capability approach. In 2011, the FAO's CFS *Round Table* on measuring food security, composed a suite of 26 indicators which relate to the four dimensions of FNS, and are further categorized into two groups of determinants and outcomes (cf. Appendix A)). Indicators have been chosen on the basis of available data for the period of time from 1990 until most recently 2012, which allows a meaningful comparison across countries, regions and time (cf. FAO, 2013b). The FAO food security database includes all countries and world regions, therefore, it represents the most comprehensive and unique database for any FNS analyses.

The USDA's Economic Research Service developed a **Food Security Assessment model** to estimate two types of food gaps. The *nutrition gap* sets the daily minimum caloric intake of 2,100 calories as baseline. Population below the baseline lacks the caloric requirements recommended by the FAO. The *distribution gap* looks at different income groups to achieve the minimum caloric requirement. A distribution gap exists if a given income group lacks food requirements. However, the disguised food distribution among the population in the first approach is addressed by the latter approach (cf. USDA, 2013).

Measurements and indicators of FNS struggle to capture a comprehensive picture of the FNS situation on different levels, and for the country, or regional specific purposes. Since the concept of FNS and its components itself are difficult to define, there is no claim to use one right measurement. It depends on the specific understanding of FNS and its dimensions, embedded in (1) the socio-organisational level, (2) the specific issues of the object on these levels, and (3) the limits of data collection.

Nevertheless, indicators can be ambiguous or unambiguous, since a certain state of FNS can indicate malnutrition but does not reveal the underlying causes of it. Consequently, there will always be an attribution gap between the theoretical construct FNS and the resulting outcomes, which have to be interpreted with caution.

2.4   Conclusion: The multidimensional concept of Food and Nutrition Security

The FNS concept evolved from the many attempts to find a rationale for persistent hunger and undernutrition in this world. Based on fundamental theories and the global discussion about solving world hunger, FNS has been defined as a problem of different magnitudes of sufficient supply, access to food, to health and nutrition. Since then, FNS has been elaborated as a multidimensional and complex concept. Despite these features, it helps to examine and to understand causes and consequences of particular issues on four different dimensions, availability, access, utilization and stability. These issues can also differ depending on the level of observation, the global, national or household level.

This holistic understanding of FNS and a detailed analysis of country specific issues regarding food and nutrition insecurity are perquisites to detect and implement respective policies. This analysis should not be narrowed by measuring methods that focus mainly on undernourishment and thereby ignoring the concept's multidimensional characteristic. Instead, the discourse of FNS should embrace the relationship and mutual influence of issues on different dimensions. Moreover, alongside the global approaches to FNS, the adequate means to improve the state of food and nutrition insecurity for households and individuals, can only be found in a national context. An international discussion on FNS, however, should not lose sight of the multidimensional and holistic characteristics of FNS.

Measuring and addressing problems of food and nutrition insecurity means to consider socio-economic, political, and environmental conditions under which these problems have developed. Particularly, it requires an examination on the national and the household level in a country or region specific context. Ultimately, it is important to detect the characteristics of national food systems and explore the relationship of policies on different socio-organisational levels, which form part of the complex and multidimensional comprehension of FNS.

Part II: Setting of the Research Object and Methodology

The Caribbean as a region and as individual countries has undergone profound social, political and economic changes in the last century. These changes shaped the diversity of these countries in the cultural, social and economic context. From the broad Caribbean region, a set of sample countries has been selected as the research object based on common socio-economic features. The Food and Nutrition Security concept serves to assess the current state of vulnerability to food and nutrition insecurity for these sample countries. The empirical-analytical approach by means of a cluster analysis is used to classify countries according to their state of vulnerability to food and nutrition insecurity. These findings serve to resume the analysis of implications deriving from the identified issues of food and nutrition insecurity in the Caribbean.

Key questions:

1. What are the underlying reasons for the current socio-economic situation in the Caribbean countries?
2. What does vulnerability mean in the context of Food and Nutrition Security and for the selected Caribbean countries?
3. What distinguishes countries and cluster of countries in their state of Food and Nutrition Security?

3. A socio-economic development analysis of the Caribbean

The Caribbean is one of the most vulnerable and diverse regions worldwide. It is often composed into the greater region of 'Latin America and the Caribbean' which in turn belongs to the American continent. The Caribbean holds one of the world's greatest systems of small islands. In terms of socio-economic development analysis, it is often aggregated to the greater region of Latin America, despite the significant dissimilarities among the countries and even within the Caribbean region itself. Hence, aggregations always require cautiousness in order to interpret any results. For Caribbean studies, a pre-analysis and definition of the countries of examination is indispensable. Therefore, a broad and significant analysis of the socio-economic development is completed in this chapter, which provides a basis for the selection of Caribbean countries for the further analysis.

The first section of this chapter provides essential background information on the history of the Caribbean region, which significantly influenced the socio-economic development of Caribbean nations. Embedded in the historical context, the development process of the respective Caribbean countries is observed from the beginning of the colonization period to their political independence. This elementary information about the history of the Caribbean is essential for an understanding of the reasons that led to the present socio-economic and demographic situation, and crucial to analyse its impacts on FNS in the region.

The second section 3.2 of this chapter discusses existing definitions of the Caribbean and narrows the Caribbean map based on common characteristics, deriving from shared historical events and socio-economic structures. In this context, chapter 3.3 critically reviews the different international classification schemes, based on the countries specific economic, social and demographic development. The results of the analysis of this chapter are the essential basis for any further examination on the FNS situation in the Caribbean.

3.1 History of the Caribbean and Caribbean development theories

The following chapter outlines the history of the Caribbean from its 'discovery' by Christopher Columbus in the 15th century till the 21st century. It is important to emphasize, that the countries of the Caribbean region share common historical experiences of colonization, slavery, economic exploitation and political domination. The historical events marked and shaped the Caribbean significantly in the way the region developed socially, politically and economically up to the 21st century.

> "The historical emphasis is not provided as […] 'passive' background material but as a concrete historical experience that informs the present which in many ways continues to provide meaning and significance for the people who inhabit the Caribbean region today" (Richardson, 1992: 3).

Therefore, it is indispensable to first outline the history of the Caribbean and explain the Caribbean countries' common and diverging geographical and socio-economic characteristics, in subchapter 3.1.1. The last subchapter 3.1.2 explores a range of development theories, which emanated in the Caribbean itself, trying to explain how and why internal disparities, persistent poverty and 'under-development', have emerged.

3.1.1 History of the Caribbean: From colonization to independence

When the New World was discovered, and the European nations conquered land and people in the yet to be discovered and underdeveloped world regions in the 15th century, the imperial powers imposed an economic concept based on the idea of mercantilism. Gaining economic and political power motivated former colonists to exploit gold reserves and other resources found in the conquered lands. The prevailing credo of the mercantilists in the 16th and 17th century proclaimed that the actual wealth of a 'first world' country resulted from excessive exploitation of land, people and resources. Consequently, battles were fought over territories in the name of kings and queens from England, Spain and the Netherlands. In 1625, Barbados became the first British colony in the Caribbean, followed by St. Kitts and Nevis in1628. In 1630 Antigua and Barbuda, Anguilla and the Virgin Islands were conquered by the British. Jamaica became the last occupied British colony in the region, in 1655. The British, Dutch and the French colonial powers obtained the control over the

Guianese and Central American part since the Spanish considered them as rather unattractive backyards (cf. Richardson, 1992).

At the beginning of the 17th century, colonization in the Caribbean was dominated by warfare between the European nations, notably Spain, England, France and the Netherlands. Meanwhile sugar cane cultivation spread throughout the region, beginning with its first extension by Spanish colonists in Santo Domingo on the island of Hispaniola (cf. Randall, 2009). Soon, sugar became the main export product for the increasing markets in Europe, grown and produced on the fruitful tropical soils in the Caribbean. European colonization and plantation foundation brought a wide range of seeds, plants and animals into the regions. The focus on the mono-cultural production of sugar cane left a serious ecological impact of natural destruction, mainly due to extensive forest clearance (cf. Richardson, 1992). In Barbados and St. Kitts, where the first British islands were introduced to plantation agriculture in 1640, the intensive production of plantation crops like cotton, sugarcane, and tobacco led to deforestation and depletion of native vegetation (cf. McGregor, 2011). The colonization not only transformed the region's economy and vegetation, but predominantly its agricultural sector, which was aimed to become a strong export-oriented sector. The agricultural production took place on the numerous plantations and was based on merely a few cash crops, dominantly sugar, coffee and tobacco. Later, further traditional export crops, such as bananas and cacao were initially cultivated by peasants on a small-scale and then on a large-scale – predominantly expanding in Dominica, St. Lucia and St. Vincent (cf. Moya Pons, 2007; Randall, 2009). The agricultural sector was of great importance, since it produced foodstuffs, beverages and tobacco, which served as a medium of exchange for imports from the metropolises.

The increase of mercantile production for external markets in the metropolis was achieved through the introduction of plantations in the colonies that were diligently controlled and administrated by the colony governments. International trade and market protection became the dominant economic policy strategy, with the aim to achieve a favourable balance of trade in the metropolis nations. Following this strategy, was meant to impose tariffs as trade barriers for imports of goods, in order to protect the domestic markets while building up state monopolies of manufactories. Particularly, Britain succeeded economic prosperity by capturing colonies and building up colony limited companies. The plantations on the islands, the forced plantation workers, and the produced agricultural output, accounted for the most valuable assets Britain possessed at that time. The essence of this profitable strategy is often described as a triangular trade between Europe, West Africa and the Americas. Required manufactured inputs produced in Europe were sent to West Africa, wherefrom forced slaves were shipped as labour inputs to the Caribbean and the Americas. In exchange tropical food, sugar and other raw material were transported back to Europe (cf. Richardson, 1992). This specific form of international trade and economic system contributed significantly to capital accumulation in the European metropolises, and established a basis for the succeeding industrialization, for which Britain was known as pioneer country.

While rivalries between the imperial powers continued in the 18th century, the 19th century was marked by political and social events that brought change to the economies in Europe as well as to the Caribbean region. On the British-Caribbean colonies, slave revolts began to arise, following the example set by the first, and most significant slave revolt in St. Dominque (later Haiti). The century was shaped by the current discussion over slavery. While massive labour import of West African slaves was initiated by the Spaniards in 1518, it later was dominated by the English, French and Dutch colonies. Slave revolts, emancipation of slaves and anti-slavery voices overseas finally led to a ban of the importation of slaves into Briton's colonies in 1807, following the final abolition of slavery in 1833, which became effective with the Abolition Act (cf. Randall, 2009).

Nevertheless, the plantation system, which refers to the „institutional arrangements surrounding the production and marketing of plantation crops" (Beckford, 1972: 8), perpetuated even in the beginning of the new era of industrialization and trade liberalization. Whereas capital flows alongside with new machinery and technology to cultivate export staples, were introduced. According to precursors of the classic liberalism like *David Ricardo,* the Caribbean should concentrate its available resources on the sugar production for the world markets, since the Caribbean states had comparative advantages in the primary production. Subsequently, free trade would benefit the trading partners, the primary exporters, as well as the *Metropolitan* import nations, which profited from low prices.

The only loser in the plantation system were the Caribbean plantation owners, who faced a shortage of labour force after emancipation, since freedmen and freedwomen could no longer be coerced to work for the planters (cf. Beckford, 1972; Best, 1968). When shortages of labour became perceivable even in the earnings for the colony administration, Britain decided to import indentured workers from its other colonies, such as

India, which later created a persistent and unique cultural diversity in the region. From 1838 until 1917 some 400,000 workers arrived mainly in British Guiana, Jamaica and Trinidad. The Dutch and the French colony administrations also imported workers from India to their colonies (cf. Richardson, 1992).

In the late 19th century the implemented international trade strategies increased the competition of other colonies for raw materials and primary products, such as unrefined sugar on the world markets. Additionally, the emerging sugar beet production in the European region was stimulated by subsidies for the industry and protectionism against competitors from the world market. Consequently, lower costs of production and increased productivity led to a crash of the world price for sugar in the 1880s (cf. Timms, 2008; Moya Pons, 2007). The sugar industries in the Caribbean were heavily afflicted by the drop in the price for sugar and, therefore, plantation owners cut their production of sugar since it became "cheaper to burn sugar cane than harvest it" (Washington Post, 1985). As a result of the economic crisis, poverty and high unemployment rates were widespread in the Caribbean region by the end of the 19th century. Population pressure alongside with unemployment forced migration within the Caribbean region to plantations where workers were paid higher salaries, or to the United States, Canada and Mexico in search of better living conditions (cf. Moya Pons, 2007). Concurrently, the introduction of other crops by peasantries reached a large-scale cultivation of cacao, coffee, tobacco and bananas, and achieved to maintain the importance of plantation systems and the reliance on cash crops for exports (cf. Moya Pons, 2007).

The following world recession in 1930 brought even more discontent to the region. Workers stroked and protested against poor working conditions throughout the Caribbean, leading to violent riots and turmoil. The call for more political freedom and better living conditions ended ten years later in the formation of workers and trade unions. Just a few years later, suddenly political parties emanated from these unions. Increasing pressure on the European powers for local control and political independence, finally led to a gradual process to grant the colonies self-government and full independence. Most of the countries gained its political freedom in the period from 1960 to 1980: Jamaica and Trinidad in 1962; in 1966, Barbados and the former British Guiana which became the independent republic of Guyana; The Bahamas in 1973, Grenada in 1974, Dominica in 1978, St. Vincent and the Grenadines and St. Lucia in 1979, Antigua and Barbuda and Belize (formerly British Honduras) in 1981, and last St. Kitts and Nevis in

1983 (cf. Richardson, 1992). Other countries in the region still remain mainly French and Dutch colonies. French Guiana, Guadeloupe, and Martinique form *départements d'outre mer* (French overseas departments) since 1946. The ABC-islands (Aruba, Bonaire, and Curaçao), Saba, St. Eustatius, and St. Marteen joined the kingdom of Netherlands in 1975 (cf. D'Agostino, 2009). Most independent countries, which formerly were governed under the British crown, are now part of the Commonwealth of Nations, a conglomerate of British former colonies.

3.1.2   Caribbean development theories and strategies

During the independence process and in the post-World War II period, the situation of Caribbean countries was precarious, since unemployment and growing poverty persisted, and impeded development. In order to explain the causes of 'underdevelopment' in the Caribbean region, expounding theories and possibly adaptive strategies to overcome these constraints emerged from economists within the region.

Caribbean industrialization and Lewis' Dual Economy Model

One of the most influential economists focusing his work on development theories to explain the causes and persistent structures of underdevelopment in the Caribbean was the Nobel laureate Sir Arthur Lewis. In his work, he proposed different models to explain underdevelopment through the well-known *Industrialization-by-Invitation* strategy for the Caribbean, and the *Dual Economy Model* (cf. Girvan, 2005). According to the latter model, the Caribbean economies are characterized by a dual economy; consisting of a large subsistence sector and a relatively small but productive capital sector. The subsistence sector is characterized by an unlimited supply of cheap labour, mostly engaged in the primary sector, e.g. agriculture. The excessive supply of cheap labour benefits the capital sector, which can easily grow and increase its profits (cf. Timms, 2008)."The result is a dual (national or world) economy, where one part is a reservoir of cheap labour for the other" (Lewis 1980: 3-4 cited in Girvan, 2005: 201).

    In the so-called 'Industrialization-by-Invitation model for development' Lewis suggested that, in the case of a dual economy, the initial focus should lie on manufacturing for exports using the surplus labour employed in the capital sector. This thought resulted from the *Ricardian theory* of comparative advantages, stating that countries, which have comparative advantages in the costs' productivity of one sector favour international trade (cf. Girvan, 2005). Moreover, if domestic capital is not available because national savings and income are low, then the foreign capital should be used temporarily for investment. By that time, the agricultural sector and other sectors of the economy start to benefit from the expansion of the capital sector in such a way that wages rise and subsequently create a higher demand for food. Lewis also found that a balanced growth in all sectors of the economy is necessary, for industrialization without the agricultural sector does not favour the economy, but would cause losses from rising food prices (cf. Lewis, 1954). Lewis' recommendations for industrialization and economic development did not result in 'developed' economies such as he aspired. In the Caribbean countries, where his strategy was entirely or just partly adopted, it created dependence on foreign capital for investment, imports of technology and potentially food imports (cf. Timms, 2008). When criticism of his theory arose, alternative development theories such as the 'Plantation Economy Theory' emerged. The main originators of this economic theory, George Beckford, Lloyd Best, Kari Levitt and Clive Y. Thomas were also Lewis' greatest critics.

Plantation Economy System and dependency

The *plantation economy theory* evolved simultaneously to the *dependencia* theories in Latin America in the 1960s. Congruently to Lewis's theory, the plantation economy theory explains the causes and the persisting structures of the 'underdeveloped' economies and societies of the Caribbean. The reasons for the backwardness of the Caribbean economies were found in the plantation system, which was installed in the Caribbean by the former *Metropolitan Economies* of the Europeans in the 17th century, and inhibited the cultivation of an integrated and independent development. The theory is embedded in the historical experiences and examines the reasons of the external dependency and the undiversified economies of the Caribbean (cf. Girvan, 2005).

George L. Beckford, Lloyd Best and Kari Polanyi Levitt, the economic thinkers and main precursors of the *plantation economy theory*, influenced intellectual thoughts and development in the Caribbean for decades. Beckford extensively explains the plantation economy system and examines the reasons for poverty and 'underdevelopment' in his comprehensive book *Persistent Poverty*. According to the 'Plantation Economy Theory', the plantation economy

> "[...] is the term we apply to those countries of the world where the internal and external dimensions on plantation system dominate the country's economic, social, and political structure and its relations with the rest of the world" (Beckford, 1972: 12).

Within the plantation system, an institutional framework was built, designed to combine resources, such as land, labour, capital, and operational tools such as management and technology. Resources remained under foreign ownership while production was orientated towards the overseas markets. Plantations were part of the world economic system producing almost solely for a *Metropolitan Centre* on which they were dependent (cf. Beckford, 1972). In the view of the Metropolitan countries, the plantation system was a successful and sophisticated export model for agricultural and primary products, and a "product of metropolitan capital and enterprise" (Beckford, 1972: 11).

According to Beckford (1972), the specificity of 'underdevelopment' derived from the misallocation of resources, causing malnutrition and poverty among the population in the colonies. Since the plantations could not absorb the abundance of labour force, and the land was under the monopolized possession of the owners, people lacked access to resources for their livelihoods. Under the condition that the best lands already were taken by the planters, and the restricted possibilities of finding work outside the plantations, the population was left with no choice of self-sufficiency or access to income and food (cf. Beckford, 1972).

Furthermore, Best (1968) argues, that the plantation production has not only led to poverty and undernutrition, but to an undiversified economy. The persistent dependency on the export of a few primary products resulted in an economy which is restricted to primary production and limited in its ability to subsequent processing of raw materials – the so-called *Muscovado Bias* (cf. Best, 1968). It is, therefore, nearly impossible for the *Hinterland* economies to transform its institutions and structures, in order to relieve themselves from dependency on exports and the traditional sector (cf. Best, 1968). To overcome underdevelopment and the one-sector dependency, the Plantation School suggested encouraging domestic agriculture production through protectionism, for at least a short period of time. Based on Best's argument, Beckford (1972) found that 'underdevelopment' can be overcome through structural change in the economic institutions (cf. Beckford, 1972).

In summary, the development of the Caribbean was dominated by the former *Plantation System* and its legacy. The different approaches and theory models argue unanimously, that the tenacious economic dependency on primary products for exports, and the legacy of the structures of the plantation systems led to poverty, inequality, to lack of access to land, and ownership of resources, unemployment and undernutrition. However, a comparison between Lewis' *Dual Economy Model and Industrialization* and the *Plantation Economy Model* shows that according to Lewis, economic development is possible through the shift of labour, whereas according to Best/Beckford/Levitt, an economic transformation is not possible without a fundamental structural change of institutions (cf. Table 1).

Table 1:   Comparison of main Caribbean development theories

	Dual Economy and Industrialization (Lewis)	Plantation Economy Model (Best/Levitt/Beckford)
Genesis	Classical *Ricardian*; aroused within the British Industrial Revolution	Structuralism; aroused within the Mercantilist era
Source of/reason for underdevelopment	Two-sector economy (modern/traditional); Surplus of labour in the traditional (agricultural) sector	Exploitation of Hinterland Economies; Muscovado Bias; Permanent dependency on the Metropolitan Economies
Consequences	Supply of labour absorbed in the capitalist (modern) sector at low wages which enables the economy to grow and 'develop'.	Surplus labour is not absorbed; Monopolization of land and misallocation of resources cause poverty and 'under-consumption' (*social costs*); *Hinterland Economies* are undiversified and dependent
Development/ Transformation Strategy	Industrialization-by-Invitation	Structural change of institutions

Source: own compilation based on Girvan (2005: 213)

3.2   Regional mapping and different classifications of the Caribbean

This chapter describes the evolvement of different definitions for the Caribbean region and countries. From this array of definitions, one is adopted for the purpose of further analysis in this thesis. Beyond the existing geological, geographical, political and historically influenced definitions, the second part of this section compares different common international classifications for the respective countries based on their methods of classification.

3.2.1 Regional mapping and a geographical definition of the Caribbean

The notion 'Caribbean' dates from the 15th century, when Christopher Columbus' on his first voyage reached the Antilles and its native inhabitants, whom he described as *Los Caribes*. Nonetheless, only in the 20th century the 'Caribbean' would become a term used to describe the region which comprises the Antilles, enclosed by the Central American land masses, and part of the North coast of South America (cf. Figure 7) (cf. Gaztambide-Géigel, 2004). The Antilles or *Antillas* (Spanish) compose the islands located in the Caribbean Sea, except for The Bahamas, which is located in the North Atlantic Ocean. The archipelago in the North consists of the Greater Antilles, including Cuba, the island of Hispaniola, which is politically divided into the Dominican Republic in the East and Haiti in the West, Jamaica, and Puerto Rico. The much smaller group of islands of the Antilles are the Lesser Antilles in the South, which again are subdivided into the southern located Windward Islands from Dominica, Martinique, Saint Lucia, Saint Vincent and the Grenadines, to Grenada. The western located Leeward Islands range from the United States Virgin Islands, the British Virgin Islands, Anguilla, Saint Martin – which is politically divided into a French and a Dutch part (Sint Marteen) – Saint-Barthélemy, Saba, Sint Eustatius, Saint Kitts and Nevis, Antigua and Barbuda, Montserrat, to Guadeloupe (cf. Britannica, 2013). Another broader perception of the geographical definition of the Caribbean region includes Central American mainland countries, the Bahamas, Turks and Caicos, Mexico's Yucatán Península, the Venezuelan and Colombian coast, as well as the three Guianas: Guyana, Suriname, and French Guiana. Before the 'Caribbean' was defined, the prevailing and oldest term to describe the region was the 'West Indies', which emerged from the false assumption that

Columbus had arrived in the Orient, and consequently named the islands *Las Indias*. It is used interchangeably with the term 'Caribbean' and refers to the entire island chain in the archipelago, including continental land masses, the Guianas and Belize.

Figure 7:   Map of the Caribbean region

Source: Encyclopædia Britannica Online (2014)

Another definition that appeared in the course of the United States (US)-geopolitical *Caribbean Basin Initiative* of the 1980s referred to the Caribbean as *Caribbean Basin*, which later was renamed to the *Greater Caribbean*. Mainly it comprises the entire basin of the Caribbean Sea, the islands states and the adjoining mainland countries, Venezuela, Colombia and Mexico. The purpose of the initiative, however, was to prevent a further spread of influence from the Soviet communism in Central America and the Caribbean, through economic development aid, preferential trade arrangements and other concessions for the region.

There has always been confusion about the definition and division of the Caribbean. Moreover, it is convenient to specify not only the term and its origin, but to understand the reasons for its present position in a global context.

However, "there is no one 'correct' definition" of the Caribbean, it rather depends on the subject of study (Girvan, 2001: 4). The definition adopted in this study, is the one proposition of Gaztambide-Géigel (2011), in which he refers to the 'insular Caribbean', synonymously with the West Indies, including the Bahamas, the two Guianas, Suriname, and Belize, based on their close historical and cultural heritages. The Latin Caribbean countries and overseas territories are excluded (cf. Gaztambide-Géigel, 2004). Therefore, this study focuses on the politically independent Caribbean countries and uses the term 'Caribbean' and 'Caribbean countries' interchangeably. Subsequently, 13 Caribbean countries are defined as the research objects for further analysis: Antigua and Barbuda, The Bahamas, Barbados, Belize, Dominica, Grenada, Guyana, Jamaica, St. Kitts and Nevis, St. Lucia, St. Vincent and the Grenadines, Suriname, and Trinidad and Tobago.

3.2.2 Different international development classifications of the Caribbean

Although the Caribbean countries have middle to high income levels, and human development in the region is ranked on a high level, poverty and inequality cannot be disguised, for they are present and impeding the development in certain areas (Stuart, 2006: 7). Even if there is no general concept or common understanding of development, on a global level, countries are classified based on different methods, indicators or criterions which determine a certain level of development or categorize them into groups, according to their level of development. The one-dimensional classification methods, which use only one criteria or indicator to classify countries, differ from the multi-dimensional methods which display the multi-facetted nature of development. The most common one-dimensional classification is set by the World Bank for an analytical classification of countries, based on the measure of per capita Gross National Income (GNI p.c.), which is calculated annually using the Atlas method. The GNI p.c. is considered a suitable variable, since the World Bank found a steady relationship between health and poverty related indicators of "such as poverty incidence and infant mortality" (The World Bank, 2013c), and the GNI p.c.. On the operational level the partition serves the World Bank's International Bank for Reconstruction and Development (IBRD) to decide on a threshold of GNI p.c., if a country is eligible to obtain a credit from the Bank (cf. Nielsen, 2011). Under this analytical and operational classification, countries are basically categorized into three groups: the high-income economies, the middle-income economies, and the low-income economies. The middle-income economies are further sub-divided into groups, the lower- and upper-middle-income economies. Countries with a GNI p.c. of US$ 1,035 or less are labelled low-income economies, the middle-income country group is sub-divided into the lower-middle-income economies with a GNI p.c. from US$ 1,036 to US$ 4,085, and the upper-middle-income economies have a GNI p.c. from US$ 4,086 to the threshold of US$ 12,615. The last group consists of the high-income economies with a GNI p.c. from US$ 12,616 (cf. The World Bank, 2013b). According to this classification scheme, the Caribbean countries are divided into three groups as follows:

WORLD BANK CLASSIFICATION FOR SELECTED CARIBBEAN COUNTRIES

Lower-middle-income economies: Guyana
Upper-middle-income economies: Belize, Dominica, Grenada, Jamaica, St. Lucia, St. Vincent and the Grenadines, Suriname
High-income economies: Antigua and Barbuda (since July 2013), The Bahamas, Barbados, St. Kitts and Nevis, Trinidad and Tobago
(cf. The World Bank, 2013b)

The majority of these countries are placed in the middle-income economies group with a GNI p.c. in 2011 ranging from US$ 3,050 (Guyana) to US$ 7,830 (Suriname). An interpretation of this classification is difficult because the indicator reflects economic capacity and 'development' and does not necessarily reflect the development status or the distribution of income within a country. Nevertheless, the World Bank itself often uses the term developing countries for low- and middle income economies, and developed countries synonymous for the high-income economies. This implies that eight out of 13 Caribbean countries have a lower level of economic capacity and 'development', and hence a lower level of well-being or development than the four Caribbean high-income and 'developed' economies. Based on this analytical classification it is not possible to make any reasonable conclusion about implications on different dimensions of development for the Caribbean countries. Neither does it disclose any distribution of the income within a country and among different income groups. Due to this analytical classification, Caribbean countries find it difficult to access development finance.

However, further classification methods used by the UNDP are based on a broader multi-dimensional understanding of development by including social and demographic indicators to its calculations. According to one of its classifications, the Caribbean countries are categorized as Small Island Developing States (SIDS). The definition 'SIDS' comprises small islands or low-lying coastal countries[11], which are due to their geographical location and economic situation, highly vulnerable to environmental and natural shocks. These specific characteristics of the SIDS are considered to impose constraints on economic and social development. The classification was first recognized by the international community at the *UN Conference on Environment and Development* (UNCED) held in 1992 in Rio de Janeiro, Brazil, identifying the SIDS special needs in the plan of action for sustainable development, captured in the Agenda 21, Chapter 17 (cf. UN, 1992). Followed by the first *Global Conference on Sustainable Development of SIDS* in 1994 and the *Mauritius International Meeting* in 2005, the *Barbados Plan of Action* together with the extended *Mauritius Strategy of Implementation* finally identified 19 priority areas to achieve sustainable development of SIDS. This can be realised through certain strategies and policies on national, regional and international level (cf. UNCSD, 2013). Further, *The Caribbean Regional Synthesis Report* for the *Third International Conference on SIDS* in 2014 emphasizes the peculiar constraints the Caribbean countries face, like climate change and environmental issues, limitation and degradation of natural resources, economic growth and financial resource constraints, and rising insecurity deriving from crime and violence. It further recognizes new challenges for the sustainable development of the Caribbean SIDS, such as Non-communicable Diseases (NCDs), the financial and economic crises, and the exploitation and management of oceans i.a. (cf. ECLAC, 2013a). Hence, the classification of SIDS emphasizes the particular social and economic structure of the countries and, therefore, enables to apply suitable strategies to address their special needs on a regional and national level.

---

11   Although Belize, Suriname and Guyana are not an island, vulnerability studies showed that the low-lying coast to sea level rise is considered to cause vulnerability (source: vulnerability assessments for the respective countries).

Still, the SIDS classification is not based on specific indicators. For further analysis in this study it has been recognized as being satisfactory, since the particular characteristics and needs of the countries are definite through this grouping.

A broader country classification method is based on the Human Development Index (HDI) constructed by the UNDP. As already outlined in chapter 2.1.2, according to the UNDP's understanding of human development the index is composed of three core elements: living standards, education, and health. Each of the dimensions is measured by a respective indicator: the GNI p.c. is used for the living standards; the mean of years of schooling and the expected years of schooling reflect the educational level and life expectancy at birth is used to measure health (cf. UNDP, 2013b). The index is ranged between 0 and 1; accordingly a higher index suggests a higher level of development. Hence, countries are classified into very high, high, medium and low human development by the HDI rank. In the recent *Human Development Report* 2013, the Caribbean countries are ranged as follows:

HUMAN DEVELOPMENT RANKING FOR SELECTED CARIBBEAN COUNTRIES

Very high human development: Barbados

High human development: The Bahamas, Grenada, Antigua and Barbuda, Trinidad and Tobago, Dominica, St. Kitts and Nevis, St. Vincent and the Grenadines, Jamaica, St. Lucia

Medium human development: Belize, Guyana, and Suriname

(cf. UNDP, 2013b)

In comparison, the World Bank classification based on the GNI p.c. which is reflected in the HDI, the additional health and education indicators influence the level of development just marginal. After all, the concept of development stays unclear and requires the inclusion of a broader range of indicators, depending on the analytical or operational context. For the continuative analysis of social and economic development in the Caribbean, it is necessary to take a look at the various indicators that designate the special characteristics and development constraints of Caribbean SIDS.

3.3   *Economic, social and demographic structure of the Caribbean*

The many attempts to merge the countries of the Caribbean into one single or various groups of countries, whether for geopolitical or economic reasons, have been a difficult challenge due to the high diversity and heterogeneity among the countries. Not only that the geological formations of the islands and mainland states, their size, and vegetation differ widely from each other, but the social, cultural, political, and economic features form a unique mosaic that distinguishes the region from other world regions. Perhaps, these specific characteristics unify the countries more than they separate them. At the same time, this uniqueness is also perceptible in the economic, social and demographic constraints and structural challenges.

> "Caribbean societies have undergone dramatic social and economic transformations in recent decades raising the standard of living and improving infrastructural development, yet large numbers of the sub-region's population continue to face rising levels of poverty, hunger and malnutrition. While the sub-region is ranked highly in terms of human development, poverty and inequality remain serious development challenges" (Stuart, 2006: 1).

These particular challenges have a significant impact on the outcome of FNS, which is analysed in the forthcoming chapter 4.1. For the purpose of identifying the main obstacles, the following chapter examines the prevalent economic and social settings of the countries. Economic and socio-demographic features partially ensue from historical and geographic characteristics of the Caribbean countries.

The first subchapter presents an overview of the current state of development related social and demographic indicators, highlighting important issues. The second subchapter analysis the current economic structure of the Caribbean countries and compares their particular performances in several economic and finance related issues. Data and information on these topics reflects the recent developments and structures of the countries.

However, it should be noted that the analysis goes as far as data is available for the respective countries, and as far as this information is relevant for further analysis in this thesis. Due to the fact that data availability for the selected countries is limited, and data is not frequently or recently collected, various data sources are used to complete this analysis. The main research data in this chapter is drawn from the World Bank's World Development Indicators (WDI), the UNDP's International Human

Development Indicators, the United Nations (UN) Department of Economic and Social Affairs, the World Population Prospect Population Data, the Economic Commission of Latin America and the Caribbean (ECLAC) statistical database CEPALSTAT, the Caribbean Development Bank (CDB) and the Caribbean Community (CARICOM) Secretariat Regional Statistics.

3.3.1 A social and demographic overview

The social and demographic overview of the Caribbean countries serves to detect different specifications of social and demographic development. Main important and relevant socio-demographic indicators describe the current state of the population and their socio-economic status.

Demographic trends

Due to its colonial history, the Caribbean is characterized by a highly diverse ethnic mixture. African, Indian, French, Spanish, Dutch and English immigrants shaped the countries cultures and religions throughout the history until the present. Based on the legacy of the colonial history, English is the official language in the majority of the countries, except for the Dutch-speaking country Suriname. Migration flows to, and from the Caribbean countries not only created multiculturalism, but also influenced the change in population numbers.

In 2010, the total population of the sample countries constituted 6.9 million people, inhabiting 435,056 km^2 (squared kilometres), which results in an estimated population density of 15.9 people per km^2 (own calculations based on CARICOM, 2013c; UN, 2013). However, the geographical size of the Caribbean countries does not naturally correlate with population numbers. While the majority of 40% of the Caribbean population lives in Jamaica on an area of 10.991 km^2, only a quarter of this population, 11% lives on the largest island Guyana, which has a size of 21.4970 km^2. The smallest part of the total Caribbean population, just 0.8% lives on the smallest islands of 269 km^2 in St. Kitts and Nevis (own calculations based on CARICOM, 2013c; UN, 2013). Consequently, population density is unequally distributed within the countries. As shown in Table 2, the highest population density can be found in Barbados with over 654 people per km^2, and the lowest in Guyana with just over 4 people per km^2 (own calculations based on CARICOM, 2013, UN, 2013).

From 2000 to 2010, the annual average population growth rate for the selected Caribbean countries was relatively low at 0.9%, showing a declining trend. In this period of time, Belize had the highest annual average population growth rate of 3%, whereas St. Vincent and the Grenadines had the lowest increase of this rate, by just 0.1% (cf. The World Bank, 2013d). (own calculations based on UN, 2013). In comparison, the current 2012 average population growth for Latin America and the Caribbean region is 1% (cf. The World Bank, 2013d).

As a comparison between the rural and the urban areas shows, higher population growth rates are registered in urban areas in the Caribbean. Urban and rural growth rates vary widely among the countries, and even reach negative rates. The average annual population growth rate of the urban population for the 13 Caribbean countries in the period of time from 2000 to 2010, is 0.8%, while the growth rate of the rural population is slightly lower at 0.6% (own calculations based on CEPALSTAT, 2013). Continuing urbanization and population growth rates are the main factors which put pressure on new housing, employment opportunities and provision of social services, particularly in Caribbean countries of more limited geographical surface and fewer resources for providing its population with these needs.

Table 2:   Socio-demographic indicators, Caribbean countries, 2010/2011

	Total population (2011)	Average population growth rate p.a. (2000–2010)	Urban population (in % of total population) (2011)	Total land area (sqkm)	Population density (people/km²) (2011)	Under 5 mortality rate per 1,000 live births (2011)	Net primary enrolment rate (2011)
Antigua and Barbuda	88,152	1.2	29.9	442	199.4	10.2	86.0
The Bahamas	366,331	1.9	84.3	13,939	26.3	17.2	97.8[a]
Barbados	281,804	0.5	44.4	431	653.8	18.8	95.1[c]
Belize	316,280	2.6	44.8	22,966	13.8	18.8	97.4
Dominica	71,401	0.2	67.2	750	95.2	12.9	98.4[b]
Grenada	105,074	0.3	39.2	345	304.6	13.8	97.5[b]
Guyana	790,882	0.5	28.4	214,970	3.7	36.3	82.7
Jamaica	2,706,500	0.6	52.1	10,991	246.2	17.3	82.4[a]
St. Kitts and Nevis	52,971	1.4	32.0	269	196.9	9.5	87.3
St. Lucia	179,271	1.2	17.6	616	291.0	17.9	88.1
St. Vincent and the Grenadines	109,357	0.1	49.3	389	281.1	23.7	98.5[a]
Suriname	529,761	1.2	69.7	163,820	3.2	21.4	92.8
Trinidad and Tobago	1,333,082	0.5	13.7	435,056	260.0	21.3	97.4[a]

Note: a 2010, b 2009, c 2008
Source: own compilation. Total population: The World Bank (2013d); Population growth: UN (2013); Total land area: CARICOM (2013c); Population density: own calculations based on The World Bank (2013d); Life expectancy: The World Bank (2013d) Child mortality, Primary enrolment: UNSD (2013a)

The slightly declining population growth rates correspond to the persistent negative trend of the net migration rate in the Caribbean countries. The net migration rate is the result of number of immigrants minus the number of emigrants and is thereby included in the population growth. Figure 8 shows that the average net migration rate for the Caribbean countries for which recent data is available has been persistently negative from 1990 to 2015. The highest negative level of net migration has been observed in the five year period from 1990 to 1995 with 221,421 people migrating. In the later period from 2010 to 2015 this figure is expected to improve to a lower negative level of 122,794 people (cf. The World Bank, 2013d).

Figure 8:   Average net migration, Caribbean countries, 1990-2015*

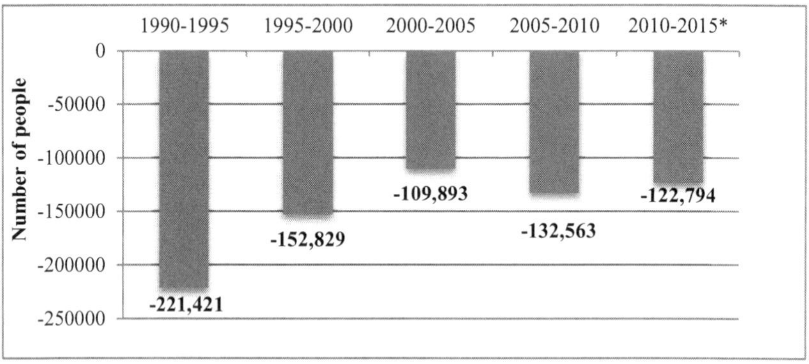

Note: *projections; no data available for Dominica and St. Kitts and Nevis
Source: own compilation. The World Bank (2013d)

Peoples' urge to migrate is associated with economic, political and social reasons and does not only play a role in the context of demographic development of the population. Ever since the emancipation movement in the Caribbean, people were allowed to move freely, and workers became motivated to migrate in search for better paid employment opportunities. In the course of the rise of the energy exploitation sector in Trinidad and Tobago, the twin-islands became a prosperous destination for workers from the nearby countries. Whereas the waves of migration have changed their directions, the original reason for migration, the pursuit of better employment opportunities, remained the same until today. In 2011, total remittances to the Caribbean countries had an amount of US$ 2.9 billion (own calculations based on The World Bank, 2013d). Especially in the case of Jamaica and Guyana, remittances count as major transnational inflow of capital, accounting for 15% of their GDP respectively (cf. The World Bank, 2013d). The United States of America (USA), Canada, the United Kingdom (UK), and the Netherlands are the most attractive destinations for migrants and, therefore, the biggest sender of remittances to the region (cf. Boswell, 2009; The World Bank, 2013a).

Education and Health

In the context of human development, the Caribbean countries have most successfully improved in the health and education status of its population. These achievements can be traced by looking at the Millennium Development Goals (MDGs). The eight goals were set at the United Nations Millennium Declaration in 2000 and signed by 189 UN member states (cf. UNSD, 2013a). The signatory countries aim to reduce poverty and hunger (MDG 1), improve the access to health and education (MDG 2 to 6), and achieve sustainable development through global partnership (MDG 7 and 8) by 2015. To assess the progress over the period from 1990 to 2015, the goals have been divided into 21 targets whose progress is measured by 60 indicators. The achievements in education are reflected in the net enrolment rates in primary education[12] which In the Caribbean countries exceed 90% in eight of the examined countries; the other five countries reach levels between 80% and 90% (cf. Table 2).

Further significant progress in the MDG achievements has been made in the health situation, reflected by the indicator 'under-five mortality rate' (MDG 4). The child mortality rate per 1,000 live births for children under five years of age, declined in nearly all the selected countries by over 50% between 1990 and 2011, except for St. Kitts and Nevis and Belize where progress has been rather slow. Barbados experienced even a reverse trend of an increased rate over 10% in the same period of time. With better access to health and healthcare services, life expectancy reached a relatively high level, an average of 74 years (cf. CEPALSTAT, 2013).

Despite the successful health outcomes in the past 20 years, progress in reducing communicable diseases like HIV/AIDS, is still halting. Among the Caribbean countries for which data is available, The Bahamas and Belize have the highest estimated HIV prevalence rate among the population aged 15 to 49 years at 3% (global rank 24) and 2% (global rank 26) (cf. UNAIDS, 2013). Data on the prevalence of HIV/AIDS for all 13 Caribbean countries is difficult to assess and, is quite insufficient. The United Nations General Assembly Special Session (UNGASS) on *HIV/AIDS Country Progress Reports,* however, discloses a worrying trend that the

---

12   The net primary enrolment rate refers to the number of children of primary school age enrolled in primary education as a percentage of the total children in the same school age (cf. UNSD, 2013b).

numbers of people living with HIV in six Caribbean countries[13] increased since the 1980s (cf. UNAIDS, 2013).

In addition to the already heavy burden of HIV/AIDS, the Caribbean countries are challenged by the increase of the (chronic) Non-communicable Diseases (NCDs) epidemic. NCDs are non-transmittable diseases such as cardiovascular disease, cancers, chronic respiratory diseases and diabetes. Further analysis on this issue has been conducted in chapter 6.

Poverty and Inequality

As described in the previous subchapter, the Caribbean countries have relatively high levels of development, measured by the GNI p.c. and the HDI. Poverty is one dimension of the multidimensional nature of development, often defined as a status of human deprivation from the lack of access to basic needs such as food, water, and shelter. Based on this understanding, poverty is a multidimensional concept. Depending on the definition and interpretation of poverty it allows different measurements to reflect either one or several of its dimensions. Due to a lack of information and data on different components of poverty, this study adopts the most common and widely used *international poverty line*, a one-dimensional income-poverty indicator. The international poverty line is defined at US$ 1.25 a day, expressed in Purchasing Power Parity (PPP) terms and, therefore, enabling comparisons across countries. The poverty headcount ratio indicates the percentage of the population living below the poverty line of US$ 1.25 and therefore, assesses the magnitude of poverty within a country. World Bank data on this indicator is only available for a small number of Caribbean countries for random years between 1990 and 2004. Poverty rates differ widely across these countries from 0.2% to 21%. In Jamaica, the headcount ratio declined from 1% in 1990 to 0.2% in 2004. Whereas in Guyana and Belize, poverty has seen a gradual increase (cf. The World Bank, 2013d). However, a meaningful inter-temporal comparison between the Caribbean countries is not possible on the basis of too few data points available for this time-series.

---

13   There is no official data available for Antigua and Barbuda, Dominica, Grenada, St. Kitts and Nevis, St. Lucia, and St. Vincent and the Grenadines.

Poverty data is also collected on national levels, using different measuring methods. National poverty data is usually collected through poverty assessments. Due to the fact that these assessments in the Caribbean countries lack an adequate and sufficient data collection, the Caribbean Development Bank (CDB) supports the countries of Antigua and Barbuda, Barbados, Belize, Dominica, Grenada and St. Kitts and Nevis, and St. Lucia to prepare *Country Poverty Assessment* (CPA) reports. Based on consumption data, national poverty lines are established, which "reflect the situation in a specific country at a certain point of time" (ECLAC, 2009: 192). However, poverty indicators based on the national poverty line can neither be compared across countries, nor can these indicators be used for inter-temporal comparisons. That is because poverty assessments are not undertaken very frequently, and poverty lines are usually adjusted over time, as they are measured based on consumption data.

Table 3 presents the most recent data available for two poverty indicators, the indigence line, the poverty headcount ratio, and the *Gini coefficient* in the selected Caribbean countries retrieved from the CPAs and additional surveys. The *indigence line* is understood as the proportion of people living in extreme poverty. It refers to the severe state of poverty when people can merely meet their basic nutritional requirements; therefore it is also called the *food poverty line*. The poverty headcount index here is specified as the percentage of the population living below the national poverty line. Although, the values of the selected indicators are not comparable across the Caribbean countries, the headcount ratio is relatively high in all 13 countries.

Additionally, the Gini coefficient is a useful indicator to measure the equality or inequality in income distribution for the population. It ranges between 0 representing perfect equality and 1, indicating the maximal inequality in the income distribution within the population. The highest inequality level is reached by The Bahamas with a Gini coefficient of 0.57, whereas the gap between rich and poor is lowest in Guyana with a Gini coefficient of 0.48. Thus, high poverty and indigence and a relatively low Gini coefficient in Guyana leads to the assumption that the average per capita income attains only a low level.

Table 3:   **National poverty data, Caribbean countries, respective CPA/report years**

	Share of population below indigence line (in %)	Poverty headcount ratio (in %)	CPA/ report year	Gini coefficient
Antigua and Barbuda	3.7	18.3	2007	0.48
The Bahamas	n/a	9.3	2001	0.57
Barbados	3.2	19.3	2010	0.47
Belize	16.0	31.0	2009	0.42
Dominica	3.1	28.8	2009	0.44
Grenada	2.4	37.7	2008	0.37
Guyana	18.6	36.1	2011	0.35[c]
Jamaica	n/a	17.6	2010	0.37[d]
St. Kitts and Nevis	1.4	21.8	2007/08	0.40
St. Lucia	1.6	28.8	2005/06	0.42
St. Vincent and the Grenadines	2.9	30.2	2007/2008	0.40
Suriname	n/a	7.5[a]	2013[b]	n/a
Trinidad and Tobago	n/a	6.2[a]	2012[b]	n/a

Note: [a] Multidimensional Poverty Index; [b] Human Development Atlas Suriname; [c] 2006; [d] 2009

Source: own compilation. CDB (2006), CDB (2007), CDB (2008), CDB (2009a), CDB (2009b), CDB (2012), CSO Trinidad and Tobago (2012), PIOJ (2012), UNDP (2013a)

Since data on poverty for the Caribbean is inconsistent or not comparable, it is important to consider the broad understanding of poverty as a multi-dimensional concept in different aspects. In the economic context, poverty results from the paucity of opportunities to generate income. In the Caribbean, high unemployment rates may also translate into high poverty rates and inequality levels. According to the Economic Commission of Latin America and the Caribbean (ECLAC), unemployment rates increased between 2007 and 2011 in the aftermath of the 2008/09 economic and financial crisis. In 2007, the highest unemployment rate was registered in St. Lucia at 14%, which increased to 21% in 2010. Unemployment rates in the Bahamas nearly doubled in the same period of time from 8% to 15%, and Jamaica also scored high rates of 12% in 2010 (cf. Alleyne et al., 2013). Data on unemployment rates is insufficient, and only available for few Caribbean countries, which limit a detailed assessment on this subject.

3.3.2 Structure of the economies and economic vulnerability

The following subchapter examines the main economic indicators, which reflect the recent economic performance and the constraints that hinder economic stability in the Caribbean countries. In addition, it examines the causes of economic vulnerability, resulting from the countries' susceptibility to external shocks.

Economic structure and economic growth

The Caribbean economies share various common characteristics and structures. They are open economies widely export-orientated, and mainly dominated by their services sectors. This narrow economic diversity and high transportation costs negatively influence economic growth and investment in the Caribbean. Furthermore, high dependence on foreign markets for goods and capital, and high financial debt levels make Caribbean economies vulnerable to external shocks.

Data on recent economic performances provides evidence for these presumptions. Due to their high dependence on external markets, the Caribbean countries were highly affected by the 2008/09 financial, economic and fuel crises. The main source of a vast bulk of capital inflows comes in form of export earnings, tourists' expenditures and remittances, which cause a high dependence on foreign capital. This financial and economic dependency becomes evident by looking at the GDP as main indicator of economic performance. Overall economic growth, constituting on just a few dominant economic sectors, decelerated significantly in the Caribbean countries in the course of the economic and financial crises in 2008/09. Figure 9 displays a retrospective view on the development of the aggregated GDP in absolute values, in million US$, and on the GDP growth rate in the Caribbean countries. While the aggregated GDP in absolute terms has been steadily increasing, the GDP growth rate, measured as the annual change rate of the aggregated GDP, shows a volatile development over the period of time from 2000 to 2011. From its highest level of 9% in

2006, the GDP growth rate abruptly dropped to its lowest level of -4% in 2009 (cf. The World Bank, 2013d). This decline resulted from the economic and financial crisis in 2008/09, which shocked the international markets for capital, goods and services. In 2009, the worst affected countries by this sharp decline of the GDP growth were Antigua and Barbuda with -12%, Grenada with -7% and St. Kitts and Nevis with -7% of negative GDP growth. After 2009, GDP growth recovered and reached an overall rate of 2% in 2012 (cf. The World Bank, 2013d). However, due to persistent weak economic performance of the USA and the European region, the Caribbean economies are merely slowly recovering from the crisis (cf. ECLAC, 2013b).

Figure 9:   GDP growth rate (in %) and aggregated GDP (in constant 2005 US$), Caribbean countries, 1990-2011

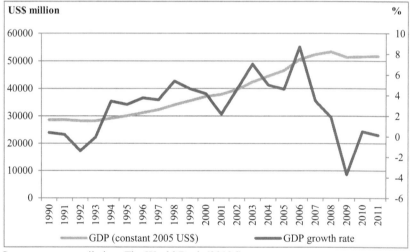

Source: own compilation. The World Bank (2013d)

In the Caribbean countries, economic growth mainly depends on the development of the countries' respective leading sector of the economy. Figure 10 presents the distribution of the economic sectors among the country's GDP for the most recent year for which data is available. This compilation of data shows that the Caribbean economies depend widely on the services sector[14] which is the largest contributor to GDP in all 13 countries. In 2010, The Bahamas share of services value added GDP, heads the figure with 97%, predominated by travel and tourism, and financial services. The second important sector, manufacturing[15] plays a minor role in all Caribbean countries but is even more significant in Suriname and Trinidad and Tobago, each constituting a share of GDP of 23%. The mining and quarrying sector[16] plays only an important role in few Caribbean countries. It is the second largest sector in Trinidad and Tobago, where it accounts for 33% of its GDP, due to its important oil and natural gas extraction industries. In Guyana, a mineral rich country, the mining and quarrying sector is dominated by mining and processing of diamonds, gold, and bauxite, contributing with 16% to its GDP. The extraction and processing of bauxite, alumina, gold, and oil also play a significant role in the mining and quarrying sector in Suriname, contributing 8% of its GDP. The agricultural sector[17] contributes to a marginal part in the majority of the Caribbean countries, except for Belize, Dominica, Guyana where it contributes to 13%, 14%, and 18% of each country's GDP, respectively (cf. CARICOM, 2013c).

---

14   Services include construction, distribution, financial services, government services, hotels and restaurants, transportation and communication, personal and community services, and other general services (cf. CARICOM, 2012).

15   Manufacturing is classified according to the International Standard Industrial Classification (ISIC) (cf. CARICOM, 2012).

16   Mining and quarrying are classified according to the International Standard Industrial Classification (ISIC) (cf. CARICOM, 2012).

17   Agriculture includes forestry, fishing and hunting (cf. CARICOM, 2012).

Figure 10:   Structure of GDP (in % of country's GDP), Caribbean countries, 2010

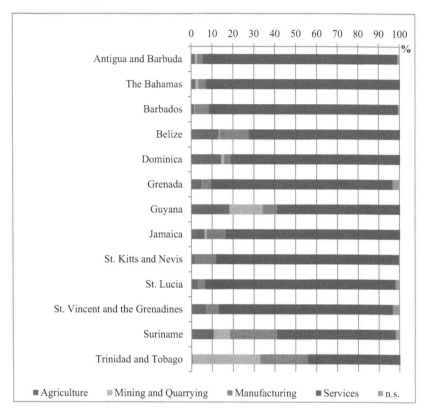

Note: n.s. = not specified
Source: own compilation. CARICOM (2012)

Due to falling prices for traditional agricultural export products and the loss of preferential access to international markets, the economic importance of the agricultural sector in the majority of the Caribbean countries declined and lost its attraction as employment opportunity. Conversely, the travel and tourism sector has emerged as the most attractive and lucrative sector, as well as the largest source of employment. In 2011, 581,500 employees worked in the travel and tourism sector in the

Caribbean countries[18]. Table 4 represents data of selected travel and tourism indicators. In Antigua and Barbuda, 72% of its total labour force has been employed in travel and tourism services, and expenditures of international tourists made up for the highest share of total exports of 80%. Notably, the travel and tourism subsector is absorbing a large part of the total labour force. Furthermore, this subsector is the major export industry in the majority of the Caribbean countries, indicated by the visitor exports as a percentage of total exports. The visitor exports account for at least 50% in seven countries. In the other Caribbean countries, such as Suriname, it merely contributes 1% to its total exports, resulting in a minor source of employment for the population, which hires just 4,900 employees, making up 3% of its total employment (cf. WTTC, 2013).

---

18   No data available for Trinidad and Tobago.

Table 4:   Travel and tourism indicators, Caribbean countries, 2011

	Total employment in travel and tourism	Employment in travel and tourism as % of total employment	Visitor exports as % of total exports
Antigua and Barbuda	19,600	71.8	80.2
The Bahamas	93,800	56.1	63.0
Barbados	49,300	38.4	60.3
Belize	39,500	29.8	27.9
Dominica	9,600	27.7	59.2
Grenada	8,800	19.0	51.0
Guyana	25,500	9.0	5.7
Jamaica	287,500	24.7	46.4
St. Kitts and Nevis	5,400	22.6	41.0
St. Lucia	29,100	40.6	56.3
St. Vincent and the Grenadines	8,500	19.8	50.7
Suriname	4,900	2.7	2.8
Trinidad and Tobago	n.a.	n.a.	n.a.

Note: n.a. = not available
Source: own compilation. WTTC (2013)

According to Thacker, Acevedo and Perrelli (2012), tourism is the major factor that has a positive effect on economic growth in the Caribbean and can even contribute to a reduction of growth volatility (cf. Nita Thaker, 2012). This would explain why most of the Caribbean countries adopted tourism as a successful development strategy, thereby benefiting from comparative advantages of this economic subsector. In this context, Lewis' theory gives an explanation for the economic shift from the traditional (agricultural) sector to the modern (tourism) sector in the Caribbean. As his theory was described previously in chapter 3.1.2, he assumed that 'development' occurs, when the re-allocation of workforce from the traditional, or agricultural sector to the modern industrial, or in this case, services sector induces a structural economic change. Whereas for Lewis this sectoral shift of resources would have meant progress or economic 'development', for the Plantation Economy School 'under-development' in

Caribbean economies persists unless structural change reduces external dependency and leads to more diversified economies (cf. ECLAC, 2013c). The Caribbean countries, however, have not experienced a significant structural change but merely a shift from the external dependent agriculture sector to the dominated services sector. Consequently, the countries are still afflicted by the persistent economic dependency on one single export sector which disregards the importance of diversification. The strong economic focus on one single sector and low levels of economic diversification create not only economic dependency, but vulnerability to external shocks. Ultimately, these shocks can adversely affect other sectors of the economy, which are directly or indirectly coupled to the leading export sector.

Trade performance

The previous data shows that for the majority of the countries, travel and tourism – as economic subsector of the services sector – is largely contributing to the total exports in the majority of the Caribbean countries. Table 5 shows that, in 2011, the services sector balance was overall positive, except for Suriname, which reached a deficit of US$ 361.71 million and Guyana with a deficit of US$ 136.11 million. This deficit is due to its lower contribution to overall exports in these economies. The Bahamas in contrary reaches the highest surplus of the services balance by US$ 1.34 billion due to the high contribution of the tourism sector to its total exports (cf. CEPALSTAT, 2013). While the majority of the Caribbean countries have a strong export services sector, the balance of goods discloses negative figures for all countries, except for the primary commodity producers, Suriname, and Trinidad and Tobago. Suriname generates a surplus of US$ 787.6 million and Trinidad and Tobago of US$ 5.43 billion, which is mirrored in their positive current account balance[19]. The current account balance comprises the goods and the services balance plus net primary and secondary income. Whereas Jamaica has the highest and most distressing deficit in the goods balance with US$ 4.26 billion, contributing to the

---

19   The current account balance comprises the goods and the services balance plus net income and current transfers.

highest current account deficit among the Caribbean countries (cf. CEPALSTAT, 2013).

Table 5: **Trade balances (in current US$ million), Caribbean countries, 2011**

	Goods balance	Services balance	Current account balance
Antigua and Barbuda	-374.57	270.67	-117.69
The Bahamas	-2132.11	1338.62	-1065.71
Barbados	-1255.05	827.73	-505.79
Belize	-170.93	168.37	-16.88
Dominica	-166.31	89.02	-71.35
Grenada	-258.14	58.83	-207.01
Guyana	-641.44	-136.11	-372.25
Jamaica	-4257.50	669.80	-2109.70
St. Kitts and Nevis	-178.28	57.84	-103.48
St. Lucia	-422.16	177.58	-243.88
St. Vincent and the Grenadines	-248.86	55.00	-198.88
Suriname	787.60	-361.71	251.10
Trinidad and Tobago	5433.00	506.40	2898.59

Source: own compilation. CEPALSTAT (2013)

In 2011, the slowdown of the global economy affected particularly the services producers among the Caribbean countries. Their existing trade balance deficits augmented due to the persistent high commodity prices of oil and gas, which triggered higher costs for imports of goods. Commodity producers, such as Suriname and Trinidad and Tobago benefited from higher commodity prices and were able to rebound the higher costs for imports of goods through higher export earnings, resulting in positive trade balances (cf. Alleyne et al., 2013). Due to its primary exports of mineral commodities, Suriname offset its negative services balance and achieved a positive balance on goods and services of US$ 452.90 million. Trinidad and Tobago was the only country with a surplus in both balances, the goods and services balance. The twin-island, therefore, reached a major surplus of its goods and services trade balance of US$ 5.94 billion (cf. CEPALSTAT, 2013). The trade balance of Jamaica indicates a high reliance on imported goods, which could not be balanced by a surplus in its services balance, thus resulting in the highest goods and services trade deficit among the Caribbean countries of US$ 3.59 billion (cf. CEPALSTAT, 2013). Overall, the Caribbean economies rely heavily on trade for export earnings, in order to purchase imports of fuel, food, and manufactured products. The trade structure thereby corresponds for the most part with the leading economic sector in the Caribbean countries, while it is limited to a narrow range of products within these sectors. The economies of the Caribbean are less diversified and, therefore, more dependent on international trade for products for which they have comparative advantages and can attain foreign exchange earnings.

Box 1:   The Caribbean Community (CARICOM)

The first attempts of regional integration efforts date back to the attainment of political independence in the Caribbean region. In 1958, predominantly the English-speaking Caribbean countries and former British colonies decided to merge their political powers under the West Indian Federation (WIF), and to assist its member countries in the process of independence. The Federation lasted only four years until Jamaica and Trinidad and Tobago withdrew in 1961/62, and the WIF was dissolved, also due to the lack of coherence and an absent sense of unity (cf. D'Agostino, 2009).
The integration movement was revived, when in 1967, the Caribbean Free Trade Area (CARIFTA) was established by the English-speaking Caribbean countries, with the aim to facilitate trade within its members, through the removal of trade barriers between them. Six years later, in 1973, the CARIFTA members decided to build a Common Market as an integral part of the Caribbean Community. With the signing of *The Treaty of Chaguaramas*, the Caribbean Community and Common Market (CARICOM) was established to foster economic integration and cooperation, improve international competitiveness, and the coordination of foreign policies (cf.Braveboy-Wagner, 2009; CARICOM, 2011b). To date, 15 Caribbean countries have gradually joined the CARICOM and are consistent members of it: Antigua and Barbuda, The Bahamas, Barbados, Belize, Dominica, Grenada, Guyana, Haiti, Jamaica, Montserrat, St. Lucia, St. Kitts and

Nevis, St. Vincent and the Grenadines, Suriname, and Trinidad and Tobago.

With the purpose to bring the economic integration forward, the CARICOM Single Market and Economy (CSME) was established in 1989 and came into effect with *The Revised Treaty of Chaguaramas*. The aim of the CSME is to completely liberalize the markets within CARICOM for the free movement of goods, services, capital, labour and people (cf. CARICOM, 2011a). While most components of the 'Single Market' have been completed, the 'Single Economy' is still left on the path with drafts and negotiations. Economic integration and the implementation of a Common External Tariff (CET) has moved slowly since then (cf. IADB, 2005). Regional integration and trade liberalization initiatives of CARICOM have always been very ambitious, although intraregional trade amounts only for a small share of total trade. For instance, in 2010 intraregional imports constituted approximately 12%, and accordingly exports constituted 18% of total trade within CARICOM Member States (cf. CARICOM, 2013c).

Currently, the future of CARICOM might be uncertain or even in crises, whereas several obstacles hinder further integration. The CARICOM faces internal loose structures, institutional weakness, and limited financial resources, which restraint the Community's capacity to handle, monitor and realize a common strategy on important issues for future development in the Caribbean Member States (cf. Stoneman et al., 2012).

Access to finance and debt accumulation

SIDS are economically disadvantaged, since they only own limited resources to attain economic development or growth, on which they can build their infrastructure by importing, capital, commodities, and technology. Mainly, this economic growth depends on their trade capacity and their earnings from exports. The constantly negative trade balances in the Caribbean countries require most importantly financing to adjust these high deficit levels. Due to the limited availability of internal financial resources, the Caribbean economies rely on external financing and investment. Consequently, they seek financing from external sources in form of credits (cf. Perez, 2007). High demands for imports and low export earnings increase the demand for credits creating high debt levels in the majority of the Caribbean countries. Persistent high debt stocks in these economies impede economic growth and complicate their recovery from the global economic crisis, which hit the services producers the most (cf. Alleyne et al., 2013).

Debt stocks can be sub-divided into *external debt* and *domestic debt.* Domestic debt comprises credits and loans obtained on the national financial markets and include private and public debt. External debt consists of multilateral, bilateral loans, supplier credits, commercial bank loans and export credits. The sum of domestic and external debt is the total debt stock.

The Caribbean economies belong to the most indebted countries in the world. External debt ratios slightly increased on an average of 42% in 2000 to 46% of GDP in 2010 (own calculations based on CEPAL, 2012). Figure 11 shows that the total debt as a sum of domestic and external debt as percentage of GDP (indebtedness ratio), in 2011, ranged widely between 24% in Suriname, and 125% in Jamaica. In 2011, St. Kitts and Nevis constituted the second highest indebtedness ratio of 120% of its GDP, mostly composed of domestic debt. In Jamaica domestic debt to GDP ratio was 68% and in St. Kitts and Nevis one of 77%. The lowest total debt to GDP ratio was observed in Suriname with 24% (cf. ECLAC, 2013b). Despite high debt levels in 2011, improvements have been noticed significantly in Guyana, which in 2008 had the highest external debt ratio among the Caribbean countries and successively reduced its total external debt from 327% in 1990 to 53% of GDP in 2011 (cf. CEPALSTAT, 2013). Debt is a major economic challenge for the Caribbean countries as it impedes long-term growth. Paying for the costs of debt services limits a country's government resources for public expenditure and disturbs its focus on the provision of public goods and services (cf. Alleyne et al., 2013; Perez, 2007).

Figure 11:   External and domestic debt (in % of country's GDP), Caribbean countries, 2011

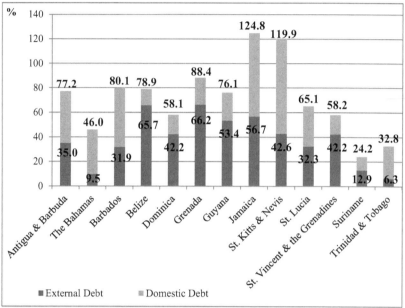

Source: own compilation based on ECLAC (2013b)

Moreover, high debt levels hinder the countries to access further financing on international markets, which they need to repay their debt services. Otherwise the Caribbean countries end in a financial trap from which they can barely escape. To repay the debt services, export earnings, and government revenues are used, but at the same time, foreign exchange is needed to buy imports. This is of major importance for the Caribbean countries that are heavily dependent on essential imports such as food, consumer, and capital goods, in order to meet the needs of the Caribbean consumers (cf. Alleyne et al., 2013). Moreover, the "growing debt burden of many Caribbean countries is generating [...] a deepening of the economic vulnerability of the region" (SIDSnet, 2013).

Economic vulnerability

Since the Caribbean countries do not have enough resources to foster 'development' and nurture themselves, they have to rely on external trade. The inherent characteristics of the Caribbean economies, such as the high dependence on trade and the high degree of concentration on a narrow range of export products, unstable economic growth, high indebtedness ratios, small domestic markets, limited natural resource endowments, remoteness, and insularity, create economic vulnerability, resulting in the exposure to external shocks. According to Briguglio et. al (2004) *economic vulnerability* refers to the *"exposure of a country to external shocks arising from intrinsic features of the economies"* (Briguglio, 2009: 3).

In the context of the Caribbean, economic vulnerability mainly results from the structure of the economies and the social and demographic constrains analysed in this chapter. Especially the inherent features and the countries' specific geographical and geological structures make a sustainable economic system indispensable to absorb and adjust to external shocks.

On the basis of Briguglio's studies on vulnerability, the *Fondation pour les Études et Recherches sur les Développement International* (FERDI) together with the United Nations Department of Economic and Social Affairs (UN DESA) built the Economic Vulnerability Index (EVI). The EVI is the arithmetic average of the *exposure index* and the *size and likelihood of shocks*. The exposure index is calculated by the weighted average of the population size, remoteness from world markets, exports concentration, and the share of agriculture, forestry and fishery in GDP. Whereas the likelihood of shocks index comprises a weighted average of the annual mean share of homeless due to natural disasters in the population, the instability in the agricultural production, and the instability in exports of goods and services (Cariolle, 2011). The EVI and the correspondent indices range between 0 and 100. The Caribbean countries show different levels for the individual indices. In 2009, high scores of the EVI, above 50, are reached by Antigua and Barbuda, The Bahamas, Dominica, St. Kitts and Nevis, St. Lucia and Suriname, which corresponds with a high level of vulnerability. The other countries reach EVI scores below 50, whereas Jamaica reaches the lowest score among the Caribbean countries with 37, corresponding with a lower level of vulnerability. Overall high levels are reached for the exposure index and the natural shock index (UN DESA, 2013). However, these indices are just one form of defining economic vulnerability and do not necessarily reflect the actual level of vulnerability in the Caribbean countries.

3.4   Conclusion: Commonality and diversity in the Caribbean

This chapter has demonstrated that a comprehensive analysis on historical, political, geo-graphical and socio-economic factors that shape the Caribbean countries is necessary to identify similarities as well as divergences between the countries.

From the 15th to the 20th century the Caribbean was dominated by a hegemonic system of external powers and resource exploitations by the British, Dutch, French and Spanish. Colonization left the people and their lands with a deteriorating system of plantations and mono-cultural export structures, which influenced not only the thoughts of the explanatory Caribbean development theories, but actually led to the development of the present economic and social structures of the countries. Due to these structures and the countries' particular geographic and geological features, various definitions of the Caribbean have evolved since their 'discovery' on the ancient world map.

On the one hand, the Caribbean countries are classified as high- and middle-income countries and achieved significant progress in human development and improvements of health and education; on the other hand, income poverty and food poverty are widely spread in the Caribbean countries, hindering the socially deprived population from adequate access to basic needs such as food, housing, and education. These are issues that have to be addressed urgently, since economic instability and vulnerability mostly affects the poor population the worst and puts them further at risk, unable to cope with the effects.

The economic analysis of this chapter, moreover, discloses that comparative advantages in exporting services such as travel and tourism have benefited the Caribbean economies significantly. However, the shifting dependency from the export of sugar and other raw materials in the past to the services sector today creates open but vulnerable economies that are prone to external shocks. Additionally, slow and volatile economic growth makes it difficult for the economies to offset financial deficits and negative trade balances.

A range of factors influence the socio-economic development of the Caribbean. Understanding the specific social, demographic and economic structures which shape the Caribbean countries in the way they evolved today, allows assessing further consequences of structural impediments.

4. A cluster analysis on vulnerability and Food and Nutrition Security in the Caribbean

Food and Nutrition Security (FNS) is frequently discussed within the context of vulnerability of Caribbean Small Island Developing States (SIDS), which struggle to overcome adverse effects of their economic, social and environmental structures.

Ever since the issue of Food and Nutrition Insecurity in the Caribbean changed from poverty- and hunger-stricken countries to the rising question of food import dependency and nutrition related diseases, so far there has been no attempt to measure FNS in the Caribbean through a suitable method of measurement. This study, therefore, tries to fill this research gap, by applying a statistical method of cluster analysis.

Based on the concept of FNS, a comprehensive examination of the four dimensions – availability, access, utilization and stability – is a requisite to assess available information on the state of FNS in the Caribbean, in the context of vulnerability. For this matter, subchapter 4.1 examines the actual issues in each dimension, and seeks to evaluate the outcomes. The second subchapter uses the information of the foregoing study on the FNS situation in the Caribbean to conduct a statistical analysis of clusters, which serves to extend the qualitative analysis of the foregoing chapter. This method is useful to highlight key issues of FNS in the Caribbean, and to discuss the outcomes by drawing a significant conclusion on this matter.

4.1 Vulnerability and Food and Nutrition (In-)Security in the Caribbean

The previous examination of the natural and socio-economic constraints in the Caribbean shows that they can limit economic as well as human development in the respective countries. FNS as multi-dimensional and complex problem is mainly an outcome of these constraints, which in turn partially root in the countries' history. There is a range of considerable factors that determine the FNS situation in the Caribbean. One of the most influential factors among others is the region's vulnerability to natural changes in the environment and external economic effects. For that reason, the FNS dimensions have to be examined specifically in the Caribbean context.

The first subchapter analyses the notion of vulnerability and its implications to FNS in the Caribbean countries. The current state of FNS in the Caribbean is analysed based on the general FNS concept of the second subchapter. The last section of this chapter discusses the practical issue of the possibility to measure this state within the Caribbean through appropriate indicators or indices. Due to the limitations of information on the specific vulnerability and FNS situation in the Caribbean countries, data is retrieved from different sources, such as the FAOSTAT and The World Bank's WDI database.

4.1.1 Vulnerability in the context of Food and Nutrition Security in the Caribbean

Vulnerability is often associated with environmental and economic conditions under which the objects – individuals, countries, and governments – are at risk and cannot cope with consequences of external shocks and their negative effects. If individuals find themselves in a situation at risk, not being able to cope with these direct or indirect negative effects, they result in a state of defencelessness, equivalent to vulnerability (cf. Dilley and Boudreau, 2001). In the extreme situation of defencelessness, vulnerability can be interpreted as "an inability to control one's own destiny" (Lappé and Collins, 1977: 182). In this case, it is important to put policies and strategies in place, so that the objects of concern gain the ability to reduce the negative impacts, and adjust accordingly to them.

Aside from the economic vulnerability described in the previous section, vulnerability in the context of Caribbean SIDS is usually linked to *environmental vulnerability*, meaning fragile natural ecological systems, affected by natural hazards such as hurricanes, tropical storms, floods, droughts, earthquakes and volcanic activities. Tropical storms and hurricanes occur frequently in the Atlantic hurricane season from June 1st to November 30th and can leave visible destructions to nature and to the population (cf. National Hurricane Center, 2013). Between 2001 and 2012, 43 tropical cyclones occurred in Antigua and Barbuda, The Bahamas, Barbados, Dominica, Grenada, Jamaica, St. Lucia, St. Vincent and the Grenadines, and Trinidad and Tobago leaving 763,235 people affected by the storms and causing a total damage of US$ 4.4 billion (cf. EM-DAT, 2009).

These destructions, due to environmental disasters, cause harm for the economies through financial losses, and damaged infrastructure, which make the countries economically vulnerable. *Vice versa*, economic vulnerability can also affect the environment, mainly through the exploitation or the misuse of resources. In the Caribbean countries, these vulnerabilities together entail the vulnerability to food and nutrition insecurity as shown in Figure 12.

Figure 12:   Economic and environmental vulnerability entailing vulnerability to Food and Nutrition Insecurity

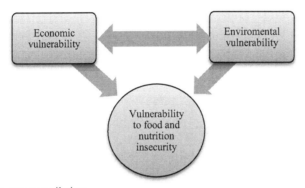

Source: own compilation

Natural disasters directly or indirectly distress food security in the affected countries damaging the provision sectors such as agriculture, and infrastructure and leave them in a destructed condition, which leads to shortages of food and water and inadequate access to water and affordable and sufficient food. In 2004, hurricane Ivan affected the entire island of Grenada, leaving agriculture and crops, livestock and fisheries damaged up to 100% and subsequent agricultural outputs at a slow recovery (cf. OECS, 2007).

From the approach of vulnerability, related to risks and hazards evolved the definition of vulnerability within the context of FNS. Formerly, vulnerability has been discussed with reference to famines and was based on the study of Sen (1981). Since then, the understanding of vulnerability has been widely accepted in the FNS literature, referring to outcomes such as undernourishment, food insecurity and no longer to causes such as hazards or shocks (Dilley and Boudreau: 233-234).

Despite existing vulnerability measurements, developed by Briguglio (2003), it is difficult to conceptualize vulnerability and incorporate it into an indicator. Nevertheless, determining, whether the object of examination is vulnerable to insecurities or risks, becomes operable by dint of measuring the outcome, which allows a subsequent and meaningful interpretation of the severity of the situation.

4.1.2   The four dimensions of Food and Nutrition (In-)Security in the Caribbean

This subchapter analyses the situation of food and nutrition (in-)security in the Caribbean countries, based on the previous examination of vulnerability, and the countries' social, demographic and economic constraints from chapter 3.3. The concept of FNS as presented in chapter 2.3 serves as a basis for this analysis, as well as means to assess the four dimensions of the concept in the context of the selected Caribbean countries.

From the previous analysis of social, demographic and economic indicators, three main factors of vulnerability can be identified that unfavourably influence FNS in the Caribbean countries (Bowell: 45-46):

1. *Natural constraints:* Caribbean SIDS are considered to be physically and economically vulnerable comprising limited physical size of land area with limited natural renewable and non-renewable resources such as land and water for (food) production.
2. *Physiological density:* Generally, there is a competition of land use for agricultural, industrial or residential purposes. When population density is already very high and arable land is scarce, pressure on land for food production increases.
3. *Poverty and income:* Poverty and/or indigence, lead naturally to lower food consumption, unequal distribution of food within households, or to consumption of lesser essential nutrients, such as minerals and vitamins, which makes people more perceptible to diseases.

These factors, inherent or not, affect the four dimensions of FNS, namely: availability, access, utilization and stability, adversely causing a state of vulnerability to food and nutrition insecurity.

Food Availability

Food availability in the Caribbean is the sum of domestic food production, and food imports. Domestic food production equals the domestic agricultural production and reflects the sector's capacity to provide a certain supply of food for the population. The increasing reliance on food imports, as already indicated, is a particular issue in the Caribbean since it has far-reaching consequences for the FNS situation and the economies in the Caribbean. The following analysis on food availability focuses on the domestic production capacity and excludes a detailed analysis of food imports, since this specific issue is discussed in chapter 5.

Due to the notable sectoral shift across the Caribbean economies, the agricultural production sector, which produces merely exclusively food for the population diminished widely or still persists on a low level of production in most of the countries. Nevertheless, the increase in food production is essential, since population growth leads to a natural increase in the demand for food. One question that needs to be asked in this section is whether domestic food production is sufficient to feed the Caribbean population.

The evolution of a countries' per capita net food production index, which reflects the relative level of the aggregate volume of the net food production[20] weighted by the average international commodity prices in 2004-2006 for each year, is represented in Figure 13. Four countries are selected, whereas the overall figure, displaying each country's food production index is found in Appendix B. The domestic food production decreased significantly in seven out of 13 countries. Figure 13 shows the negative evolution of the per capita net food production index for selected countries in the period from 1990 to 2011. From a very high food production index of 301.4 points in 1990, St. Lucia experienced the steepest decline of the index to a level of 95.6 points in 2011. St. Kitts and Nevis reaches the lowest level of food production among all 13 countries with a value of just 36.3 points in 2011, a decline from 126.7 points in 1990 (FAOSTAT, 2013). Despite the drastic decline of food production in St. Lucia and St. Kitts and Nevis, the other Caribbean countries experienced a rather slight downward drift of the food production index. In six out of 13 countries the net food production index per capita increased in the same

---

20   Inputs such as seed and feed are subtracted (cf. FAOSTAT, 2013b).

period of time. The biggest growth of the index has occurred in Guyana, from 49.4 points in 1990 to 113.3 points in 2011. Overall, the highest level of food production among all 13 countries was achieved by The Bahamas at 128.9 points in 2011, an increase from the 73.1 points in 1990 (FAOSTAT, 2013). In addition, the evolution of the index shows an extensively volatile movement for some countries. There were significant jumps from one year to the other which has several economic reasons, and were due to environmental impacts on the food production sector.

Figure 13:   Per capita net food production index (2004-2006=100), Caribbean countries, 1990-2011

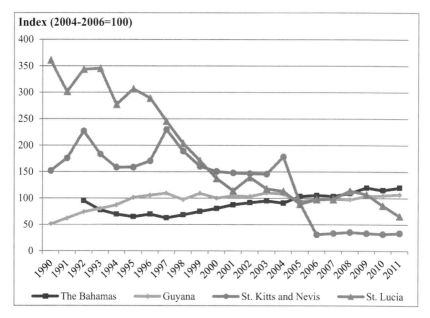

Source: own compilation based on (FAOSTAT, 2013b)

Despite some signs of an increase in food production, external effects and internal constraints affecting agricultural production negatively, endanger the stable domestic food production in the long-term. The problem of food availability is not one of scarcity, but one of the capacities to grow food on a domestic level, to provide for the population adequately, and to guarantee a reasonable stable domestic supply.

The Caribbean has a long history of an important agricultural sector which formerly produced a small but significant variety of crops for the export market, such as sugar, coffee, bananas, tobacco, and cacao. On a mostly small-scale, it provided food for the domestic markets, and agricultural production has played an important role in the domestic food security (Boswell, 2009). Nevertheless, a range of factors such as increasing prices for agricultural inputs, favourable prices for food on the international markets, the lack of marketing and distribution, and the insufficient access to financing, contributed to the decline in small scale production and countries moved gradually from net exporters, to net importers of food (cf. Beckford and Campbell, 2013). Consequently, the agricultural sector has been increasingly depending on the international market for raw materials, and intermediate inputs, while food imports balance the increasing demand for food and the lower domestic supply on the Caribbean markets.

Nevertheless, the importance of the agriculture sector has been undermined in the Caribbean, since the sector's productivity is inefficient. The negligence of this sector leads to further impediment of investment, and hence to the containment of the possibility of an increase in productivity. The sectors regeneration is important since agriculture plays a significant role in providing healthy and nutritious food for the population.

Although, food production in the Caribbean shows some arguable constraints of sufficient domestic production, availability of food, as the sum of domestic food production and food imports, is also partially represented in Food Balance Sheets (FBS), which shows the availability of calories and proteins for the population.

FBS are a useful tool to display the total supply of commodities available during a period of time or the exact year (FAO, 2001). FBS are provided by the FAO Statistic Division (FAOSTAT) and are based on national data. The total domestic supply of food is calculated for a certain period of time and equals the food produced on a domestic level, plus the total of food available through trade (imports minus exports), adjusted by stock changes (increase or decrease) (FAO, 2001).

$$Total\ domestic\ supply$$
$$= production + imports - exports + changes\ in\ stocks$$

$$Domestic\ supply\ per\ capita$$
$$= \frac{production + imports - exports + changes\ in\ stocks}{population}$$

If the total domestic supply is divided by the total population, FBS display specific data of per capita food supply, and more specifically they provide estimates of the availability of energy measured in kilocalories (kcal), fats in grams and proteins in grams per capita and per day. The FBS for the Caribbean countries show a sufficient supply of energy, fats, and proteins for the population. All sample countries meet the Average Dietary Requirement (ADER) in kcal per capita per day (cf. FAO, 2013b).

Nevertheless, FBS lack the ability to represent comprehensive data on food availability. It is not possible to identify if the source of nutrients derives from domestically produced or imported foods. Further, FBS do not reveal any information about the distribution of the available food across countries, or even among members of the same household. If incomes are unequal distributed among the population, the supply of food is also more likely to be unequally distributed due to the lack of sufficient access to food for the poor population. The *Gini coefficient* shows that income across the Caribbean countries is mostly unequally distributed (cf. Table 4, chapter 3.3.2). This conclusion leads to the examination of the second dimension of FNS, the access to food.

Access to food

Physical and economical access to food is essential for adequate nutrition of the population. The *economic access* of food depends primary on the level of household or individual income. Among the Caribbean countries' population, the *Gini coefficient* indicates an unequal distribution of income, and relatively high levels of poverty are prevalent. Additionally, high food prices aggravate the situation and hinder adequate access to affordable food, especially for the poor population.

A common measurement of assessing the number of people suffering from poverty and undernutrition, the 'food insecure' population, is the *food poverty line* – also known as the indigence line – which for Caribbean countries, based on the country assessment reports, is calculated by the minimum cost of a food basket, meaning the minimum expenditure necessary to meet basic nutritional requirements.

A review of the country poverty assessment (CPA) reports, the living condition surveys, and the human development atlas, shows the most recent quantity of the proportion of the population that is vulnerable to FNS, as access to food is restricted by low income. Although, data is not comparable, since it is based on different methodologies, food poverty seems to be an important issue among all the countries for which data is available (cf. Table 3).

The biggest concern in this context, however, is the price level of food. On the macro level, an increase in the world market price for food induces an increase of the national food import bill, consequently putting a financial burden on the food import dependent countries. The same applies to the micro level for households and individuals. Higher world market prices for (imported) food pervade the prices for food on the domestic and local markets. The shares of income spent on food, increase with higher prices, especially in the case of the poor and vulnerable population which already spends a significant high proportion of their income on food. In the Bahamas, poor households spend 37% of their budget on food, which is relatively low compared to the other countries of the Caribbean (cf. Government of The Bahamas, 2004). In Barbados, the escalating costs of food and housing, triggered an increase in food expenditure per capita, so that nutritious food items were substituted by cheap and less nutritious food items to cut back on expenditure for food (cf. CDB, 2012). Jamaica reports higher rates of poverty since 2007 due to the subsequent effect of the higher prices for food and fuel (cf. PIOJ, 2012).

If higher prices for food are not adjusted by increasing the income, or lower prices for other basic needs, food price inflation is inevitable. The population of the Caribbean countries was affected significantly by the inflation of prices for food items during the last 5 to 10 years. The Consumer Price Food Index (CPFI) inflation reflects the change rate of food prices from one year to the previous year. The increase in the CPFI inflation for the Caribbean countries ranged from 40% to 93% in a ten-year period from 2001 to 2011 (own calculations based on FAOSTAT, 2013b). Figure 14 shows that, among all the countries, the inflation rate recorded its lowest point at -7% in The Bahamas in 2007. However, two years later, the CPFI inflation reached its peak in Jamaica at 31% in 2009 (own calculations based onFAOSTAT, 2013b). This was also the year in which all countries reached the highest inflation rates noticed in the ten-year period, due to the economic crisis. The CPFI measures the annual increase or decrease of the food prices on the basis of the year 2000 (2000=100). The CPFI continuously increased throughout the Caribbean countries in the ten-year period from 2001 to 2011. In some countries the CPFI recorded a severe increase, such as in Trinidad and Tobago, where food consumer prices increased over 449%, in Jamaica over 241%, and in Suriname over

218%, in 2011. The lowest increase has been noticed in The Bahamas with 23% (FAOSTAT, 2013b).

Figure 14:   Consumer Price Food Index (CPFI) (2000=100) and CPFI inflation, Caribbean countries, 2001-2011

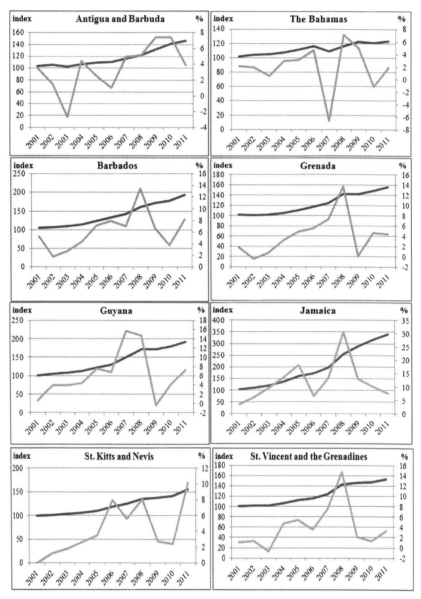

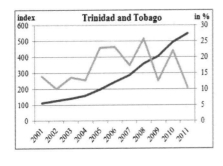

———— Consuer Price Food Index (CPFI)

======= Consumer Food Price (CFP) inflation

Source: own compilation. Own calculations based on FAOSTAT (2013b)

Whereas economic access to food can be displayed through various observations, *physical access* to food is difficult to measure or to identify. Physical access to markets for consumers as well as producers is mainly provided through roads and physical infrastructure. Throughout the Caribbean countries, there has not been noticed any significant improvement in this area. On the islands, the density of paved roads is extremely high, reaching from 50% to 99% – in Dominica 50%, in Jamaica 73%, and Barbados 99%, whereas, on the larger mainland countries, the density is notably low, such as in Guyana at 7%, Belize at 17% and Suriname at 26%. Even so, the density neither increased nor decreased for a long time. Except for Jamaica, paved road density appears to correlate negatively with land size. However, improved physical infrastructure can facilitate the access to food, which is true in the case of Guyana, e.g., where the construction of farm-to-market roads improved the supply of food and even contained food price inflations (cf. Government of Guyana, 2011).

Food consumption and utilization

Nutrition or malnutrition is the outcome of food consumption and utilization. With reference to the three forms of malnutrition, under-nutrition, over-nutrition, and micronutrient deficiencies, the main concern in the Caribbean countries are relatively high rates of under- and over-nutrition. Nevertheless, micronutrient deficiencies also count to apparent health and nutrition problems in the Caribbean countries. Most common are Iron

Deficiency Anaemia (IDA) and Vitamin A Deficiencies (VAD). Data from country studies conducted by the World Health Organization (WHO) show relatively high levels of anaemia due to iron deficiency among children, ranging from moderate levels around 11% to severe levels between 34% in Dominica (1997), and 56% in Grenada (1992) (cf. CFNI, 2007). According to the WHO, anemia prevalence of pregnant women and pre-school-age children is a severe public health problem in Belize, Guyana and Jamaica, whereas it is a moderate health problem in the other 10 sample countries (cf. WHO, 2008)[21].

Figure 15 shows that the Prevalence of Undernourishment (PoU) decreased on average in seven countries in the period of 2000-2002, and 2008-2010, whereas in Barbados and Dominica there has not been any notable change in the prevalence rate and remains under 5%, the lowest level among the countries. In The Bahamas, Belize, Jamaica and St. Lucia the prevalence increased rather slightly. Nevertheless, the highest rates are represented by Antigua and Barbuda and Grenada each constituting 21% (cf. FAO, 2013b).

---

21 "Anemia is more prevalent in pregnant women and young children" (WHO, 2008: 1).

Figure 15:   Prevalence of Undernourishment (PoU), Caribbean countries, 2000-2002 and 2008-2010

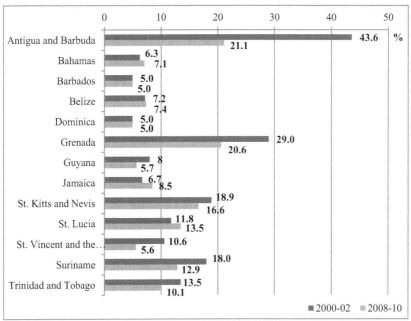

Source: own compilation. FAO (2013b)

Undernutrition is just one side of the coin, resulting from poverty, unequal distribution of food, a lack of adequate access, and supply of food. On the other side, unhealthy diets, poverty, as well as biological factors might cause overnutrition. Additionally, it is important to recognize that lifestyles and cultural habits influence the consumption and utilization of food significantly (cf. Bhargava, 2008). In the Caribbean, consumption patterns have changed notably in an unhealthy way over the last decades. The increased availability of a variety of and greater access to affordable food due to higher food imports may have led to this transformation. Consequently, several factors such as adapting to North American lifestyles and the consumption of cheaper but less nutritious food, and food items that contain an excess of fats and sugars aggravate the tremendous change of consumption patterns in the Caribbean.

The dietary supply of energy, fats and proteins exceeds the dietary requirements of these nutrients. In terms of the dietary energy supply adequacy, calculated as the Dietary Energy Supply (DES) as percentage of the ADER[22], all Caribbean countries exceeded the maximum level of 100% in 2009-2011 and, therefore, fulfilled the requirement (cf. FAO, 2013b). Since data of energy, fat and protein supply is retrieved from FBS, it must be mentioned that based on this data, actual consumption can be below the availability levels represented in the FBS. Nevertheless, the high availability of energy dense food allows the assumption that food consumption is led by the supply and access of food.

In order to conclude how and what people eat, and to assess the nutritional status of households and individuals, detailed information about food consumption is indispensable. This information is collected through food consumption surveys. In the case of the Caribbean countries, these kinds of surveys are not conducted recently or frequently, so that (recent) information about actual food consumption and diets is insufficient. However, country studies on nutrition and health, point out, that unhealthy diets in the Caribbean are a cause of concern due to the rapid increase in diet-related diseases, which in turn have long-term consequences for the health of the population, and the economies through the loss of productivity. In this context, chronic Non-communicable Diseases (NCDs) have risen with epidemiological transitions and became a major public health problem in the Caribbean today. Further analysis and discussion on diet-related diseases and the economic and social impact of NCDs follows in chapter 6.

Stability

The food systems in the Caribbean are mostly the result of the legacy of the plantation food production systems. Since then, plantation farming and large scale production were replaced by peasant and family farms in the food production system. Food production, therefore, was concentrated first and foremost to provide food for the peasant families and the nearby neighbourhood; food production surplus was sold on local markets in small quantities (cf. Beckford and Campbell, 2013). This small but vital food production system nourished the people in the Caribbean and supported families and small-scale farmers. With trade liberalization and the

---

22   Average Dietary Energy Requirement (ADER) for the Caribbean region ranges between 2240 kcal and 2520 kcal (cf. FAO, 2013b).

establishment of food retailing operations (supermarkets, groceries, etc.) the former traditional system was no longer efficient to provide the population with adequate, affordable and stable supply of food.

Since the capacity of small-scale production is on a low productivity level to cope with risks and natural disasters, food supply is exposed not only to seasonality, but to unforeseeable external events. Further, food price volatility causes instability in food supply and directly affects the economic access to food for consumers. Domestic farm production which is in the case of Trinidad and Tobago e.g. aimed for local markets lack guaranteed output prices and risk reduction support measures often applied only in the case of production for exports (cf. Løvendal, 2007).

Stability of FNS often refers to the dimension of food availability and stable food supply. In the Caribbean countries, stability is probably the most debatable dimension because it is impaired by economic and environmental vulnerability.

4.1.3 Measuring Food and Nutrition (In-)Security in the Caribbean

The objective of this section is to examine whether current indicators and measurements of FNS already reviewed in chapter 2.4, are suitable to measure the FNS situation in the Caribbean and if there are other methodological options for its assessment or not. On the basis of the vulnerability and food and nutrition (in-)security situation in the Caribbean some measurements and indicators seem to be less relevant and others more significant for the purpose of the subsequent analysis.

From the reviewed indicators and indices, The Global Hunger Index (GHI) compiled by IFPRI is the only one which found data for at least some of the Caribbean countries such as Guyana, Jamaica, Suriname and Trinidad and Tobago, indicating a low to moderate severity of hunger. The Global Food Security Index (GFSI) does not reveal any score for not one of the selected countries. The use of the USDA Food Security Assessment model for the Caribbean case is difficult. Especially the assessment of a *distribution gap* is not feasible, since data availability on respective income groups in the Caribbean is inadequate. Whereas the calculation of a *nutrition gap* according to the suggested minimum caloric baseline of 2,100 calories, can be excluded since the dietary energy supply adequacy in the Caribbean countries are above the threshold.

As the GHI shows, food and nutrition insecurity often indicates 'hunger' or undernourishment as an outcome indicator. The Caribbean countries, however, are not considered to show severe levels of the prevalence of undernourishment. These indicators and measurements undermine the necessity to apply further indicators retrieved from the other dimensions of FNS, which in the case of the Caribbean are more important for an assessment of the specific FNS situation in the countries. Most certainly, the various approaches and aggregate measures aim to provide a broad, and eventually a global perception of the food and nutrition insecurity situation and its outcomes.

Further, most indices release data for aggregated regions such as for Latin America and the Caribbean (LAC), which includes mainly the Latin-Caribbean countries for different reasons one of which is the paucity of data for the Caribbean SIDS. Consequently, the values of indicators for the LAC region have to be interpreted with caution, since data for excluded countries could bias aggregated values on the regional level.

Moreover, macro indices such as the GHI are reasonable, if there is a large sample of countries, to allow a comparison between countries or regions. Thus, for a relatively small sample of 13 Caribbean countries, global or macro indices are less feasible due to the selected indicators the countries might reach very similar scores. From the reviewed global measurement methods of FNS arise the importance to measure FNS in the Caribbean through a more adequate and specific approach which identifies significant and relevant factors that influence FNS in the Caribbean. Ultimately, the main reason for measuring the state of FNS derives from the strategic consideration to appropriate policies and strategies, with the aim to mitigate negative outcomes and to identify the underlying factors that influence FNS.

FNS measurement is a difficult operational procedure because the multi-dimensional concept of FNS requires a set of indicators rather than just a single indicator to capture a broad understanding of each of the dimensions and to reflect a country's or regions' specific issues on FNS. In order to use a suitable indicator or index for FNS measurement in the Caribbean, data has to be available for a certain time or period of time. It has to be emphasised, that data collection in the Caribbean is already insufficient in certain areas, and the availability of reliable or even time-series data on FNS issues is limited and difficult to obtain. The challenge of assessing the FNS situation of the Caribbean through a suitable measurement method is not only to use a comprehensive data set which indicates changes over time, but also to enable a meaningful comparison across countries.

The FAO's comprehensive set of food security indicators presented in chapter 2.3.3 also comprises the PoU indicator for which time-series data on the Caribbean countries is available. However, the application of one single indicator does not reflect the complexity of FNS in the Caribbean.

In 2012, the Committee on World Food Security (CFS) Round Table on hunger measurement of the FAO compiled a core set of indicators which cover the dimensions availability, access, utilization and stability, and are divided into input and output indicators. The FAO's data set of food security indicators serves to choose indicators from different dimensions and categories which can be used for a broader FNS analysis in the Caribbean in a certain period of time.

4.2   A cluster analysis of Food and Nutrition Security in the Caribbean

The results from the previous section show that it is difficult to determine or to choose indicators or indices that could reflect the multifaceted FNS situation in the Caribbean. So far, the discussion about FNS in the Caribbean has focused on the undernourishment issue of only a few sample countries in the broader region. The specific circumstances under which the Caribbean evolved as a region of high social, economic, cultural and environmental diversity, requires a region-specific or even country-specific approach to assess the FNS situation in the selected sample countries. For this purpose, this subchapter uses a cluster analysis and explains the procedure and methodology which has been chosen to classify the selected Caribbean countries according to their similarities or differences. The first step was to identify the countries on the basis of certain classification criteria, based on the examination from chapter 3.2. The second section of this chapter presents the selection of three suitable indicators, reflecting the particular situation of FNS in the Caribbean. In the subsequent sub-section 0 describes the employment of the method chosen for the procedure cluster analysis. In the last section of this subchapter, results are presented and discussed thoroughly. Finally, these results serve for any further discussion on specific issues regarding FNS in the selected sample countries.

General objectives of the cluster analysis

To identify groups of countries according to particular features, this study employs a cluster analysis and uses data for 13 Caribbean countries. Three indicators for which time series data is available have been selected from the comprehensive set of FNS indicators provided by the FAO. Cluster analysis is a statistical method used to classify a sample of cases[23] and merge them to a limited number of groups, based on a set of selected variables. It serves to identify groups, each of which share some degree of similar features, and identify disparities between these groups and the group members. Grouping a variety of countries, which share common issues and disparities, is a useful method. It allows combining countries with similar characteristics into groups or making discrepancies between groups of countries visible. For this matter, countries and groups can be classified according to their outcomes of the FNS, in order to draft relevant strategies and policies for addressing specific problems for each respective group of countries.

4.2.1   Selected Caribbean countries

From the previous analysis of different country classifications and the search of a reasonable definition for the Caribbean results the determination of 13 Caribbean countries as objects of examination (cf. chapter 3.1 and 3.2). Moreover, additional criteria which are crucial to conduct the cluster analysis, endorse the selection of the Caribbean countries. The following two criteria have to be considered for this analysis and evaluated in the context of the Caribbean countries.

1. Data availability: Adequate data of the indicators should be available for a certain period of time, and retrieved from reliable data sources. Data collection in the Caribbean is challenging due to institutional and financial limitations. This issue has been partially addressed by regional institutions such as the CARICOM secretariat, and various regional institutions or organizations, responsible for collecting data on special issues, and provide

---

23   Subsequently, and throughout this study, cases refer to countries; variables refer to indicators.

open access databases. Data collection and provision is certainly an imperative to policy makers and governmental organizations, in order to transpose sound policies to address particular issues based on sufficient and reliable data.

2. Homogeneity/heterogeneity criteria: The Caribbean countries share a common history and have similar socio-economic and demographic features. Alongside a significant diversity of their economic structures and performances, cultural differences and the variety of languages and cultures, the countries can be sub-classified into smaller groups of countries according to their proximal common characteristics, in order to make differences between the groups visible. In the context of FNS, diversity within commonalities has to be identified on the basis of suitable indicators.

The following analysis and further examinations will be conducted based on 13 selected Caribbean countries: Antigua and Barbuda, The Bahamas, Barbados, Belize, Dominica, Grenada, Guyana, Jamaica, St. Kitts and Nevis, St. Lucia, St. Vincent and the Grenadines, Suriname, and Trinidad and Tobago.

4.2.2 Underlying data and indicators

The selected set of indicators is based on the theoretical concept of FNS explained in detail in chapter 2.3. There are numerous indicators and indices, which can be used to measure FNS, and in particular the four dimensions availability, access, utilization and stability on the macro or national level, and on the micro or household level. It is necessary to identify the relevant dimension(s) for this study and include suitable indicators to avoid redundancy.

In this analysis, the indicators should represent a specific and broad view of the situation of food availability, and access to it for each group of countries. The quantity of indicators is limited by the statistical assumption, that the number of variables[24] should not exceed half of the number of cases[25], and to avoid redundancy. Consequently, the selection

---

24   Calculations in SPSS refer to the notion 'variables' which in this study are 'indicators'.
25   Calculations in SPSS refer to the notion 'cases' which in this study are 'countries'.

of 13 countries for this study, leads to the limited number of indicators of six.

From the FAO's dataset of 26 food security indicators, divided into 'Static and Dynamic Determinants' and 'Outcomes', three out of six possible indicators, for which data is available for all 13 countries, are identified for this study (cf. FAO, 2013b). Data from 2000 to 2011 reveals the cluster evolution and reflects the present state of food availability and access in each country and group of countries. Two of the three indicators represent the dimension availability: the Value of Food Production (VoFP) per capita and the Dietary Energy Supply (DES) in kilocalories (kcal) per capita and day. One indicator belongs to the outcome indicators of the dimension access: the Prevalence of Undernourishment (PoU). In order to avoid further distortion of variations in the indicators for the ten-year period, the arithmetic, and accordingly the geometric mean is calculated for each indicator respectively. Results for each country can be found in Appendix D.

From the availability dimension of FNS, the **Value of Food Production (VoFP)** per capita represents the total value of food production for each year, expressed in International Dollars (Int$) and divided by the total population. Its calculation allows a comparison of the relative economic size of the food production sector in the selected countries (cf. FAO, 2013b, 2012c). An examination of the data shows variations in the food production values for the investigative period of time from 2000 to 2011. These variations may result from external effects on world markets such as price fluctuations, environmental factors such as natural hazards, and economic policies, which can directly or indirectly influence the domestic food production. However, the VoFP does not reveal, whether the production of food is aimed for domestic consumption or exports.

The second indicator, the **Dietary Energy Supply (DES)** is measured in kcal per capita and day. It indicates the amount of kcal available for a person to meet her or his daily Minimum Dietary Energy Requirement (MDER), provided solely through domestic food production and/or imports of foodstuff (cf. FAO, 2013b). This indicator does not reveal, whether the calories available derive from a great variety of foodstuff or just one main source of energy provider. Further, the DES does not capture the whole range of the essential nutrients such as proteins, minerals and micronutrients, necessary for the body to function. Both indicators together, the VoFP and the DES represent a broad picture of the per capita level of food available on a national level.

On the contrary, the **Prevalence of Undernourishment (PoU)** indicator represents the proportion of the total population suffering from undernourishment. The PoU is an outcome indicator and measures the proportion of the total population, whose energy intake is below the recommended threshold of the MDER (cf. FAO, 2013b). A more detailed discussion on the indicator is given in chapter 2.3.3. The DES and the PoU can be analysed together as they disclose, whether food insecurity is due to a relatively low level of food availability, or due to a particular problem of the absence of adequate national distribution policies in the context of poverty (cf. FAO, 2013b). A short summary of the indicators is represented inTable 6. Complete data for these indicators are listed in Appendix D.

Table 6:   Food and Nutrition Security Indicators used for the cluster nalysis

Access Indicator	Definition
Prevalence of Undernourishment (PoU)	Proportion of the population with a level of dietary energy consumption below the threshold of the minimum dietary energy requirement.
Availability Indicators	**Definition**
Value of Food Production per capita (VoFP)	Total value of food production within a country divided by the total population, expressed in Int$.
Dietary Energy Supply (DES)	Dietary energy supply derived from different sources of food in kilocalories per person and per day.

Source: own compilation. FAO (2013b)

4.2.3 Methodology

Data management and analysis was performed using SPSS Statistics 21. Basically, there are three kinds of clustering procedures: the hierarchical, the two-steps, or k-means cluster analysis. The two latter methods are employed in the case of a high number of cases. Due to the relatively low number of cases in this study, a hierarchical cluster analysis is employed to generate a FNS profile for the selected 13 countries and groups. The algorithm of the hierarchical method can be either agglomerative or divisive. Agglomerative hierarchical clustering starts with each case being a cluster itself. In the next step, successive clusters with the shortest distance to another are merged together, until all cases are joined in one single cluster. The divisive method begins with all cases in a single cluster, and then separates them according to the longest distance between cases, until every case belongs to an individual cluster. The proximities between scores are measured through employing the squared *Euclidean Distance* (ED), which is the most common used distance measure. It calculates the distance between two cases x and y in n-dimension(s) – with n representing the number of variables (n=3). With the cases' coordinates (X_i, Y_i) the *ED* formula is (cf. Bühl, 2012):

$$ED\ (x, y) = \sqrt{\sum_{i=1}^{n} (x_i - y_i)^2}$$

In order to eliminate the bias caused by differences in the scales of the variables – that can be scaled as interval, ratio or value – they are converted and standardized into z-scores (cf.Hair, 2010). In the next step, the calculated distances between the one and the other case are represented in a proximity matrix, which serves as the basis for merging cases into clusters. Clusters are merged together in a stepwise procedure. In order to measure the distance or similarity between clusters, different algorithms can be employed. In this study, the cluster algorithm of *Ward's method* is applied. This method uses the squared ED and measures similarities within clusters by minimizing the variance of the total sum of squares across all variables within all clusters (cf. Eugenio Diaz-Bonilla, 2000; Hair, 2010). "Clusters are joined together as to minimize the variance at each step" (Eugenio Diaz-Bonilla, 2000: 11).

The next step of the cluster analysis requires the determination of the optimal number of clusters. SPSS produces traceable results at every step of the procedure. The solutions from this procedure are interpreted and discussed in the subsequent section.

4.2.4   Results and discussion

The agglomerative hierarchical clustering produces n-1 cluster solutions according to the number of cases (n=13). SPSS computes several possible cluster solutions from which the 'optimal' number of clusters has to be determined. The determination of the optimal number of clusters results rather from a subjective selection on the basis of particular criteria, than from any objective procedure; the determination of the optimal number of clusters is, therefore, based on an evaluation of meaningful cluster memberships. However, there are some approaches that have been identified to be practical. One procedure is to interpret the variations in the value of the distance measure (ED), the so-called *agglomeration coefficient*. Table 7 represents the *agglomeration schedule,* which displays the 12 stages at which clusters are combined; it also shows the agglomeration coefficient according to the squared ED of the dedicated z-variables. An increase of the agglomeration coefficient indicates growth in heterogeneity within a cluster, and accordingly a decrease of similarity within a cluster (cf. Hair, 2010). The smaller the number of clusters is computed, the higher the heterogeneity within a cluster. The distance measure increases with every step of the cluster agglomeration procedure. The selected number of clusters depends, i.a., on an acceptable level of heterogeneity within a cluster. Table 7 below shows that there is a significant increase of the coefficient between the 10th and 11th stages. The agglomeration of clusters should not be continued after the 10th stage; otherwise a smaller number of clusters would be generated with a higher degree of heterogeneity. A solution with a relatively low heterogeneity level among the group members would accordingly result in three clusters (cf. Bühl, 2012).

Table 7:   Agglomeration Schedule (WARD's method)

Stage	Cluster Combined		Coefficients	Stage Cluster First Appears		Next Stage
	Cluster 1	Cluster 2		Cluster 1	Cluster 2	
1	8	11	,002	0	0	4
2	10	13	,027	0	0	5
3	9	12	,224	0	0	10
4	3	8	,429	0	1	8
5	2	10	,770	0	2	8
6	1	6	1,260	0	0	10
7	4	7	1,821	0	0	9
8	2	3	2,938	5	4	11
9	4	5	5,146	7	0	11
10	1	9	7,450	6	3	12
11	2	4	16,402	8	9	12
12	1	2	36,000	10	11	0

Source: calculated and generated with SPSS based on FAO (2013b)

Another method subsidiary to determine the optimal number of clusters is given by a graphical solution of the *dendrogram*, which illustrates the agglomeration process in a tree-like graph. The value of the agglomeration coefficient converted in real value is displayed in the horizontal scale, ranging from zero to 25, labelled as rescaled distance cluster combination (cf. Hair, 2010). The dendrogram in Figure 16 shows that, in the beginning, the coefficient value is zero, and increases as clusters are merged together. The dendrogram displays the number of clusters ranging from two at a scale of 25 to six clusters, at a scale between zero to five. It becomes visible, that the agglomeration coefficient increases in large jumps after generating four clusters. At the point of five of the rescaled distance cluster combination, three clusters are formed as the plotted line indicates. From the previous observation a three clusters solution becomes a possible and actually a reasonable result, demonstrated in the graphical solution of clustering by dint of the dendrogram.

Figure 16:   Dendrogram using WARD Linkage

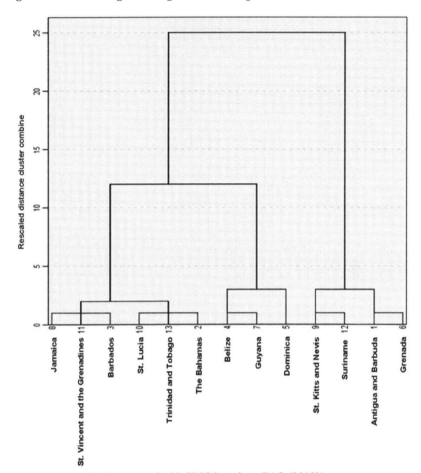

Source: calculated and generated with SPSS based on FAO (2013b)

The results computed with SPSS are found in Appendix D, while the cluster membership and country classification are displayed in Table 8. The first cluster comprises the four members, Antigua and Barbuda, Grenada, St. Kitts and Nevis, and Suriname. The second cluster consists of six countries, The Bahamas, Barbados, Jamaica, St. Lucia, St. Vincent and the Grenadines, and Trinidad and Tobago. The remaining three countries, Belize, Dominica, and Guyana are grouped into the third cluster.

Table 8:   Cluster membership of Caribbean countries

Cluster	Countries
Cluster I	Antigua and Barbuda Grenada St. Kitts and Nevis Suriname
Cluster II	The Bahamas Barbados Jamaica St. Lucia St. Vincent and the Grenadines Trinidad and Tobago
ClusterIII	Belize Dominica Guyana

Source: own compilation

Characteristics and relationship of the indicators

The general characteristics of the groups according to the three selected indicators can be analysed by means of scatterplots, which can also be used to produce a graphical cluster result. First and foremost, this practice allows identifying countries with similar features and further to examine the relationships between at least two variables. Instead of an examination of three variables in a three-dimensional graph, results are more reasonable and evident in a two-dimensional graph. Subsequently, three possible combinations of pairing two variables lead to clearer results, which then can be interpreted in combination according to the clusters' characteristics.

  (a) Value of Food Production (VoFP) and Prevalence of Undernourishment (PoU)
  (b) Value of Food Production (VoFP) and Dietary Energy Supply (DES)
  (c) Prevalence of Undernourishment (PoU) and Dietary Energy Supply (DES)

The analysis of each relationship (a) and (b) raises two complex questions:

1. Does food and nutrition insecurity result from insufficient food availability, indicated by a low level of the VoFP? Is inadequate access to food indicated by high levels of PoU or low levels of the DES?
2. Is food and nutrition insecurity a particular problem of poor national distribution policies related to income and poverty?

However, the relationship (c) between PoU and DES should not reveal any unexpected results since a low PoU naturally correlates with a higher level of DES. Nevertheless, the following results reveal a predominantly clear cluster membership of the first two relationships (a) and (b). Detailed data of each indicator and the related clusters can be found in Appendix D.

The relationship between the VoFP and the PoU is shown in Figure 17. According to the countries' geographical distribution in the scatterplot, countries can be merged into clusters. Considering the findings of the previous examination, the results also show a solution of three clusters. From the comprehensive FAO dataset and the resulting mean for each indicator and each country, reasonable baselines are determined for each indicator. According to the average values in rounded figures, the baseline for the VoFP is at Int$ 300, the PoU at 15% and the DES at 2700 kcal per capita and per day. The graph is divided into four squares, according to each baseline of the indicators, showing that countries are located in three squares and, therefore, grouped in three clusters. Characteristics of each cluster can be interpreted on the basis of the values and the relationship between the VoFP and PoU indicated by the geographical location of each country.

Cluster I, which compromises Antigua and Barbuda, Grenada, St. Kitts and Nevis, and Suriname, appears to be vulnerable to food and nutrition insecurity, since all four countries show the highest level of the PoU above the threshold of 15%. Antigua and Barbuda heads the scale at 31%, whereas the PoU level in Suriname is relatively low at 16%. Additionally, the countries of this first cluster mark a low level of the VoFP, which reaches a level below the threshold of Int$ 300 per capita. Cluster II consisting of The Bahamas, Barbados, Jamaica, St. Lucia, St. Vincent and the Grenadines, Trinidad and Tobago has a similar low level of the VoFP, reaching the highest level at Int$ 200. However, the PoU indicator differs from the first cluster significantly as its level lies below 15% and reaches its lowest point at 7.2% in Jamaica. Accordingly, the second cluster can be labelled as moderately vulnerable to food and nutrition insecurity. Overall,

Belize reaches the highest level of the VoFP at Int$ 574, a member of the Cluster III, together with Guyana and Dominica, which reach a VoFP level notably above Int$ 300. Considering their low level of PoU, which lies even below 10%, Cluster III can be labelled the most food secure cluster of all sample countries. In this case, a high level of food availability through domestic food production correlates with a simultaneously low level of the proportion of people suffering from undernourishment. The opposite is true for the first cluster, where a low level of VoFP shows a positive relationship with a high level of PoU. An exception is the second cluster of countries, where a similarly low level of VoFP correlates with a likewise low level of PoU.

Figure 17:   Resulting relationship between the Value of Food Production (VoFP) per capita and Prevalence of Undernourishment (PoU), Caribbean countries

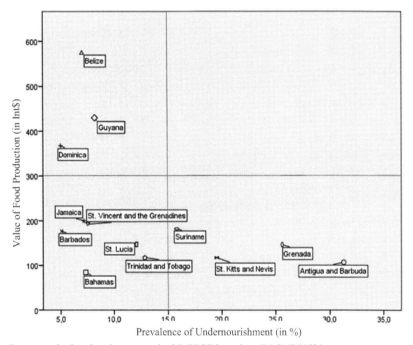

Source: calculated and generated with SPSS based on FAO (2013b)

The final interpretation of the cluster characteristics can only be drawn until the relationship (b) between the VoFP and the DES is examined. This relationship is drawn in Figure 18. In this scatterplot, the Cluster III, which from the previous relationship (a) was identified as the most food secure cluster, proves its label through a relatively high level of the DES, headed by Dominica with 3086 kcal per capita and per day. Hence, a high caloric supply in these three countries may result from an efficient domestic food production sector, since the VoFP for this cluster is on a high level as already asserted in the previous relationship (a). Conversely, in countries of Cluster I where the domestic food production is low, DES is even below the threshold of 2700 kcal per capita and per day. The second cluster, which is moderately vulnerable to food and nutrition insecurity, repeatedly indicates low levels of VoFP correlating with high DES levels above 2700 kcal per capita and per day. This intriguing relationship leads to the assumptions that the high caloric supply is derived from external resources other than from domestic food production, or the domestic food production sector produces predominantly energy dense foods.

Figure 18:   **Resulting relationship Value of Food Production (VoFP) per capita and Dietary Energy Supply (DES), Cribbean countries**

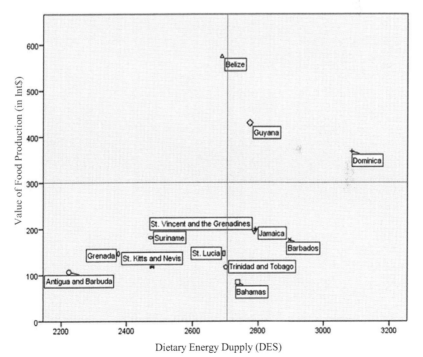

Source: calculated and generated with SPSS based on FAO (2013b)

The expected results from the relationship of the PoU and the DES plotted in Figure 19, reveal that a high DES level correlates with a low PoU level. For clusters where the DES level is lower, the PoU level is relatively high. Although, Antigua and Barbuda reaches the lowest level of the DES at 2223 kcal per capita and per day, it still achieves the MDER, which is at an average of 1880 kcal per capita and per day. The other three countries of the Cluster I, which are located in the lower half of the scatterplot, have relatively low levels of DES, however, exceeding the MDER respectively. The third scatterplot does not serve as a graphical cluster result, for it rather shows an obvious correlation ensuing from the previous findings of the relationships (a) and (b).

Figure 19:   Resulting relationship between the Prevalence of Undernourishment (PoU) and Dietary Energy Supply (DES), Caribbean countries

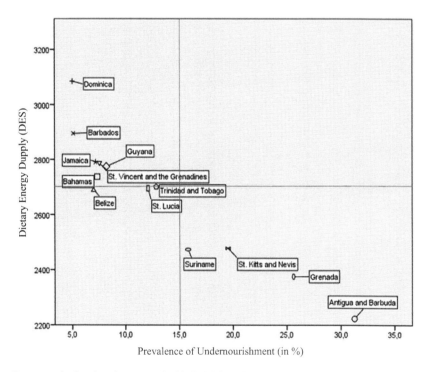

Source: calculated and generated with SPSS based on FAO (2013b)

4.2.5 Final results and conclusion

Table 9 and Table 10 summarize the results from the graphical cluster analysis in a matrix, presenting the different levels of the indicators' baselines. These cluster results reflect certain state of vulnerability to food and nutrition insecurity.

Table 9:   **Relationship (a) VoFP and PoU, cluster results**

	High level VoFP (> 300 Int$)	Low level VoFP (< 300 Int$)
High level of PoU (> 15%)	n.r.	Most vulnerable Cluster I
Low level of PoU (< 15%)	Least vulnerable Cluster III	Moderately vulnerable Cluster II

Note: n.r. = no results
Source: own compilation

Table 10:   **Relationship (b) VoFP and DES, cluster results**

	High level VoFP (> 300 Int$)	Low level VoFP (< 300 Int$)
High level of DES (> 2700 kcal/p.c.)	Least vulnerable Cluster III	Moderately vulnerable Cluster II
Low level of DES (< 2700 kcal/p.c.)	n.r.	Most vulnerable Cluster I

Note: n.r. = no results
Source: own compilation

The resulting relationships (a) VoFP and PoU and (b) VoFP and DES reveal two important assumptions. First, food and nutrition insecurity in the Caribbean is an issue of insufficient availability, and results from the low levels of domestic food production, as demonstrated in two of three clusters. Therefore, in the majority of the countries, the level of the VoFP is below the average baseline of Int$ 300.

Secondly, in countries, where the value of food production is low, food imports might be crucial in order to meet the domestic demand for food. Both assumptions apply to **Cluster I** and **II**, which are characterized by low levels of domestic food production. Additionally, the results for **Cluster I** show that countries from this cluster are most vulnerable to food and nutrition insecurity due to relatively high prevalence of the population suffering from under-nutrition, and a low caloric supply per capita (cf. Table 11). As already indicated, the low DES in these countries is still above the MDER, although it appears that a relatively large share of the population suffers from under-nutrition, hence does not meet the MDER. Consequently, this fact leads to a third assumption that the lack of access to food reflected by the high PoU may result from an unequal distribution of food or income among the population. On the macro level, these results may indicate that overall food supply for these countries is low due to a low level of domestic production, and a low level of food purchased through imports. Countries in Cluster I therefore, can be labelled as most vulnerable to food and nutrition insecurity.

Conversely, the countries of **Cluster II** reach high levels of the DES per capita and a low level of the PoU, and together indicate that sufficient food is available on the domestic level, and access to food is a minor, but not an insignificant problem in these countries. However, the supply of food in Cluster II may not necessarily derive solely from domestic food production indicated by the countries' low level of food production value. Food supply, therefore, may depend on external sources such as food imports. Based on these assumptions and results, Cluster II can be classified as moderately vulnerable to food and nutrition insecurity (cf. Table 11).

Cluster III is classified as least vulnerable to food insecurity due to its high levels of dietary energy supply and the low prevalence of undernourishment (cf. Table 11). It is, moreover, the only cluster that reaches high levels of the food production value. The food production sector in these countries – which each produces over Int\$ 300 per capita – indicates high levels of food availability on the domestic level. As a result, the excess of the food production may even be exported, while food imports do not contribute significantly to the overall supply of food in the countries.

Table 11:   Food and Nutrition Security cluster results, Caribbean countries

Cluster	*Countries*
Cluster I – most vulnerable	Antigua and Barbuda Grenada St. Kitts and Nevis Suriname
Cluster II – moderately vulnerable	The Bahamas Barbados Jamaica St. Lucia St. Vincent and the Grenadines Trinidad and Tobago
ClusterIII – least vulnerable	Belize Dominica Guyana

Source: own compilation

The cluster analysis results represent an important component of the FNS situation in the Caribbean countries. A detailed examination on the implications of this study is made in chapter 5 and 6.

4.3   Conclusion: The Caribbean Food and Nutrition Security situation revealed

This chapter analysed the FNS situation in the selected 13 countries in two steps. The first step consisted of the assessment of FNS issues on each of the four dimensions, availability, access, utilization and stability. It was guided by the region-specific examination of the driving forces and underlying reasons of the distinctive socio-economic development in the Caribbean countries resulting from chapter 3. From this previous study it infers, that food and nutrition insecurity in the Caribbean is a consequence of the limited capacity of the domestic food production sector to provide the population with a sufficient supply of food, despite the increase of the food production index. Food imports may serve to balance the increasing demand for food, but concurrently impede the development of and investments in the agricultural sector, which certainly would help to boost domestic food production in the Caribbean countries. Additionally, high food prices and persistent high poverty and inequality levels limit the individual's access. This may lead to a tendency to shift from consumptions of nutritious food to a low-cost food basket consisting of high energy- and fat-dense foodstuffs. Evidently, over-nutrition in the Caribbean increased with the growing risk of the incidence of nutrition related diseases, while the countries made significant progress in the reduction of the prevalence of undernourishment indicator.

From the Cluster analysis, it derives that availability of food is an emergent issue, particular in the countries of Cluster I and II, but a less alarming issue for the countries of Cluster III. Moreover, the limited access to food and the lack of an equal distribution of income or food may be an impediment to FNS for the countries of Cluster I which is labelled as most vulnerable to food and nutrition insecurity. The vulnerability aspect in this examination emphasizes the need to consider the overall socioeconomic situation of the sample countries and the factors which impact FNS. The multidimensionality of the concept itself and the particular features of Caribbean SIDS have to be included into the discussion of FNS in the Caribbean. Limiting the cluster analysis to three indicators and two dimensions of FNS due to technical feasibility of the study shows that the results lead to further implications, which have to be discussed. These cluster results allow the understanding of the diversity of the FNS situation in the sample countries and reveals significant differences between them.

Part III: Problem Analysis and Implications

Based on the previous analysis in Part II, in which the problems of food and nutrition insecurity in the Caribbean has been identified, Part III of this thesis examines their causes and consequences in a socio-economic context. Two main issues have been identified in the context of Food and Nutrition Security: high food imports and nutrition related health risks. Both issues have different but far-reaching implications on the Caribbean socio-economic and financial situation. The aim of this part is to detect differences between clusters concerning the double burden of high food imports and health risks. Concomitantly, this leads to a comprehensive assessment of the major causes and consequences of the double burden. Ultimately, this last part answers the main research question: What are the implications of food and nutrition insecurity in the Caribbean?

Key questions:

1. What are the underlying causes and main consequences deriving from the low levels of food production in the Caribbean countries?
2. Which implications can be drawn from the food import structure and dependency for different clusters?
3. What are the causes and consequences resulting from health risks in the Caribbean countries?

5. Implications of food imports on Food and Nutrition Security in the Caribbean

From the previous analysis, it became obvious that some Caribbean countries are struggling to secure an adequate supply of food, and to make it accessible for the population. Three clusters have been identified. Countries of Cluster I are vulnerable to food and nutrition insecurity; whereas Cluster II and Cluster III are characterized as moderately vulnerable and least vulnerable to food and nutrition insecurity. The availability of food on a national level depends mainly on domestic food production and on food imports. FNS in the Caribbean is commonly discussed in the context of the relatively low capacity of the agricultural sector, and the countries' dependence on food imports to secure a steady supply of food. Both issues are the result of different reasons but may influence one another. The underlying reasons ensue among other factors from the limited economic diversity of the small and vulnerable countries. However, food imports in general are not a problem itself, since countries around the world import a large share of their food to ensure a steady and sufficient supply of food, and to increase the variety of food products available on national markets. This leads to the main question of this chapter: What implications do food imports and food import dependency have on the FNS situation in the Caribbean countries? In order to address this question, differences between countries and clusters have to be evaluated and examined – based on to their state of vulnerability to food and nutrition insecurity.

This chapter aims to investigate the causes and effects of food imports through a macroeconomic approach, on the basis of trade data from the investigative period of time from 2000 to 2011. The first subchapter explores the specific underlying causes of the development of food import dependency in the Caribbean, which constitutes in the weak capacity of the domestic food production sector, and the general tendency to rely on external trade for foodstuff. Why are food imports an emerging issue in the Caribbean countries? Food imports as a share of total merchandise imports on average[26] constitute 37% in the Caribbean countries (own

---

26 The simple average (mean) is used.

calculation based on UN COMTRADE, 2010) providing industries and the local food supply sector with raw, semi-processed and processed food products. These imports have different implications on the national and the individual level for different groups of the population, which will be discussed in subchapter 5.2.

The last subchapter 5.3 examines the total value of food imports and the reason for its increase in the period of time from 2000 to 2011. High values or quantities of food imports are mirrored in the so-called Food Import Bill (FIB). Despite the fiscal and economic implications of food import dependency and the FIB, these issues will be discussed in a broader context of the FNS situation in the Caribbean countries and clusters.

Results from the previous cluster analysis serve to examine differences between the clusters and common constraints based on the degree of dependence on food imports and the size of the FIB, respectively for the three clusters. For this chapter, data is inevitably drawn from different data sources. The United Nations Commodity Trade Statistics Database (UN COMTRADE), the Food and Agriculture Organization Statistics Database (FAOSTAT), the statistics database of the World Trade Organization (WTO) and the World Development Indicators (WDI) of the World Bank serve as main data sources to compile a set of comparable data for the selected Caribbean countries. In the figures and tables used in this chapter, countries are distributed according to their cluster membership and not by any alphabetic order, or order of scale.

5.1   The causes of food import dependency in the Caribbean

Food production in the Caribbean takes place in the agricultural sector, which almost exclusively is dedicated to the production of food and primary products for domestic consumption and the export market. Ever since the rise of the flourishing services sector and the global price fall for export commodities such as sugar, the agricultural sector in the Caribbean got crowded out, mainly by the services sector in the majority of the countries – and accordingly in Suriname and Trinidad and Tobago by the oil, gas and mining industry. Partially, these events caused a reduction of the domestic food production and led to a rising dependence on food imports. The Caribbean countries made a rapid transition from net agricultural exporters to net food importers.

The first section of this subchapter explains the underlying causes of the decline of the agricultural food production and the rise of food imports which inversely can be both: main cause and leading consequence. A decline of the food production may have occurred due to a rise in food imports, which its part may have led to a decline of domestic food production amplifying the effect of the food import dependency. Different degrees of dependency reveal the severity of the food and nutrition security or insecurity for the three clusters in the last sub-section of this chapter.

For the following study it is important to discern the notions 'agriculture' and 'food' produce. The latter term derives from agricultural production and refers to a narrow range of items, which are aimed for direct or indirect consumption and have a nutritious value. Agriculture comprises all products, emanating from this sector and not necessarily aimed for food consumption. Nevertheless, the agricultural sector plays a significant role in the capacity of domestic food production. A further reason for this distinction between 'agriculture' and 'food' is to reveal the food groups in the Caribbean destined for exports, and which of these food groups rather used for domestic consumption. Although the majority of beverages are produced domestically within the Caribbean countries, according to a FAO study (2011), there is no production data of the amount or values of beverages (cf. Silva et al., 2011). Thus, beverages in this analysis are excluded.

5.1.1 Agricultural trade and domestic food production in the Caribbean

"Plenty can only be produced by encouraging agriculture; and agriculture can be encouraged only by making it gainful" (Samuel Johnson cited in Murphy, 1832: 538).

Agriculture in general has different functions for the society, the economy and the environment (cf. IAASTD, 2009). In the Caribbean, agriculture has changed significantly and in the recent context, it provides – to different extents – employment and income, rural livelihoods, earnings from exports, it contributes to domestic food supply and can protect the environment (cf. Beckford and Campbell, 2013).

In the context of trade and food security, it is often argued that trade liberalization is beneficial to countries, which do not have the capacities to grow sufficient food, and thus filling the food gap through food imports. The controversy over the effects of trade on economic growth is widely discussed in literature and economic theory since the *Ricardian* theory of trade liberalization and its expansion through the *Heckscher-Ohlin-Theorem* (cf. FAO, 2003). In particular, the differences in productivity and costs of agricultural production result in comparative advantages, while the factor endowment of capital and labour of trading countries, determine the prices of production factors on the world markets. Trade liberalization of agricultural products, therefore, results in favourable prices for the consumers, and thus food becomes accessible.

However, the argument that developing countries or Small Island Developing States (SIDS) can benefit from trade liberalization, indirectly through economic growth or directly through lower prices for food, is disputable.

> "However, the impact of liberalization on SIDSs appears to be negative — welfare gains for SIDSs are expected only under the compensatory scenario. [...] It is apparent that gains from agricultural liberalization to SIDSs are more limited compared to other groups of countries" (Monge-Roffarello, 2003: 17).

According to Briguglio (2009), the high degree of economic openness, export concentration on a narrow range of products, and the dependence on strategic imports make especially developing countries and SIDS susceptible to external shocks, constituting their vulnerabilities (cf. chapter 3.3.2) (cf. Briguglio, 2009).

In the last decades, Caribbean countries opened their markets to the world market, either through regional or bilateral trade agreements, for instance with the European Union (EU), the USA, Canada. This progressive trade liberalization does not necessarily benefit the countries or the region under the CARICOM. Prices for commodities such as sugar fell sharply, and thus rapid adjustment of the agricultural production could not be made due to various constraints, whereas external debt, the lack of investment, poor infrastructure and weak institutions aggravated the situation. The domestic market and the export market for food are barely able to compete with low world market prices, which result from cost-effective and efficient food production sectors of the competitive countries. Thus, the agriculture and food production sector in the Caribbean countries suffers from the negative consequences of trade liberalization.

In the 1980s, Structural Adjustment Programs (SAPs) were promoted by the World Bank and the IMF for the developing world, including the Caribbean, in order to obtain further loans for tackling high national debt burdens. In exchange, the countries had to comply with the conditions of the SAPs such as the facilitation of trade liberalization. Later, when the

Caribbean countries joined the World Trade Organization (WTO) in 1995/96, further liberalization was induced by the agreement to lower agricultural trade tariffs (cf. WTO, 2013). Thus far, agricultural imports have grown consistently faster than agricultural exports. Imports increased steadily from US$ 1.5 billion in 1995 to US$ 2.6 billion in 2011, whereas agricultural exports rose in a more volatile manner from US$ 1.2 billion to US$ 2.2 billion in the same period of time as shown in Figure 20. In 2011, these figures result in a negative agricultural trade balance of US$ 423.48 million, for all the sample countries (own calculation based on FAOSTAT, 2013b).

Based on the data from Figure 20, agricultural imports and exports are dominated by the main five products shown in Table 12. Country data is aggregated for the main products and measures trade values in US$ 1000. The main agricultural trade items differ according to their state of processing. In general, the price of raw agricultural products is more volatile than that of processed items. A further detailed analysis on price changes of food is made in the up-coming chapter 5.3.1. The composition of agricultural exports of the Caribbean countries concentrates on just a few traditional agricultural products and relies mostly on commodities (cf. Table 12).

Figure 20:   **Agricultural exports and imports, aggregated for the Caribbean countries, value based quantity (in US$ 1000), 1990-2011**

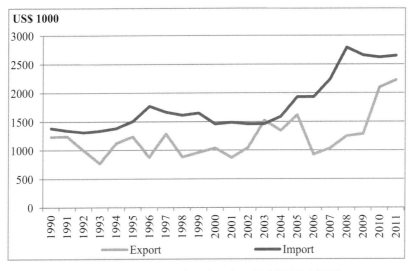

Source: own compilation. own calculations based on FAOSTAT (2013b)

Table 12:   Top five agricultural imports and exports, Caribbean countries, 2011

Agricultural Imports	*Agricultural Exports*
Food preparations n.e.s.	Sugar raw centrifugal
Wheat	Beverages, distilled alcoholic
Meat, chicken	Beverages, non-alcoholic
Beverages, non-alcoholic	Beer of barley
Maize	Juice, orange, concentrated

Note: n.e.s. = not elsewhere specified
Source: own compilation. FAOSTAT (2013b)

The agricultural sector's contribution to GDP in some Caribbean countries is significant. Table 13 displays the agriculture value added in percentage of GDP, which in Dominica and Guyana accounts for double-digit figures of 14% and 21% respectively in 2011. In the other countries, this contribution is lower due to other sector's higher contribution to GDP (cf. chapter 3.3.2). Overall in the Caribbean the value added agriculture contribution to GDP almost halved, declining from 14% in 1990 to 7% (own calculation based on The World Bank, 2013d). However, the measurement of agriculture production value added GDP, merely includes the output of the sector and refers to primary production including fishing, forestry, hunting and livestock production. Further stages of the agriculture food sector, as well as interlinked activities such as food processing, business and financial activities, and transport, are not included in this measurement, and sometimes underestimate the contribution of the agricultural sector to the national economies as a whole (cf. Brathwaite, 2009). The strong export orientation of the agricultural sector on international markets derives from its role as source for foreign exchange that is determined and shaped by the legacy of the plantation economy system explained previously in chapter 3.1. Although, agriculture production partially shifted from the dominant sugarcane plantation cultivation to other traditional cash crops such as bananas, coffee, rice and nutmeg, its mono-cultural characteristics are still persistent. These primary agricultural products, for which tariffs are usually lower than for processed agricultural products, are mainly traded outside the region; approximately two-thirds of all agricultural products are destined for the US and the European markets (cf. Ford and Rawlins, 2007). Accordingly, only a small quantity is traded within the region due to internal constraints, and persistent trade barriers and transaction costs (cf. Chesney and Francis, 2004). However, analysing the intra-regional trade of agricultural and food products in the Caribbean is not the scope of this study. A considerable amount of studies and reports have been published on trade-related issues in the CARICOM, which analyse trade and intra-regional trade flows.

Table 13:   Agriculture related indicators, Caribbean countries, 2011

	Agriculture value added (in % of GDP)	Net agriculture production, per capita (in Int$)	Agriculture trade balance (in US$ 1000)	Total employment in agriculture[1]
Cluster I				
Antigua and Barbuda	2.3	111.30	-59,704	8,000
Grenada	5.3	122.75	-3,068	9,000
St. Kitts and Nevis	1.8	42.17	-14,941	5,000
Suriname	9.7	178.29	-79,083	33,000
Cluster II				
The Bahamas	2.3	95.29	-242,561	4,000
Barbados	3.0[a]	161.65	-171,605	4,000
Jamaica	6.6	203.55	-519,424	212,000
St. Lucia	3.4	85.94	-66,369	17,000
St. Vincent and the Grenadines	6.3	199.64	-23,026	11,000
Trinidad and Tobago	0.6	121.12	-420,806	46,000
Cluster III				
Belize	12.1[b]	479.75	89,968	31,000
Dominica	13.8	371.22	-29,784	6,000
Guyana	21.4	431.68	287,757	49,000

Note: [1] original data in thousands; [a] 2009, [b] 2008
Source: Agriculture GDP: The World Bank (2013d); Net agriculture production: own calculations based on (FAOSTAT, 2013b) (The World Bank, 2013d); Agriculture trade balance: own calculations bases on FAOSTAT (2013b); Agriculture labour force: UNCTADSTAT (2013).

Domestic food production faces economic constraints, as well as environmental ones. The former plantations partially destroyed the ecosystem through intensive farming and cultivation practices on suitable land, which led to soil depletion and erosion on various islands of the Caribbean (cf. IICA, 2012; McGregor, 2011). Another issue that derives from the plantation system is that the land, which was formerly occupied by large plantation estates, later has been left abandoned due to labour scarcities and decreasing profits. Although, former plantation land later became available for a small-scale or even large-scale production, it has not been re-cultivated, it has been rather left fallow or re-used for housing or tourism purposes (cf. IICA, 2012).

Nevertheless, large mono-cultural cultivation of permanent crops for exports occupies mostly the best fertile and arable land, which provokes a competition between land for agricultural export production, and domestic production. Domestic agricultural production is often conducted by small-scale farmers[27], which have to deal with far less fertile soils, cultivation on hillsides or landslides. Small-scale farmers in the Caribbean countries also depend largely on export markets but mainly concentrate on mono-cultural production practices. The role of small-scale farming for domestic food supply is guided mostly by local diets and the capability to grow food under the local conditions of soil, weather and the access to resources (cf. Beckford and Campbell, 2013; Graham, 2012). Although, the small-scale production of food crops in the Caribbean is based on traditional and local crops and, therefore, did not change significantly, cultivation for domestic markets is more diversified than for export markets (cf. Graham, 2012). However, small-scale producers struggle to integrate into the domestic food supply chain, since they have to compete with high volumes of imported food with low prices. Imported foodstuff is mostly destined to the domestic supply for supermarkets and retail seller for the final consumers, as well as hotels and restaurants. Small-scale farmers face various production constraints such as lower efficiency because of high costs of production, low technological and labour-intensive practices, impeding their capacity to compete with large food producers and food imports (cf. Beckford and Campbell, 2013; Graham, 2012).

---

27   According to the Census of Agriculture, a small-scale farmer in the Caribbean is a famer who operates on under two hectares of land, including landless farmers (cf. Graham, 2012).

The implications of trade liberalization on FNS in the Caribbean are far-reaching. Agricultural trade liberalization has negatively affected the local and small-scale producers, hardly being able to compete with the cheap global food supply, which is highly subsidized and available at lower prices (cf. Beckford, 2012). Low prices on the world markets and higher productivity, on the one hand, led to higher competitiveness, which primarily has been achieved through technology advancements and higher productivity, on the other hand. The contrary is true for the Caribbean countries, having lost competitiveness in the agricultural sector due to falling commodity prices, weak infrastructure and the lack of research and development in the agricultural sector. This could stimulate investment in the sector and eventually be conducive to productivity (cf. Ford and Rawlins, 2007). Further studies revealed that the efficiency of infrastructure influences the costs of imports and exports (cf. FAO, 2003; Pinnock and Ajagunna, 2012). Caribbean ports, technically conducting exports and imports, lack efficiency and increase the costs of trade through high cargo shipping costs and poor port infrastructure (cf. Pinnock and Ajagunna, 2012). FAO data shows that investments in form of a change in the agriculture capital stock has been stagnant or merely slightly increasing in the last years for the Caribbean countries (cf. FAOSTAT, 2013b). The agriculture and food production system faces different constraints in the selected Caribbean countries. That is attributable to the fact that the availability of land for agricultural production is limited, because of the small size of most of the Caribbean countries.

Nevertheless, in countries such as Belize, Dominica and Guyana (Cluster III), the value of agriculture production per capita shows high levels and agriculture contribution to GDP makes up for double-digit figures in this cluster, as displayed in Table 13. In the other two clusters, these figures vary widely from Int\$ 42.17 value of agriculture production in Suriname (Cluster I) and Int\$ 203.55 in Jamaica (Cluster II). Countries from Cluster I and II, nonetheless do not reach such high values as the countries from Cluster III. However, it is difficult to assess, whether the domestically produced agriculture output is also consumed domestically or rather destined for the export markets. The agriculture trade balance is negative in all sample countries, except for Belize and Guyana. A positive agriculture trade balance means that countries are Net Agricultural Exporters (NAEX). In countries where the agriculture trade balance is negative, agriculture production is focused on the domestic market, and it is not efficient enough to meet domestic demand – since import values are higher than export values. These countries can be labelled as Net Agricultural Importers (NAIM). Jamaica constitutes the highest agriculture trade deficit of Int\$ 519,424, although its agriculture production value per capita and agriculture's share of GDP is the highest in Cluster II. Since agriculture production comprises a great variety of products including food, animal feed, the reason for high imports may also be that these imports are in large part composed of inputs for production, such as seed and fertilizer. Labour force in agriculture compared to the labour force working in travel and tourism, is significantly lower for some countries, due to the fact that working in agriculture, in the Caribbean countries is not as attractive as working in other sectors offering better opportunities and salaries. Agriculture employment is mostly associated with poor livelihood and working in rural areas and, therefore, may leave this sector with a higher demand for labour than available supply in the Caribbean.

Analysing challenges and potentials of the agriculture sector in the Caribbean countries shows that costs for labour, machinery, and inputs such as fertilizer and seeds are relatively high, while investments into the sector are poor. The traditional role of agriculture was to provide the population with a sufficient supply of food and labour, serving as a major source of income and economic growth. However, this role changed significantly in the Caribbean countries. Agricultural food production contributes only marginally to economic growth fails to offer attractive employment opportunities for the population or to provide sufficient food. A discussion on the reasons for agriculture's weakness and its declining importance for the economy, therefore, can be differentiated into causative supply-side and demand-side factors.

Box 2:   **The Jagdeo Initiative for Agricultural Development in the Caribbean**

In the context of a long-standing discussion about the weakness of the agricultural sector in the Caribbean, in 2003, the Caribbean Community (CARICOM) on behalf of the Caribbean countries, agreed on the *Jagdeo Initiative on Agriculture*. The initiative was introduced by the former president of Guyana, Mr. Bharat Jagdeo, and identifies nine key binding constraints to the development of the agricultural sector in the Caribbean. On the basis of these identified constraints, corresponding mechanism and initiatives should be implemented in order to strengthen the agricultural sector and boost its growth (cf. FAO, 2011b).

Jagdeo Initiative Key Binding Constraints (KBCs):
(1) Inadequate financing and investment in the sector
(2) Inefficient and outdated agriculture health and food safety regulations
(3) Inadequate land and water resource management and distribution system
(4) Deficient and uncoordinated disaster risk management
(5) Market and marketing development and its linkages
(6) Ineffective research and development
(7) Lack of skilled human resources
(8) Disorganized, un-coordinated private sector
(9) Inadequate transportation system

Aside from these rather structural constraints of the agricultural sector in the Caribbean countries, natural resource constraints are hardly considered as KBCs. Issues such as land distribution, land ownership regulations, little arable land area, sloping lands, poor soil quality, hillside agriculture, and land degradation should be seriously considered as general weaknesses (cf. Table 14). Moreover, climate change poses a great threat on the agriculture and the fisheries sector (cf. UNEP, 2008). The fisheries sector, however, deserves a particular analysis in this context, since constraints differ in some areas from the agricultural sector.

A country specific assessment of existing constraints is more adequate to address specific issues on a national level and to foster potentials in a collective region-wide framework, such as proposed by the CARICOM under the *Revised Treaty of Chaguaramas* Article 56, the *Community Agricultural Policy* (CAP). The following table lists main challenges and potentials of the agricultural sector for the selected sample countries. This information is mainly based on accessible information from the Ministries of Agriculture, CPA reports and IICA.

Table 14:   Identified challenges of the agriculture sector in the Caribbean countries

Country	Main agriculture product	Challenges
Antigua and Barbuda	Banana, cotton, coconut, cucumber, hot pepper, mango, pineapple	Soil depletion, drought, groundwater shortages
The Bahamas	Avocado, banana, cabbage, cassava, coconut	Little arable land, low soil fertility, limited technology, low institutional capacity
Barbados	Cotton, cucumber, sweet potato, squash, sugarcane, tomato	Reduced quantities of land, lack of affordable water, high input costs, exposure to natural hazards
Belize	Banana, citrus, sugarcane, black beans, rice, corn	Exposure to natural hazards, drought, floods, steep slopes, poor drainage, high input costs, absent land titles for small farmers, lack of access to affordable credit
Dominica	Banana, plantain, cocoa, coffee, root crops	Land distribution underutilization of arable land, exposure to natural hazards, mountainous areas, hillside slopes, lack of technology, praedial larceny
Grenada	Banana, cocoa, citrus, golden apple, mango, nutmeg	Adapting irrigation technology, drought, land distribution, praedial larceny, obsolete farming systems, insufficient research and development, lack of access to affordable credit
Guyana	Banana, coconut, cocoa, citrus, sugar, rice, tobacco, vegetables	Climatic conditions, high labour costs, potentials of expanding production

Country	Main agriculture product	Challenges
Jamaica	Banana, coffee, cocoa, citrus, pumpkin, yams	Soil erosion, high input costs, inadequate irrigation, poor infrastructure, exposure to natural hazards, deforestation, limited application of modern technology, praedial larceny
St. Kitts and Nevis	Banana, cotton, coconut, livestock, rice, sugarcane, yams	Distribution of land, hillside farming, erosion, lack of technical knowledge and skills, low diversification
St. Lucia	Banana, cocoa, coconut, citrus fruits, livestock	High input and labour costs, distribution of land, limited land availability, poor soil conditions
St. Vincent and the Grenadines	Arrowroot starch, banana, cassava, coconut, eddoe, dasheen, pineapple, sweet potato, yam	Exposure to natural hazards, praedial larceny, soil erosion, land distribution, water pollution
Suriname	Banana, citrus, rice	High soil tillage costs, labour intensive production, lack of suitable irrigation and drainage facilities, floods
Trinidad and Tobago	Breadfruit, cassava, cocoa, coffee, mango, pumpkin, rice, sweet potato	Poor water management, flood control, poor infrastructure, lack of labour supply, poor post-harvest storage, alienation of agricultural lands

Source: own compilation based on public information from the respective Ministries of Agriculture, CARDI (2011), CARICOM (2013c), IICA (2013)

Although there are natural and structural constraints of the agricultural food production, the Caribbean agriculture sector is capable of an ample domestic food production, at least on a regional level. Since adequate food production depends on various economic and environmental factors, the agricultural sector faces different surmountable as well as insuperable constraints. Imports of food products and agricultural inputs enhance the availability of food in the countries, but at high costs, which will be discussed in the forthcoming chapter 5.3. The weakness of the domestic food production, which is the case for at least the majority of the selected countries, is the result of internal factors such as the increasing demand for food, changing consumption patterns and the high costs for unstable and low-level domestic small-scale food production. These factors led to an unsustainable increase of a wide range of raw, semi-processed and final-processed food imports. On the other hand, the decline of the agricultural food production is the consequence of external influences that considerably transformed the sector. Changing trade policies of liberalization led to wide open small Caribbean economies, and to a considerable decline of the agricultural and food production output, since the sector is not very competitive or efficient. Food imports are mostly demand driven by different sectors of the economies and the final consumers. The main drivers are distributers in the retail sector, the final consumers, tourism, and gastronomy establishments. The increasing demand for a variety of food products determines the import structure.

5.1.2 Food import structure and food balances

On a large and a small-scale, the agricultural sector in the Caribbean produces food for domestic consumption and export. This food production, however, is not sufficient to meet domestic demands. In addition, food production concentrates merely on the production of primary and less processed foodstuff. In this case availability of food is limited, which results in a national food gap between the domestic supply and the domestic demand. In this case, food imports can fill this gap and expand the variety of food products of different processing stages.

In order to examine the actual food gap and the magnitude of imported foods, this sub-section presents the food trade structure of five main food groups. While food production data for specific food groups is measured in quantities (in tonnes), food trade data is measured in values (in US$). For this analysis, data was drawn from the UN DESA COMTRADE database using the Standard International Trade Classification, Revision 3 (SITC, Rev.3) for selected and eligible food groups of the divisions 01 to 06 and 09: 'Meat and meat preparations' (01), 'Dairy products and birds' eggs' (02), 'Fish, crustaceans, molluscs and aquatic invertebrates, and preparations thereof ' (03), 'Cereals and cereal preparations' (04), 'Vegetables and fruit' (05), 'Sugars, sugar preparations and honey' (06), 'Miscellaneous edible products and preparations' (09).[28] These food groups have been selected due to confining food trade from agricultural trade

---

28   These food groups are different from the food groups used by the FAO, which does not include 'fish' into its classification of food.

which also includes the sections 'Live animals' (00), 'Coffee, tea, cocoa, spices, and manufactures thereof' (07) and 'Feeding stuff for animals' (08) (cf. UNCTAD, 2013). A detailed table of the SITC classification of all food commodities is given in Appendix E.

In order to identify the value of each of the imported food groups for each of the three Clusters for the Caribbean countries, data has been aggregated for the investigative period of time from 2000 to 2011. Food import and export data has not been steadily reported by every country throughout this whole period of time. Therefore, in order to avoid miscalculations, for every country annual data has been aggregated first and then averaged by dividing the total value by the number of years for which data is available. In the second step, these one-year average values have been aggregated for each cluster and then calculated as simple (mean) average. Given that it is important to record the values of imports and exports for each country individually, trade flows of food within a cluster are not excluded. However, re-imports and re-exports are excluded, in order to avoid double counting of products. Food trade data is presented in transaction values (in current US$) and not in quantity as in the case of production data, due to the compilation of international trade statistics based on transaction values. This method is useful, since food imports and exports measured in value terms also mirror accordingly the level of global food prices. Trade data, however, does not reflect domestic food consumption. Food consumption data is not easily available and is usually collected through microeconomic household surveys. Chapter 6 deals with the analysis of food consumption patterns in the Caribbean based on available information.

In Figure 21, five selected food groups are presented in aggregated and one-year averaged values, expressed in nominal values (in US$ million) for the three clusters. Cluster II imports the greatest value of all seven food groups resulting in a total amount of US$ 296.51 million annually, in the period of time from 2000 to 2011. Within this cluster, the larger economies, The Bahamas, Barbados, Jamaica and Trinidad and Tobago contribute up to 93% to the total amount of imports. Cereal products record an annual import value of US$ 68.70 million in this cluster. Within all food groups, Cluster III also imports mainly cereals of a total annual amount of US$ 18.51 million, and the smallest amount of meat with an annual value of US$ 5.38 million. Imports of fish, vegetables and fruits, and sugar merely account for a small share of total imports for Cluster III, which indicates that these food groups are rather produced domestically in the countries of this cluster. In total, Cluster III has an annual import value of all food groups of US$ 66.27 million. The total import value of all seven food groups account for a slightly lower annual value of US$ 63.33 million in Cluster I (own calculations based on UN COMTRADE, 2010). Overall, these figures show that the Caribbean food imports are mainly composed of cereal products.

Figure 21:   **Imported food products, values (in US$ million), one-year average, Cluster I, II, and III**

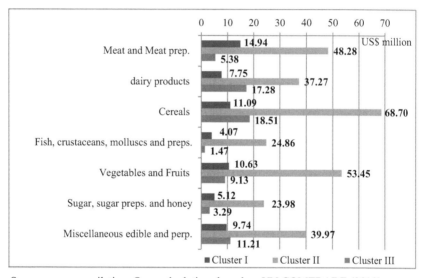

Source: own compilation. Own calculations based on UN COMTRADE (2010)

These results unfold that Cluster II, which is moderately vulnerable to food and nutrition insecurity, imports a large share of its food to meet domestic demand. Cluster III, which is the least vulnerable group of countries, imports much less of the listed food items, since its level of domestic food production, as well as its net agricultural production, is relatively high compared to other clusters. Nevertheless, the lowest value of food imports is reached by Cluster I, the most vulnerable cluster to food and nutrition insecurity, although having the lowest level of food production value. The previous results from the cluster analysis already indicated a lower supply of food in Cluster I, since the dietary energy supply is at a lower level, and the undernourishment levels are higher compared to the other Caribbean countries and clusters. The above results for Cluster I

164

could be a sign of low capacity to import food, therefore, resulting in a food supply deficit and probably in a large food gap on the domestic level. Further examination of the food import dependency and the food import bill in the upcoming subchapters will reveal the severance of vulnerability to food and nutrition insecurity for the clusters.

According to the above results, the import structure of all three clusters covers a relative broad variety of foods from all seven food groups, compared with the food export structure, which is less diversified and in total values smaller than the total import value. Figure 22 displays the one-year average values for each food group and cluster. From this figure, it becomes apparent that, Cluster II and III export a large value and amount of sugar, which is the top agricultural export commodity in the Caribbean (cf. Table 12); Cluster III records an annual sugar export value of US$ 67.00 million and Cluster II of US$ 22.35 million. These figures indicate a persistent dependency on this traditional commodity in Cluster II and III; whereas Cluster II exports an even slightly higher annual value of vegetables and fruits constituting for US$ 22.76 million. The highest export values in Cluster I are recorded for cereal products with an annual total of US$ 7.18 million. Meat and dairy exports are exclusively low in all three clusters, and account for higher import than export values, as shown in the previous Figure 21. Overall, Cluster III reports the highest values of food exports with an annual value of US$ 189.66 million, whereas Cluster II and I reach lower annual values of US$ 76.96 million and US$ 11.77 million respectively (own calculations based on UN COMTRADE, 2010).

Figure 22:   Exported food products, values (in US$ million), one-year average, Cluster I, II, and III

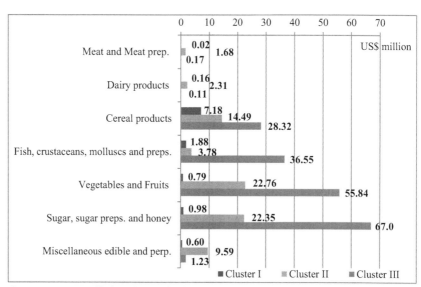

Source: own compilation. Own calculations based on UN COMTRADE (2010)

The low food export values and high food import values suggest that food trade balances (export minus imports) are negative. In total, the annual food trade balance of the 13 Caribbean countries yields in a deficit of US$ 1.48 billion. Cluster I, which shows the lowest levels of food imports and food exports, suffers from an annual food trade deficit of US$ 51.56 million. Cluster II reaching the highest annual value of food imports, but in comparison much lower levels of food exports, suffers from the greatest annual food trade deficit of US$ 219.55 million. Solely Cluster III reaches a surplus in its annual food trade balance of US$ 123.39 million, due to its high food exports (cf. UN COMTRADE, 2010). Cluster I and II, therefore, can be labelled as Net Food Importing (NFIM) cluster, whereas Cluster III can be labelled as Net Food Exporting (NFEX) cluster.

According to the FAO study *Reducing the CARICOM Food Import Bill and the Real Cost of Food: Policy and Investment Options*, the deficit in the food trade balances in the Caribbean economies increased since the 1960s, with a steep increase from 2003 on (cf. Silva et al., 2011). Food and agricultural exports decreased while imports for food, as well as for agricultural products augmented rapidly since 2003/04 (cf. Figure 20). However, at the same time, Guyana and Belize exhibit steady surpluses of their food trade balances (cf. Silva et al., 2011). In this respect, a differentiation between the food trade balance and the agricultural trade balance may be necessary, since agriculture or food products differ in their definition.

The main sources of food imports for the above selected food groups, in the investigative period of time from 2000 to 2011, for all the sample countries are the USA, Canada, Trinidad and Tobago, and Europe, particularly the UK and the Netherlands (cf. UN COMTRADE, 2010). Trinidad and Tobago also counts as one of the main food suppliers for most of the Caribbean countries, due to its larger food processing sector, which nonetheless depends highly on imported food and agricultural inputs for processing and export.

In order to examine the actual amount and significance of trade in food, food imports are calculated as share of total merchandise imports. The share of food imports as a percentage of total merchandise imports for the Caribbean countries arranged in clusters is illustrated in

Figure 23. Total food imports are calculated by aggregating the values of to the seven relevant food groups for the whole period of time from 2000 to 2011. Food imports, as well as merchandise imports, are calculated as simple (mean) average sum of the investigative period of time. These shares vary widely among the countries and within the three clusters. In addition, it has to be noted, that the value of food imports in comparison to merchandise imports decreased from 2000 to 2011. Albeit food imports increased to an overall high level in some countries merchandise imports also increased, but at a faster pace in the same period of time. With a growing GDP and rising importance of food processing industries, the demand for corresponding inputs and imports of non-food products such as machinery, energy and fuel increased significantly (cf. Silva et al., 2011). In smaller and less populated countries, such as The Bahamas, Dominica, Grenada, St. Kitts and Nevis, St. Lucia, and St. Vincent and the Grenadines, the values of merchandise imports are overall higher. Consequently, food imports reach relatively high levels ranging from 12% to 19% (cf. Figure 23). Conversely, in Antigua and Barbuda, Barbados, Belize, Jamaica, Guyana, Suriname, and Trinidad and Tobago, total merchandise imports reach the highest values among all countries; therefore, food imports make up for a smaller proportion of total merchandise imports. A cluster comparison for these results does not reveal any significant differences between clusters.

**Figure 23:   Food imports (in % of total merchandise imports), aggregated
                    average, Caribbean countries, 2000-2011**

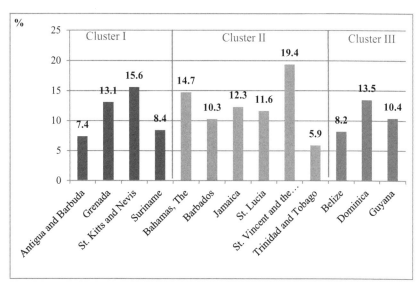

Source: own compilation. Own calculations based on UN COMTRADE (2010);
UNSD (2012)

In comparison to the above definition of 'food', the definition 'all food
and beverages' includes all categories of section '0' (food and live animals) and '1' (beverages) (cf. UNCTAD, 2013). Figure 24 shows these
food import ratios for the Caribbean countries, for which most recent data
is available. According to the most recent data on imports, the highest
share of 'all food' as a percentage of total merchandise imports, in 2012
was recorded to be 24% in Antigua and Barbuda. This high figure for Antigua and Barbuda indicates that imports of beverages and other foods
from the previous excluded categories constitute a much greater share of
total merchandise imports than just 'food' imports. This high figure is followed by Grenada, St. Kitts and Nevis, Barbados, and St. Vincent and the
Grenadines, where the food import ratio reached similar high levels;
whereas Trinidad and Tobago had the lowest share of 10% (cf. UN
COMTRADE, 2011). This comparison between the two definitions of
food and 'all food' imports is important, since discussions on the high dependence on food imports in the Caribbean, often include 'all food' and
'beverages'. For further analysis, and in order to assess the dependence on
food imports for all Caribbean countries, data of 'all food' and 'beverages'

will be used accordingly. Information and detailed analysis of the import ratio of each food group can be found in Silva et.al (2011).

Figure 24:   **All food and beverages imports as percentage of total merchandise imports, Caribbean countries, 2011**

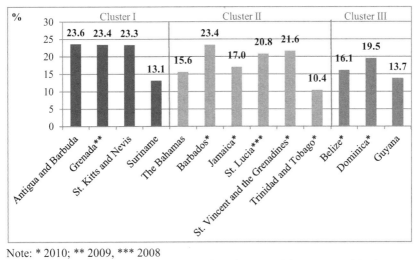

Note: * 2010; ** 2009, *** 2008
Source: own compilation. own calculations based on (UN COMTRADE, 2011)

Moreover, total merchandise exports have drastically decreased in most of the Caribbean countries, except for Trinidad and Tobago, and Suriname. This has occurred due to the shift to export industries from traditional agricultural exports, or to a partial shift from the manufacturing sector to the services sector[29], constituting for the vast bulk of total exports in the Caribbean countries – particularly the travel and tourism sector (cf. Table 4, p. 102). Thus, food imports can make up a high share of total merchandise exports, which means that an unsustainable high share of export earnings is used to purchase food imports. Consequently, Caribbean countries are not only dependent on food imports, but also on a few and dominant export sectors. The following subchapter examines whether high levels of food imports can be sustained through export earnings, or whether food

---

29   Services exports are not included in the merchandise trade data. Data of this sector is collected separately in the UN Services Trade database.

import dependency levels are high due to a higher degree of capacity to import foodstuffs in the economically resilient Caribbean countries.

5.1.3 Food Self-Sufficiency, Food Import Capacity, and Food Import Dependency

The objective of this section is to assess the food import dependency status in the Caribbean countries and for the three clusters, as well as critically discussing the implications of food imports on the vulnerability to food and nutrition insecurity. The main question in this context is whether the dependency on food imports is higher for countries of Cluster I and II, which are vulnerable to food and nutrition insecurity.

To assess the dependency of food imports, descriptive indicators are used, which provide evidence of the former examination on high food imports in Cluster I and II. The results of the indicators used for the assessment of food import dependency reveal the key relationship between domestic food production and food imports. These results serve as a basis for further discussion on the implications of food import dependency on FNS in the Caribbean countries and clusters in the up-coming chapter 5.2.

In order to provide comparable data, production as well as export and import data is drawn from the FAOSTAT database and aggregated for the investigative period of time from 2000 to 2011. Since a broad variety of food is imported and exports concentrate mostly on just a few primary products, the calculation of the indicator includes not simply one single food commodity but 'all food' items, to reflect the general situation on food import dependency in the Caribbean countries. However, comprehensive production data is just available for six sample countries. Therefore, meaningful interpretations of results for the three clusters are not feasible in the case of the Self-Sufficiency Ratio (SSR), and the Import Dependency Ratio (IDR).

The food Self-Sufficiency Ratio (SSR)

In the context of food security, food self-sufficiency is a hypothetic assumption that a country could provide food for its own population solely through domestic food production without the need of food imports. The concept and its major critique are explained in chapter 2.2.1. However, one major limitation of this concept has to be mentioned at this point: it does not provide any information about food adequacy. Even if domestic food supply is totally or in a large part composed of domestic food production, overall food supply may be, in fact, insufficient or inadequate to satisfy the population's needs of an adequate nutrition.

If domestic food production is not able to satisfy the demand, food imports can fill the food gap. The higher the share of domestic food production of the total supply, the lesser a country has to rely on food imports to fill its food gap. Subsequently, the country is considered to be more self-sufficient.

The food *Self-Sufficiency Ratio* (SSR) is calculated as quantity of food production in relation to domestic supply (cf. FAO, 2001):

$$SSR = \left[\frac{Production}{Domestic\ Supply}\right] \times 100$$

Whereas domestic supply is defined as:

$$Domestic\ Supply = Production + Imports - Exports$$

The higher the SSR (in %), the more self-sufficient a country is and hence depends lesser on food imports. The SSR of 100% means that a country reached total self-sufficiency of food meaning that domestic production entirely covers domestic supply. For the calculation of the SSR for the Caribbean countries, food production, food import and export data is provided by the FAO and retrieved from the FAOSTAT database, using data of 'all food' products (values in US$) to avoid distortions caused by different definitions and data values. In order to compare the ratios between the countries, data was aggregated for the period of time from 2000 to 2011. The major problem of this calculation is that the production data is not available for all Caribbean countries of the sample; therefore a meaningful comparison between the clusters is not feasible.

The results obtained from this calculation for the six Caribbean countries for which complete data is available is presented in Table 15. It is apparent from these figures that there are significant differences of SSRs between the countries. The only country which seems to be self-sufficient is Belize (Cluster III), reaching the highest ratio above 176%. This remarkably high figure indicates that Belize's food production even exceeds domestic supply; in that case food exports are higher than imports. Belize

exports over 80% of its food production which mostly consist of traditional export crops such as sugar and bananas (own calculations based on
FAOSTAT, 2013b). Due to lower levels of food imports and higher exports, total domestic food supply in Belize is relatively low, in comparison
to Barbados, Jamaica and Trinidad and Tobago from Cluster II, and in
comparison to Suriname from Cluster I. Jamaica and Suriname also reach
extraordinary high ratios of 85% and 71% respectively. Food imports for
these countries may account for a smaller share of total food supply due to
a high level of domestic production. In Barbados and Trinidad and Tobago
domestic food production accounts for nearly 50% of total food supply
and just 30% in Antigua and Barbuda (own calculations based on
FAOSTAT, 2013b).

Table 15: **Self-Sufficiency Ratio (in %), six Caribbean countries, 2000-2011**

Country	*SSR*
Antigua and Barbuda	30.0
Suriname	71.3
Barbados	49.9
Jamaica	85.2
Trinidad and Tobago	45.0
Belize	176.2

Source: own calculations based on FAOSTAT (2013b)

These figures and the short analysis on the food SSR clearly show that
even if a country is considered to be self-sufficient, domestic food supply
may not be adequate. Food imports may be necessary to fill the supply gap
of food or to satisfy the consumer demand for different food items which
cannot be produced domestically.

Food Import Dependency Ratio (IDR)

Food can be made available either through food imports or domestic food
production, or both. If food imports account for a high share of overall
food supply, which is the case in some Caribbean countries, it is more
likely that food import dependency is an issue in these countries. The extent to which countries depend on food imports can be calculated for any
food commodity or all food commodities by the *Import Dependency Ratio*
(IDR).

The IDR is defined as follows:

$$IDR = \left[\frac{Imports}{Domestic\ Supply}\right] \times 100$$

Whereas domestic supply is defined as:

$$Domestic\ Supply = Production + Imports - Exports$$

It reveals whether domestic supply is high due to domestic production or due to a greater reliance on food imports. The IDR reaches a scale from 0 to 100. An IDR of 100 implies that the whole supply of food is produced domestically. The lower the IDR scale, the more dependent on food imports a country is (cf. FAO, 2001).

Table 16 presents the results obtained from the calculation of the IDR for the six countries, Antigua and Barbuda and Suriname from Cluster I, Barbados, Jamaica and Trinidad and Tobago from Cluster II, and Belize from Cluster III. Two very different results occur in Cluster II, where 76% of the food in Jamaica derives from domestic production whereas merely 20% of food comes from domestic production in Trinidad and Tobago, which is obviously more dependent on food imports than Jamaica. Suriname obtains 50% of its food from domestic production, while Antigua and Barbuda, Barbados and Belize reach similar high levels of dependency on food imports up to 71%, since a relatively small share of food derives from domestic production (own calculations based on FAOSTAT, 2013b).

Table 16:   **Import Dependency Ration (IDR), six Caribbean countries, 2000-2011**

Country	IDR (in %)	Food supply (in % of domestic food production)
Antigua and Barbuda	71.1	28.9
Suriname	50.2	49.8
Barbados	68.7	31.3
Jamaica	24.2	75.8
Trinidad and Tobago	80.5	19.5
Belize	67.9	32.1

Source: own compilation. Own calculations based on FAOSTAT (2013b)

Comparing the results from Table 15, Belize, which has the highest SSR is also relatively high dependent on food imports, since merely 32% of its food derives from domestic production (own calculations based on FAOSTAT, 2013b). This suggests that food imports may not be necessary to fill the food gap but to satisfy consumer demands or due to the fact that domestic food production may not be adequate. Conversely, Antigua and Barbuda from Cluster I which is less self-sufficient, heavily relies on food imports, merely 29% of domestic production is imported (own calculations based on FAOSTAT, 2013b). A high dependency on food imports, in this case, suggests that food imports are indispensable to compensate low domestic production and to meet national requirements.

Data for the rest of the sample countries is not completely available to analyse SSR or IDR values in terms of food for all Caribbean countries and compare cluster results. However, the above results provide, even for a smaller sample of countries, significant conclusions that can be used for further discussion on food import dependency.

Food Import Capacity Index (ICI)

The capacity to import food is determined by economic parameters such as export and foreign exchange earnings. The Caribbean economies rely on foreign exchange earnings from exports of a narrow range of products. Although export earnings from services or oil and mineral sectors grew substantially and contributed significantly to the economic growth, these export earnings are volatile due to the economies' susceptibility to external shocks on the world market. While the amount of food imports is not correlated to exports or export earnings but to the national demand, changes in export earnings can have a significant impact on the capability to import food which, on the other hand, can have adverse economic and social effects.

On the basis of available data on food imports and total exports, the food *Import Capacity Index* (ICI) can be calculated. For this study, the averaged investigative period of time allows a comparison between clusters and reveals if the Caribbean countries have the capacity to stabilize their food demands through food imports in the long term.

Valdés and McCalla (1999) defined the index as the ratio of the value of food imports to the total value of merchandise exports as follows (cf. Valdés and McCalla, 1999):

$$ICI = \frac{Value\ of\ Imports\ M}{Value\ of\ Merchandise\ Exports\ X}$$

In the sample of their study Valdés and McCalla (1999) found that the food ICI is usually higher for Caribbean SIDS and lower for bigger and less food import dependent countries. The higher the food ICI, the less capable is a country to purchase food through earnings from merchandise exports and consequently burdens its trade balance. The authors suggest that high ratios lie above 0.25, which indicates that countries are vulnerable to food and nutrition insecurity (cf. Valdés and McCalla, 1999).

Table 17 compares the results obtained from the calculation of the food ICI within all 13 Caribbean countries. Since food import data is not consistently available for all countries through all years of the investigative period of time, available data has been averaged for the corresponding years. It is apparent from this table that all countries except for Suriname from Cluster I, Trinidad and Tobago from Cluster II and Guyana from Cluster III have levels above 0.25. These countries depict exceptionally low scores due to their profitable oil or mineral rich industries that are strongly export orientated. A calculation of the simple average of the indicator for each cluster reveals interesting results. Cluster I has the highest mean score of 0.84, confirming its low capability to purchase food through merchandise exports. Cluster II scores also a certainly higher mean of 0.53, indicating a low food import capacity due to its moderate state of food and nutrition insecurity. What is interesting in Cluster III is that there are two opposed results of the food ICI: Guyana, which has a high food import capacity; and Dominica having a low capacity with an index value of 0.64. The simple average of the food ICI for Cluster III, therefore, shows a balanced result and the lowest figure of 0.39 (own calculations based on FAOSTAT, 2013b).

However, these results have to be interpreted with caution since Suriname, Trinidad and Tobago and Dominica are outliers in each cluster and values differ within clusters. Further, a taxonomy according to the index values shows that the food import capacity is higher in larger countries such as Belize, Guyana, Suriname and even Trinidad and Tobago and lower for smaller island states such as Grenada, Antigua and Barbuda and St. Kitts and Nevis. Larger Caribbean economies tend to have higher merchandise exports, which can be explained in part by their greater resource endowments and broader production capacities.

General caution has to be made at this point of interpreting the food ICI in the context of the Caribbean countries since the indicator specifically does not include services exports that for some countries account for a relative great share of total exports. Therefore, it may underestimate the actual food import capacity. Incorporating the value of services exports reveals significant differences particularly for countries and the smaller islands for which services contribute to a large part to their GDP. However, there is no significant change between the food ICI without services exports and the food ICI with services exports for Suriname, Trinidad and Tobago and Guyana. For these countries, services exports account only for a marginal share of total exports (cf. chapter 3.3.2). On the basis of this calculation only Jamaica and Grenada have a low capacity to import food since both reach figures above 0.25, whereas the rest of the sample countries have a higher capacity to import food.

Table 17:   **Food Import Capacity Index (ICI), Caribbean countries, 2000-2011**

Cluster	*Country*	*Food ICI*	*Food ICI (with services exports)*
Cluster I	Antigua and Barbuda	1.01	0.15
	Grenada	1.28	0.27
	St. Kitts and Nevis	1.00	0.22
	Suriname	0.08	0.07
Cluster II	The Bahamas	0.65	0.11
	Barbados	0.54	n.a.
	Jamaica	0.43	0.36
	St. Lucia	0.68	0.18
	St. Vincent and the Grenadines	0.87	0.20
	Trinidad and Tobago	0.05	0.04
Cluster III	Belize	0.31	0.13
	Dominica	0.64	0.20
	Guyana	0.16	0.13

Note: n.a. = not available
Source: own compilation. Own calculations UN COMTRADE (2010); UNSD (2012)

Furthermore, one major drawback of this index is that values of imports and exports differ and change with price variations on the world market. If food prices increase or higher valued food products are imported, the ratio of food imports to total exports increases and the capacity to import food declines. This means that adjustments cannot be made through higher exports. Although exports of services and mineral and oil products may sustain large food imports over the investigative period of time, foreign exchange earnings from these sources may not be stable since prices for exports of primary tend to fluctuate. As long as domestic food production stays on a low level, food imports exceed domestic food production, making countries dependent on food imports to meet national demands of food. However, much of the discussion on the increase in food imports has neglected factors on the demand side such as population growth, population density, urbanization, income increase, changing consumption patterns, and the increased activities in the travel and tourism industry. These factors most probably can lead to an increase in food demand and more importantly precipitate a shift of the consumer demand for local production to imported foodstuff.

A comparison of the two results from the food IDR in Table 16 and the food ICI without services exports in Table 17 reveal that food import capacity and food import dependency are negatively correlated. Antigua and Barbuda seems to depend on food imports to a relatively large degree, while its share of food imports of total domestic production is relatively low at 30%. Its food import dependency results from the low level of domestic food production and a low food import capacity – the lowest food ICI among the sample of Caribbean countries. The capability to import food is very high for Suriname although it merely imports 50% of its food, which may be due to its high SSR (own calculations based on FAOSTAT, 2013b). As already observed, Trinidad and Tobago has the lowest food ICI and, therefore, the highest capacity to import food. It seems that Trinidad and Tobago exhausts this capacity by depending strongly on food imports. Conversely, Jamaica is less dependent on food imports due to its higher food SSR while its capacity to import food is also low.

These results suggest that in countries which obtain a larger share of their food from domestic production are less dependent on food imports, and hence their food import to total exports ratio is lower. Conversely, it could be argued that due to a minor export sector which could finance necessary food imports, the food import capacity of a country is lower, leading to a lower dependency on food imports and a higher share of domestic production. In this argument lies the essential causality between food imports and the capacity of domestic food production. The question remains, whether low domestic food production induces higher food imports or if lower food imports would have a positive effect on the food production sector to trigger higher investments into the agricultural sector. The Caribbean countries show differing capacities to produce and to import food. Therefore, the importance of using different indicators and the comparison of all three indicators is that the results reveal the complex situation of the food import dependency for the sample countries. This information allows drawing implications for policies and strategies which can be adapted for different clusters or countries.

Studies and a long list of government and non-government proposals showed that the Caribbean countries have the potential to increase domestic food production. Thereby they could reduce the risk of vulnerability to food and nutrition insecurity and the risk of food shortages from which the countries could have escaped during the food crisis, in 2007/08.

A high import dependency on food is naturally coupled with high expenditures for food imports which can burden a country's trade and its current account balance. Consequently, high food imports entail negative financial and socio-economic impacts. However, the dependency on food imports per se is not a problem as long as a country has the capacity to balance its food gap through imports without undue economic dislocation. Low agricultural capacity to produce sufficient food for domestic supply drives countries into increased levels of food imports to ensure an adequate supply of food for their population, or it may lead to a higher pressure on agricultural production to increase the level of domestic food production. Thus, food imports can support countries that are not able to produce a sufficient amount of food to satisfy the domestic demand.

5.2   *Implications of food imports in the Caribbean countries*

From the previous subchapter results that the Caribbean countries' weak capacity of agricultural and food production, in combination with trade-related factors and structural constraints. It has been the leading cause of an increase in food imports into the region. Consequently, this economic condition in most of the Caribbean countries, in combination with high food import levels can lead to a state of dependency on food imports, and accordingly on exports of goods on services for foreign exchange. This dependency does not implicitly affect the Caribbean economies negatively, if deficits in the food trade balances can be adjusted by earnings from exports to avoid a negative balance of payments.

Food and nutrition insecurity is a complex and serious concern, particularly in countries, where food import dependency impedes development of and in the agricultural sector. Furthermore, dependency on food imports have far-reaching effects on the domestic markets, where farmers eventually have to deal with higher prices for inputs and consumers with higher prices for food products.

This subchapter describes direct and indirect effects of high levels of food import dependency in the Caribbean countries. These implications are based on the previous examination of the leading causes for this dependency and the cluster-based results of the identified indicators measuring the degree of dependency in the sample countries. The first section of this subchapter describes the potential effects of agricultural trade and low food production capacity on the Caribbean economies. The last section assesses economic and social effects of food imports on the consumers and producers in the Caribbean countries.

5.2.1 Implications of agricultural trade liberalization in the Caribbean

Trade liberalization of agricultural products aims to separate the competitive agricultural producers from the less productive producers, and concomitantly benefits consumers through favourable prices. With the process of agricultural liberalization, the Caribbean countries lost preferential access to world markets for most of their traditional agricultural export products. This loss was due to multilateral policies and trade liberalization under the WTO, or because of multilateral trade agreements such as the *European Partnership Agreements* (EPA)[30] between the CARICOM and the EU. These circumstances contributed to a reduction of economic activity in the affected industries. In addition, less diversified countries such as St. Kitts and Nevis and St. Lucia, where the agricultural export sector heavily depends on preferences, also failed to make adjustments to protect their sector from losses (cf. Conforti and Ford, 2007). Despite the negative

---

30   The CARICOM-EPA was signed in 2008. Thereby preferential access at lower tariffs for the CARICOM countries have been removed (cf. CARICOM, 2013a).

effect of agricultural trade liberalization, this does not only create new competition for domestic suppliers but enlarges the domestic market through a greater availability and variety of goods. Nevertheless, Caribbean countries can improve their benefit from agricultural trade liberalization and mitigating adverse effects through investments. This would include simulative investments into key sectors, to foster domestic food production, coupled with investments into infrastructure and new technologies through enhanced activities in research and development. These specific investments in turn could stimulate investments in other purviews of the economy, through forward and backward linkages (cf. Ford and Rawlins, 2007).

Trade policies of larger, higher diversified and more competitive Caribbean countries comprise measures, such as export subsidies and protection of local markets through import tariffs. Hence, these countries can increase their productivity in a larger scale, whereas the other Caribbean countries are exposed to these market conditions, under which high productive global food suppliers offer cheaper and higher quality products. In the face of the drastic decline of the agricultural sector, Caribbean countries adopted national policies to overcome persistent constraints in this sector, but failed i.a. due to the lack of important financial and technical resources (cf. Ford and Rawlins, 2007). In 2005, these failures led to the *Jagdeo Initiative*, which identified key constraints impeding agricultural development and suggesting appropriate interventions to overcome main obstacles, such as the lack of competitiveness confronted by agricultural producers in the Caribbean countries (cf. chapter 5.1.1).

The role of the agricultural sector in the Caribbean goes beyond its economic functions as a contributor to economic growth, exports and employment. The agricultural sector plays an important role to FNS and rural livelihoods, especially in small and vulnerable economies. A dwindling of the agricultural sector – lower output prices, and higher costs of production – put family farms and small-scale farmers in rural communities at risk of falling into poverty and food and nutrition insecurity (cf. IAASTD, 2009). Additionally, farmers in the Caribbean, currently have to deal with inhibitive effects of climate change and access to land, water and irrigation.

Since small island states are price-takers on the world markets, volatile prices for export products constitute "an important factor of high vulnerability for some small, vulnerable economies" (WTO, 2005). Moreover, economies that heavily rely on foreign exchange earnings, in order to balance high expenditures for food imports are vulnerable to any fluctuation of prices, leading to a decline of their Terms of Trade (ToT). Particularly Caribbean countries are prone to significant changes in ToT, due to the narrow range of export products on which they depend (cf. FAO, 2003). When prices of export commodities such as prices of traditional agricultural exports tend to increase, decline, or even fall, and prices for imported manufactured products increase concurrently, the exchange ratio of import and export prices, translated in ToT, eventually decline. Foreign exchange earnings are a binding constraint for the Caribbean countries and significantly determine the capacity to import food. The important question is to what extent foreign exchange earnings can sustain high levels of food imports.

5.2.2 Implications of food imports and food import dependency

In some countries in the Caribbean, food that is readily available in every supermarket, market and restaurant, does not necessarily derive from domestic production and processing, but is becoming increasingly available through food imports. The results from the previous subchapter 5.1 revealed that the sample countries can be classified as Net Food Importing (NFIM) countries and Net Food Exporting (NFEX) countries.

- *Net Food Importing* (NFIM) countries: Antigua and Barbuda, Grenada, St. Kitts and Nevis, Suriname (Cluster I); The Bahamas, Barbados, Jamaica, St. Lucia, St. Vincent and the Grenadines, Trinidad and Tobago (Cluster II), Dominica (Cluster III)
- *Net Food Exporting* (NFEX) countries: Belize and Guyana (Cluster III)

The food trade balance is positive for NFEX countries and negative for NFIM countries, it burdens the NFIM countries' financial and trade balances and requires foreign exchange earnings from exports to balance the outlays for food imports.

High and ever growing levels of food imports can have far reaching consequences for the Caribbean economies. On the supply side, cheaper and higher quality food imports can trigger a 'crowding out' of domestic production which has significant negative economic and social effects (cf. Silva et al., 2011). The *economic effects* of high food import levels in the

Caribbean result from the evidence of regional studies and the previous findings in this chapter.

- **Market shift and 'crowding out'**: Regionally produced foodstuff is being substituted with imported foods (cf. Silva et al., 2011); e.g. regionally produced cassava and cassava flour are substituted with imported wheat flour, whereas wheat is consumed in high quantities, but production accounts to zero (cf. ECLAC, 2009; Silva et al., 2011). Import substitutions lead to a decline of domestic markets, which in turn affect the local producers, since locally produced foodstuff becomes less capable to compete with imports.
- **Loss of productivity**: Local agricultural producers are affected by lower output and profits, higher costs for inputs and lower private and public investment; consequently, unemployment rises, making higher government expenditures for social support programmes necessary (cf. Silva et al., 2011).
- **Increase of the food import bill**: When foreign exchange earnings are not sufficient to compensate expenditures for imported foodstuff, the financial burden will rise; consequently, impeding government expenditure for other areas such as for social safety nets, education and public health.

Social effects of high food import levels affect different groups of the population on the supply as well as on the demand side.

- **Loss of rural livelihoods**: In some Caribbean countries, labour force in agriculture is high (cf. Table 13, p. 155), which means that agriculture plays a significant role to rural livelihood and families. They depend on their farming activities first and foremost, for their means of subsistence (cf. Beckford and Campbell, 2013; Ford and Rawlins, 2007; Silva et al., 2011).
- **Migration to urban territories**: Loss of employment and poor rural living conditions may cause migration into urban areas, where housing, employment and security are already under stress, particularly in population dense states such as Barbados.
- **Rising poverty levels and food and nutrition insecurity**: High food prices, unemployment and higher poverty rates affect the poor and vulnerable population which already spends up to 37% of its income on food (cf. Government of The Bahamas, 2004) (cf. chapter 3.3.1).

- **Changing consumption patterns:** Local diets shift towards readily available and cheaper foodstuff that is mostly imported and different from the local food. The population thereby adopts more global diets of processed and ready-to-eat foodstuff; diet-related diseases and health problems are related to these changes (cf. Ford and Rawlins, 2007). Further analysis on this topic follows in chapter 6.

Both, causes and effects of food imports lead to a double-sided dependency on imports and exports. For the Caribbean countries, imported food is needed to meet consumer demands, but is also used as input for the production of semi-processed and processed food products, such as wheat for bakery products. In this context, import substitution is discussed as a possible strategy to overcome food import dependency, but may not be an aspiring objective, given the particular resource endowments of small island states and the consumer tastes (cf. Kendall and Petracco, 2003). However, food import dependency is not insurmountable, as long as a country is capable of sustaining high levels of food imports through foreign exchange earnings, and as long as it has still the capacity to extend domestic food production and increase productivity. NFIM countries heavily depend on foreign exchange earnings through exports of agricultural, as well as non-agricultural goods and services, which create this double-sided dependency and aggravate their vulnerability to external shocks. Valdés and MacCalla (1999) point out those small and vulnerable NFIM economies do not have the resources or the capacities to surmount their dependency on food imports. Hence, they would need food or financial aid, preferential access to world markets for their main export products, or the implementation of liberalization adjustment and diversification strategies (cf. Valdés and McCalla, 1999).

The implications of food import dependency are severe for the economy and the societies of the Caribbean countries. The economic and social structures of these countries lead to low capacities and development of the agricultural food production sector, aggravating the vulnerability situation of food and nutrition insecurity in the Caribbean countries. Economic and social effects of food import dependency are more harmful for the Caribbean countries, where neither the economies can absorb the negative effects nor the social structures can mitigate social costs.

5.3   The burden of the Caribbean Food Import Bill

Increasing food imports and a soaring Food Import Bill (FIB) are major concerns in the Caribbean, since several countries are highly dependent on food imports. Alongside with structural and fiscal constraints, this leads to macroeconomic vulnerability and in the worst case it leads to an economic crisis. The low domestic food production capacity causes a diversion to food imports, which in turn may aggravate the dependency of the Caribbean countries on external trade for foreign exchange. In combination with a rising FIB, the consequences are affecting the Caribbean economies and its population. Ultimately, it is the Caribbean consumer who may have to pay higher prices for food, determined by world market prices. The low levels of domestic food supply and higher prices for food, hence, threaten FNS in the Caribbean.

The first subchapter 5.3.1 focuses on the costs of food imports, which are determined by global food prices. Import and export values are indicated in nominal terms, in order to depict the development of the FIB and mirroring changes in food prices. The second subchapter focuses on the economic and fiscal implications of the increasing costs of food imports for the Caribbean countries. Based on previous analyses on economic features and trade structures of Caribbean economies, the high FIB may have an exacerbating effect on the macroeconomic vulnerabilities in various sample countries.

5.3.1 The high costs of food imports

Real costs of food imports are reflected by changes in the Commodity Terms of Trade (ToT), which represent the relationship between the price for imports and the price of exports, expressed in price indexes. Costs for food imports may rise as a result of a relative increase in import prices to export prices. A decline of both, exports and foreign exchange earnings lead to a decline of Commodity ToT, thus resulting in a low capacity to import food. Due to their seasonality, world food prices are extremely volatile. The small and open economies of the Caribbean countries are price-takers on the world market and are immediately affected by any price change of food commodities or export commodities (cf. FAO, 2003). According to a FAO study on the CARICOM FIB and the costs from 2011, the value of food imports in CARICOM countries increased gradually since the 1960s, due to steadily increased world market prices for food (cf. Silva et al., 2011). Based on previous results from chapter 5.1, it can be estimated that the Caribbean countries approximately import 50% to 60% of their food. This makes the affected countries highly vulnerable to price increases that are ultimately mirrored in the high levels of the FIB.

The impacts of global food prices

Alongside with the most recent global food crisis in 2007/08 and according to the FAO Food Price Index (FPI), world food prices peaked in 2008 and latest in 2011. The effects of food prices increases on producers and consumers – small-scale producers are also referred to as consumers – are controversially discussed in literature and among experts. It is argued that high food prices benefit producers more than consumers, since they can expand their food production and export their production output on the world markets at higher prices, thus attaining higher yields. In the Caribbean, only in a few countries, high prices might have been beneficial for producers, for instance, rice producers in Guyana have benefited from the global food price increase (cf. FAO, 2011b). It is more likely that only NFEX countries (Guyana and Belize) benefit from high food prices, through improving their Commodity ToT, continuously expanding food production, and subsequently increasing food exports. However, this is a critical argument, since particularly small-scale farmers cannot easily or rapidly respond to high output prices through boosting cultivation, because agriculture production is confronted with a time lag between cultivation and disposal. Moreover, the volatility of food prices, particularly for the NAEX countries (Antigua and Barbuda, Guyana and Belize) may have adverse effects on their agricultural trade balances and increase the risk for small-scale producers regarding unpredicted levels of future income (cf. ECLAC, 2011).

Conversely, NFIM countries are mostly afflicted by high food prices, since they have to sustain higher costs of food imports through foreign exchange earnings. High food prices almost provoked an economic crisis, spiralling higher world market prices for food which translated into domestic food price inflation, and, as a result, into higher consumer prices. These effects of the global food crisis in 2008 increased the concern of the FNS situation of the population in the Caribbean countries, because food prices triggered a subsequent and almost unbearable increase in the costs of living. For the consumers in NFIM countries the consequences of high food prices are severe, since an increase in global food prices of imported food items translates into higher costs for domestically available food. The higher the dependence on food imports, the higher the transmission of global food prices. The extent of the transmission of high food prices to domestic food prices depends on various macroeconomic factors and is more serious for Caribbean countries where exchange rates are flexible such as for Guyana, Jamaica, Suriname and Trinidad and Tobago with floating exchange rates regimes (cf. CARICOM, 2013d).[31]

In the Caribbean countries food expenditure accounts for a significant share of the overall consumption basket ranging from 12% in The Bahamas to 54% in St. Vincent and the Grenadines, food and non-alcoholic beverages make up the greatest weight in the Consumer Price Index (CPI) (cf. CARICOM, 2013c; FAO, 2011b; Lora et al., 2011). As the previous analysis in chapter 4.1.2 showed, high food prices and thereby a steady increase of the Consumer Price Food Index (CPFI), in 2008 and in 2011 rushed inflation of the CPFI in nearly all Caribbean countries. In addition, the CPFI inflation was notably higher than the CPI inflation in both years of the food price escalation. The differences between the CPI inflation and the CPFI inflation are shown in Table 18. Inflation rates were significantly lower in 2011 than in 2008. In 2008, Jamaica reached the highest inflation rates with 22% CPI inflation and over 30% of CPFI inflation (cf. CARICOM, 2013c; FAOSTAT, 2013a). Suriname, St. Vincent and the Grenadines and Trinidad and Tobago also had the highest CPFI inflation rates in 2008. In the case of Jamaica, Suriname and Trinidad and Tobago which have flexible exchange rates, a rise in global food prices may have passed inflation to the domestic CPFI. On the other hand fix exchange rates may have helped to stabilize domestic prices in the other countries (cf. Alleyne and Lugay, 2011; ECLAC, 2008). Notably, Antigua and Barbuda has the lowest CPFI inflation rate of 5% and the lowest difference between the CPI inflation and the CPFI inflation rate in 2008. In 2011, nearly all countries, for which data is available, reached single digit inflation rates, in both indices. The Bahamas seems to have the most stable

---

31   Fixed exchange rates prevail in the countries Antigua and Barbuda, The Bahamas, Barbados, Belize, Dominica, Grenada, St. Kitts and Nevis, St. Lucia, St. Vincent and the Grenadines (cf. ECCB, 2013).

prices (consumer and food) reaching the lowest level of CPFI of 2% in the same year (cf. CARICOM, 2013c; FAOSTAT, 2013a).

Table 18:   Consumer Price Index (CPI) inflation rate and Consumer Price Food Index (CPFI) inflation rate, (2000=100), (in % change), Caribbean countries, 2008 and 2011

	2008		2011	
	CPI inflation rate[1] (% change)	CPFI inflation rate (% change)	CPI inflation rate[1] (% change)	CPFI inflation rate[2] (% change)
Cluster I				
Antigua and Barbuda	4.7	5.2	3.5	3.9
Grenada	5.2	13.7	2.4[a]	4.4
St. Kitts and Nevis	5.3	8.0	5.8[a]	10.2
Suriname	15.2	25.9	n.a.	10.5
Cluster II				
The Bahamas	4.6	7.1	3.2	1.9
Barbados	8.0	13.5	9.4	8.2
Jamaica	22.0	30.6	7.5	7.7
St. Lucia	5.6	14.7	1.5[a]	3.3
St. Vincent and the Grenadines	10.1	24.6	n.a.	16.6
Trinidad and Tobago	12.1	25.9	5.1	10.5
Cluster III				
Belize	n.a.	13.3	n.a.	n.a.
Dominica	6.0	11.7	n.a.	n.a.
Guyana	8.1	14.7	n.a.	7.24

Note: n.a. not available; [1] different base years; [a] excludes data for the month of December
Source: own compilation. CPI inflation: CARICOM (2013c); CPFI inflation: own calculations based on FAOSTAT (2013b)

Various factors such as the fluctuation of exchange rate, monetary and fiscal policies, domestic food production and supply explain the variation of inflation rates among the countries. However, a detailed examination on the determinants of the CPI and CPFI inflation for each country would require precisely explaining the differences of inflation rates between the countries. Such an investigation is beyond the scope of this thesis.

The costs of the food import bill

The rise in global food prices is reflected in CPI and CPFI inflation, and thereby in the FIB, which represents total costs of food imports at nominal levels expressed in import values (in US$). Relatively high import values and subsequently high costs of food imports arise from not only from an increase in global food prices, but from prices that indirectly influence global food prices such as prices for fuel and energy. The FAO's global Food Price Index (FPI) measures the monthly and annual average of global food price changes of five food commodities: cereal, vegetable oil, dairy, meat, and sugar (cf. FAO, 2013e).[32] The global FPI is subject of annual and monthly variations. Global food prices for these commodities increased steadily from 2000 to 2011. Figure 25 shows the total value of imports of 'all food'[33] commodities, which is defined as the total FIB for the Caribbean countries, positively correlates and steadily increases with the global (nominal) FPI in the investigative period of time from 2000 to 2011. In order to adjust missing data for some countries in different years, the annual simple (mean) average of the total FIB was calculated. The reason for this correlation of the FPI and FIB derives from the assumption that the Caribbean food import basket mainly consist of the FPI food basket items. Starting from a relatively low point of 91.1 (FPI), and US$ 118.16 million (FIB), both, the FPI and the level of the Caribbean FIB peaked in 2008, when the FPI reached 201.4 points, and the average FIB reached US$ 240.28 million. Afterwards, both values rapidly declined until 2009. In 2011, when global food prices escalated and reached their overall high, the FPI outstripped its former peak and reached 230.1 points, while the FIB increased more slightly and reached an average value of US$ 255.22 million (cf. FAO, 2013a; UN COMTRADE, 2010).

---

32   The average of five food groups (representing 55 quotations) is weighted with the average export shares of each of the groups for 2002-2004 (FAO, 2013a).

33   Refers to the division '0' of the SITC, Rev. 3 in the COMTRADE data.

Figure 25:   **Correlation between average Caribbean Food Import Bill (FIB) (in US$ million) and global Food Price Index (FPI) (2000-2004=100), 2000-2011**

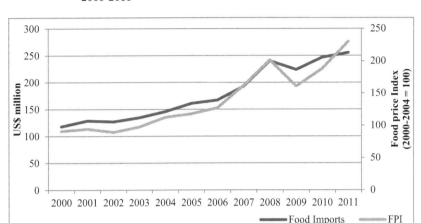

Note: FIB data is incomplete for Antigua and Barbuda, Grenada and St. Lucia
Source: own compilation. FPI: (FAO, 2013a); FIB: own calculations based on (UN COMTRADE, 2010)

The escalation of food prices recently in 2011, also lead to an increase of the total FIB for all countries compromising 'all food' items reached approximately US$ 3.1 billion[34]. Including beverages imports, the total food and beverages import bill accounted US$ 3.5 billion, in 2011 (own calculations based on UN COMTRADE, 2010). This is an alarming figure, since the FIB value doubled since 2000, when it amounted US$ 1.5 billion (own calculations based on UN COMTRADE, 2010). This increase within the observed years has been experienced differently in the respective sample countries. As Figure 26 shows, the highest increase of the FIB between 2000 and 2011 can be observed in Jamaica, where FIB levels increased from US$ 447.82 million to US$ 938.38 million and in Trinidad and Tobago from US$ 241.25 million to US$ 622.40 million. As already discovered, both countries were severely affected by the increase of global food market prices, triggering domestic food prices and CPFI inflation. The smallest rise of the national FIB is found in Dominica, where

---

34   There is no data for Dominica, Grenada, St. Lucia and Trinidad and Tobago for the year 2011. Alternative data for 2010 and 2009 serves as reference value for calculating the total FIB.

it increased about US$ 13 million within 10 years. What is interesting in this figure is that countries from Cluster I and Cluster III have overall lower levels of their total national FIBs, than countries from Cluster II, except for Suriname and Guyana, which both are outliers here. For Cluster I the reason of lower FIB levels may lay in the lower capacity to import food (cf. Table 17, p. 176). A possible explanation for the low levels of the FIB in Cluster III is that Belize and Guyana of this cluster are NFEX countries. Together with Dominica, which also has a high agriculture production value, they have higher levels of domestic food production, than countries from the other clusters. Nevertheless, the overall FIB on national levels reached an unsustainable and alarming high level in the Caribbean countries threatening its FNS. The fiscal and socio-economic impacts of high FIB levels and the resulting burden will be accordingly discussed in subchapter 5.3.2.

Figure 26:   Food Import Bill (FIB) (in US$ million), Caribbean countries, 2000 and 2011

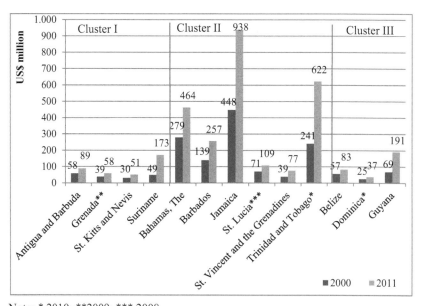

Note: * 2010; **2009; *** 2008
Source: own compilation. UN COMTRADE (2010)

Obviously, there are various factors that nurture the growth of the FIB: low domestic food production, increasing demand with higher incomes, or increasing demand of food that is not produced domestically, population growth, and the rise of international food prices. These factors can lead to an increase in the volume of food imports and the costs for imports, both reflected by the level of the FIB. Konandreas (2012) examined both, the effect of volumes and the effect of prices on the cereal FIB for two groups of different countries, which he defined as Net Food Importing Developing Countries (NFIDCs) and Least Developed Countries (LDCs). His results show that the effect of a price increase was much higher than the effect of increased imported food volumes on the overall cereal import bill, for the examined NFICDCs. The study also drew results for some Caribbean countries. For instance, the price effect in Barbados was nearly 100%, for Grenada and St. Kitts and Nevis this effect was over 60%, while for Dominica, St. Lucia, St. Vincent and the Grenadines, Trinidad and Tobago it was nearly 60%, and for Jamaica the price effect was nearly 50% (cf. Konandreas, 2012). Evidently, the increase of the FIB in the Caribbean countries was driven by food prices, rather than by the volume of (cereal) food imports, the latter may have still increased, but at a low or even marginal level. Consequently, an increase of the domestic demand for cereals might have either stimulated domestic food production, or led to a supply shortage and higher price levels for cereals.

The diversity of the geographical size and population in the Caribbean determines the demand for food and the structural and economic constraints determine the low capacity of domestic food production. However, calculating the FIB per capita proves that there is no positive correlation between the level of the FIB and population or the geographical size of a country. High per capita FIB levels are found in countries, where total FIB levels are already high: The Bahamas (US$ 6492), Barbados (US$ 2442), and Trinidad and Tobago (US$ 3472). This may be due to agricultural constraints (cf. Table 14, p. 160) or because of the economic structures of the countries (cf. chapter 3.3.2). Additionally, Barbados and Trinidad and Tobago have a high food IDR ratio at nearly 70% and 80% (cf. Table 16, p. 173). The lowest per capita FIB levels are found in Dominica (US$ 70) and St. Lucia (US$ 40). Although Jamaica has a high SSR level of 85% and a relatively low IDR of 24% , its total FIB is the highest among the sample countries, whereas its per capita FIB accounts for US$ 1186 (own calculations based on UN COMTRADE, 2010; The World Bank, 2013d). For Jamaica these figures reveal that its food import basket might be composed of food items, which are not produced domestically or not in sufficient amounts to meet domestic demand. For this reason, the Jamaican

Ministry of Agriculture (MoA) aims – through its campaign "Grow What We Eat, Eat What We Grow" – to subsidize food imports for food items, which most certainly can be produced domestically (cf. Jamaican MoAF, 2013). Such a policy requires specific knowledge of the composition of the total national FIB.

The Caribbean food import basket

Based on the previous analysis of the food import structure in chapter 5.1.2, data for the period of time from 2000 to 2011 depict that cereal imports accounted for the heaviest weight in total imports (in real values). Based on COMTRADE data, the recent total food import basket of all Caribbean countries is dominated by six food groups, in 2011: cereals, meat, vegetables and fruits, dairy and fish displayed Figure 27 each by the size of their shares of the total FIB. Cereals and cereal products make up the largest share of imports within these food groups, constituting 21% of the total FIB. Cereals such as grains and wheat are not produced on a domestic level in the Caribbean. In contrary, fruits and vegetables are produced in a great variety within the countries (cf. Table 14, p. 160), but make up the second largest share of the food import basket with 15%. This might be another proof for the low output of the domestic agricultural sector. Meat makes up for the third greatest share of the Caribbean food import basket with 15%, indicating an increasingly high demand on the domestic level (own calculations based on UN COMTRADE, 2010).

Figure 27:   **Import structure, food imports (in % of total FIB), Caribbean countries total, 2011**

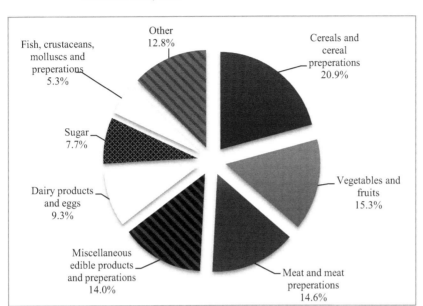

Source: own compilation. Own calculations based on UN COMTRADE (2010)

Silva et al. (2011) found that of the different food categories, food preparations[35], dairy, wheat, and maize were the most imported food items within the CARICOM region. The authors further ascertained that the value of processed food increased at a faster pace since 1990, and in fact currently dominates the food import basket in the Caribbean (cf. Silva et al., 2011). Certainly, the drastic increase of the imported value of processed food is driven by changes of the FPI and prices for transport and energy, but it also leads to the assumption that it is driven by changes in consumption patterns which drive the demand of foodstuffs such as cereals, meat or processed food.

---

35   Food preparations are not elsewhere specified in the COMTRADE trade section.

5.3.2 Financial and economic concern related to the Caribbean food import bill

Driven by high food prices, there is no sign that the FIB will decline, if prices remain to stay on high levels or even continue to rise. The fiscal imbalances and high debt levels already impose a high burden on the Caribbean countries (cf. chapter 3.3.2). In addition, expenditures on food imports exacerbate the precarious financial situation of the economies. Food trade balances are negative for all Caribbean sample countries (cf. chapter 5.1.2), except for NFEX countries – Guyana and Belize – negatively affecting their Balance of Payments (BoP). The BoP is sub-divided into the current account[36] and the financial[37] and capital account[38]. Imbalances and high debt levels (cf. Figure 11, p. 108) in the Caribbean countries are reflected in relatively high deficits in their current account balances, displayed as share of GDP in Figure 28. Trinidad and Tobago and Suriname are the only countries reaching a surplus in their current account balances, whereas Trinidad and Tobago reaches a higher figure of surplus of 12% of GDP (own calculations based on The World Bank, 2013d). Although having one of the highest FIBs among the Caribbean countries, Trinidad and Tobago's FIB share of GDP is the lowest at 0.2%. This low level emerges from high export revenues from the oil and gas industry, which contribute to the highest GDP among all the sample countries. A comparison with the total debt levels from chapter 3.3.2, Figure 11 also shows that Suriname and Trinidad and Tobago have the lowest debt to GDP ratios. Debt and capital and financial account deficits can be adjusted through a surplus in the current account balance. In that case, the low FIB to GDP levels do not affect their macroeconomic stability. Conversely, countries with higher deficits and high debt levels are more likely to be vulnerable to a financial crisis, due to high and increasing FIB levels. Antigua and Barbuda and Barbados seem to be the most vulnerable countries in this context, since both feature debt levels over 70%, high BoP deficits, and relatively high FIB to GDP ratios of 2% and 1% respectively (own calculations based on UN COMTRADE, 2010; CEPALSTAT, 2013; The

---

36 The current account includes trade of goods and services, income and current transfers.
37 The financial account includes direct and other investments.
38 The capital account comprises capital transfers, including government debt forgiveness.

World Bank, 2013d). In addition, St. Vincent and the Grenadines, Guyana and Barbados have the highest deficits in their BoP, which threatens their macroeconomic vulnerability. Countries less vulnerable are St. Kitts and Nevis, The Bahamas and Belize, which have positive capital and financial account balances. The surplus in their capital account balance, however, can barely make up for adjustments of large deficits in their current account balance – except for Belize, where the current account deficit of 1% of GDP is balanced by a surplus of 1% of GDP in the capital and financial account (cf. The World Bank, 2013d). Overall, high deficits in the BoP and a relatively high FIB to GDP ratio additionally put pressure on the capacity to sustain an increasing FIB and unsustainable high debt levels; which may be labelled as macroeconomic crisis in the Caribbean countries.

Figure 28:   **Balance of Payments (BoP) and Food Import Bill (FIB), (in % of country's GDP), Caribbean countries, 2011**

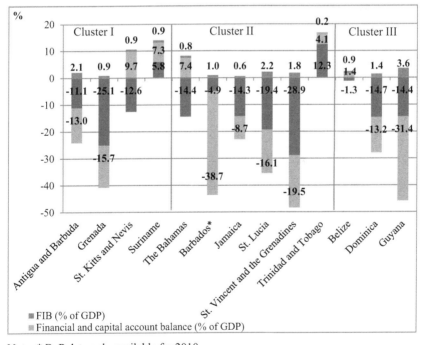

Note: * BoP data only available for 2010
Source: BoP in % of GDP: own calculations based on The World Bank (2013d). FIB in % of GDP: own calculations based on UN COMTRADE (2010), The World Bank (2013d)

Financial resources and foreign exchange are indispensable to pay for the FIB. Caribbean countries are at risk that chronic national debt levels will further increase if they lack financial resources or foreign exchange to pay for imported food; additionally compressing their food import capacity. This also puts pressure on government expenditures for risk-coping strategies reducing negative effects of food price increases and inflation on the population's welfare. FNS measurements that increase governmental expenditure have been implemented in the event of the global food price crisis in various Caribbean countries. For instance, such measurements included price subsidies on staple foods in St. Lucia, free food distribution programs in Grenada, expanding social safety nets programs in Jamaica, and removal of the Value Added Tax (VAT) from basic food items in Trinidad and Tobago (cf. Silva et al., 2011). These expenditures are important to improve unequal distribution of income and food, and to hinder poverty levels to rise, in short-term crises situations and the long-term. Nevertheless, the additional costs or financial burden, which may decrease government revenues and possibly curbing economic growth in the short-term, may have a positive impact on human development and consequently on the economy in the long-term. However, fiscal imbalances and debt levels determine the scope of implementation of such policies (cf. Canuto, 2011).

The importance of the agricultural and food production sector for the Caribbean economies has decreased with the change of their economic structures. Thus, its contribution to the countries' economic growth has become marginal. An increase of food imports and higher FIB levels can affect the economies through different macroeconomic channels, increasing economic vulnerability and limiting the capacity to cope with crises and external shocks. Economic vulnerability of Caribbean countries results mainly from structural constraints and the lack of economic diversification (cf. chapter 3.3.2). Furthermore, deficits in the BoP and continuous high debt levels may aggravate the weak and vulnerable economies. In the case of NFIM countries which depict a double deficit in the food trade and agricultural trade balances – except for Antigua and Barbuda – two implications arise. First, food imports cannot be paid by earnings from agricultural exports, and second, in times of high food prices, countries are not able to substitute food imports with domestically grown and processed foodstuff.

The magnitude of the impact of food crises and an increase in food imports depend on long-term public and private expenditures and investments in key sectors. Higher expenditure and investments can improve FNS and mitigate negative effects in the Caribbean economies. Various reports and publications from non-governmental institutions emphasize the absence of public and private investments and the lack of financial resources (cf. Carmichael et al., 2009; Silva et al., 2011). A high dependence and unbearable costs of food imports restrain incentives to invest in domestic food production and to diversify the Caribbean economies. Gross National Savings (GNS) in relative terms of GDP decreased in the majority of the sample countries, from 2002 to 2010 (cf. Appendix F). The drop of savings was most obvious in 2008, whereas some countries experienced a second drop in 2010, due to the late and subsequent effects of the economic and financial crises (cf. CARICOM, 2013b).

Low investments, the weak financial capacity of the government to provide and support the population with social safety programs, and persisting structural constraints may lead to a deterioration of the vulnerable economies, thereby threatening FNS in several Caribbean sample countries. Despite serious economic and fiscal implications of the high FIB, the consumers have to pay the costs at higher consumer prices. As already analysed, price increases directly affect the consumers in their expenditure decision, but also in their food consumption choices. When prices for certain food items increase, consumer may spend a larger share of their income on food, and concurrently shift their consumption to cheaper food items, which leads to either a drop in calorie intake or a less adequate nutrient intake.

5.4   Conclusion: The high burden of food imports in the Caribbean

This chapter explored the main factors that led to high food imports in the Caribbean countries and the implications on different socio-organizational levels. Similar and sometimes divergent results within single clusters prove that there are significant differences in the features of the Caribbean economies, but also common issues regarding the causes of food imports. A summary of the study findings from this chapter is displayed in Table 19.

The result from this analysis of agriculture and food production in all sample countries clearly finds that food import dependency is lower for all NFEX countries and countries from Cluster III, because of their higher agricultural/food production capacity. For NFIM countries from Cluster I, import dependency is low, since these countries have weak export sectors. Subsequently, these countries fall short of foreign exchange which leads to a lower import capacity. Cluster II shows different results for this analysis, relying on exports of agricultural or primary materials, having a higher capacity to import food, depending on food imports, and thus, displaying high FIB levels. Consequently, dependency on exports for foreign exchange and imports of food increase economic vulnerability in all 13 sample countries in the Caribbean. Dependency on food imports results from a weak agricultural sector and unfavourable trade policies.

"It can be argued, with some justice, that the dependence of a country on importing food from abroad for the survival of its own population can be a major source of vulnerability for the country [...] the desire to be less dependent on outsiders for the most basic necessity of life is easy to sympathize with" (Drèze and Sen, 1989: 166).

On the basis of these and previous findings in this thesis, FNS is a complex supply-side issue. The Caribbean countries experienced rapid and intensive economic change during the last six decades, in which the fundamental economic transformation has been displaced by undiversified and weak economies. The persistently low domestic food production and the lack of resources, such as of fertile land, employment, inputs and investments, led to higher dependencies on food imports and on exports of services and primary products. Hence, the decline in agricultural production and an increase in food imports may be both, consequences of the same series of events, mutually determining each other. The Caribbean countries recognised and identified various constraints in the agricultural sector, but only recently since the food crisis in 2008, small measures were taken to mitigate serious socio-economic impacts of food import dependency.

Moreover, policies that could cushion the negative external effect on the domestic level require adequate financing and investments into the food production sector. In addition, public social safety nets are necessary to support the affected population. This makes the conceptualization of adequate policies difficult, but not impossible, if the discussion about addressing the regional FIB (within the CARICOM) also considers country-specific needs and priorities in the Caribbean countries.

Table 19:   Summary of cluster and results of the burden of food imports analysis, Caribbean countries

		NAEX	NAIM	NFEX	NFIM	SSR	IDR	Food ICI[a]	FIB (in US$ million)[b]	FIB (in % of GDP)[b]
Cluster I	Antigua and Barbuda	X			X	low	high	high	89	2.1
	Grenada		X		X			high	58	0.9
	St. Kitts and Nevis		X		X			high	109	2.2
	Suriname		X		X	high	moderate	low	173	0.9
Cluster II	The Bahamas		X		X			high	464	0.8
	Barbados		X		X	moderate	high	high	257	1.0
	Jamaica		X		X	high		high	938	0.6
	St. Lucia		X		X			high	51	0.9
	St. Vincent and the Grenadines		X		X			high	51	1.8
	Trinidad and Tobago		X		X	low	high	low	622	0.2
Cluster III	Belize	X		X		high	high	high	83	0.9
	Dominica		X		X			high	37	1.4
	Guyana	X		X				low	191	3.6

Note: a Food ICI without services, b 2011

Source: own compilation based on study findings; FIB (in US$ million): UN COMTRADE (2010); FIB (in % of GDP): own calculations based on UN COMTRADE (2010), The World Bank (2013d)

6. Economic and social burden of nutrition related diseases in the Caribbean

In the Caribbean, food and nutrition insecurity results from an array of various internal and external constraints on the supply side. On the one hand, the consumers' demand determines the supply of food. On the other hand, consumers are directly and indirectly affected by changes on the supply side, channelled through availability and access of food, and thereby influencing their consumption patterns. Both, the supply-side and the demand-side are exposed to economic and demographic changes. The previous chapters explored the economic and social settings of the Caribbean countries and examined the reasons and consequences of the main constraints on the supply side. This chapter subsequently analyses the demand side, representing the dimension 'consumption and utilization' of the FNS concept. Results from the previous examination showed that food import dependency and succeeding high levels of food imports lead to an economic burden of high costs for the Caribbean countries. Ultimately, the consumers are directly and indirectly affected by these costs and changes in the availability of imported foodstuffs. Therefore, an examination on main issues on the demand side is indispensable to complete the analysis of FNS in the Caribbean.

Chapter 6.1 examines the food consumption patterns in the Caribbean on the basis of available data, reflecting changes in the availability and utilization of essential nutrients. Based on the understanding of the past and current socio-economic conditions, consumption patterns changed over time, determining the current health status of individuals and the population in the Caribbean. In this context and based on available data and information, chapter 6.2 provides an overview of the incidence and prevalence of nutrition related diseases[39], identified as Non-communicable Diseases (NCDs) in the Caribbean countries. The drastic increase of health risks related to NCDs leads to higher mortality rates, which partially over exceeded the high mortality and prevalence rates of communicable diseases in the investigated countries. However, the increase in NCD

---

39 Here this term refers to chronic diseases related to overnutrition.

prevalence rates has negative effects on the social life of affected individuals and the economy, due to the loss of productivity and higher expenditures for healthcare service. This essential analysis is made in chapter 6.3 and leads to the question, which countries and population groups are the most affected by this epidemic and what implications for the healthcare systems in the Caribbean countries can be drawn from this analysis.

Data for this chapter is mainly drawn from the World Health Organisation (WHO) and its regional office, the Pan American Health Organisation (PAHO). Data availability on this issue in the Caribbean countries is limited. Consequently, clear and visible differences between clusters cannot be detected so that a reference to the cluster will only be made at the end of this chapter.

6.1   *Food consumption and nutrition related diseases in the Caribbean*

Food consumption is determined by the availability of food and the access to it. As long as individuals have access to food and can consume "sufficient, safe and nutritious food that meets their dietary needs and food preferences", they are healthy – depending on biological factors and physical conditions of each person (FAO, 1996). This chapter focuses on the utilization and consumption dimension of the FNS concept. In this context, it is important to consider particular factors, such as food quality and safety, cultural factors, preparation and eating habits, which determine nutritional outcomes and reflect consumption patterns. Ideally, household surveys for detailed consumption data and information of households and individuals would reflect changes of consumption patterns over time. This infomation is essential to assess the impact of consumption patterns on nutrition related health risks and diseases in the Caribbean countries. Since information and data on food consumption based on household surveys is scant, this chapter uses available information on national levels and country studies respectively for the other sample countries.

6.1.1   Caribbean consumption patterns

Early studies on food consumption found that consumption patterns are not static, but change over time. These changes are driven by various cultural, social, political and economic factors such as migration, inter-societal imitation, marketing and advertisement, trade liberalization, availability and accessibility of food (cf. Mintz and Du Bois, 2002). Measurement and observation of the effects of each factor on consumption patterns is difficult and barely feasible, however, important in order to assess the actual change of consumption patterns. In the Caribbean, the combination of these factors led to a change of consumption patterns within the last 20 to 30 years (cf. Carmichael et al., 2009). Therefore, a combination of data on food supply, utilization, and observable general information on the FNS situation in the Caribbean countries serve to assess changes in consumption patterns and evaluate possible impacts of social, economic and political factors. Changes in consumption patterns can also be observed by comparing intra-generational consumption patterns – meaning the patterns between different age groups within a population. Younger population groups are more perceptible to food consumption trends, passed through by advertising, media and 'external influences' (cf. Carmichael et al., 2009).

Since consumption patterns and habits are also influenced by cultures, they are exposed to cultural changes, which in turn can be induced by different external and internal influences. The Caribbean countries are one of the world's most culturally diverse regions, having evolved as such in a short, but intensive period of time, and consistently being influenced by migration. Food has not only played an important role as economic good, but it is embodied in the Caribbean countries' local and authentic cultures (cf. Richards-Greaves, 2012; Wilson, 2012). Therefore, cultural dietary habits can be influenced by economic forces of globalization. Increased reliance on food imports may have induced a shift of diets, from traditional diets consisting of nutritious food towards modern diets including processed, cheap, and imported food, that may be less nutritious and high in sugar, fat and salt (cf. UN SCN, 2004).

Changes in food consumption patterns can be assessed by means of relevant socio-economic information on the national and household level over time. Data on the micro or household level is usually collected in consumption surveys, which for Caribbean countries are scant, or not continuously and recently conducted. This makes a detailed and quantitative analysis of current or changing consumption pattern for the sample countries difficult. A selection of various country specific studies and reports, however serve to mirror the current consumption patterns for the Caribbean countries. This chiefly country specific information and data can be used to some extent for explaining the main conspicuous facts of current dietary habits representative for all the sample countries.

- Consumption of **fruits and vegetables** lies below recommended levels of the WHO[40] associated with an overall low intake of micronutrients and a lack of diet diversity (cf. Carmichael et al., 2009; PAHO, 2007, 2008a, 2008b).

- Dietary energy intake from **protein and fat** is high and above WHO recommended levels for the Caribbean countries;[41] Over 25% of energy consumption alone derives from fat, and 16% from proteins (cf. FAO, 2005a).

- **Energy-dense** consumption is more prevalent among the younger and middle-aged population (< 50 years) than among the older groups; indicating a dietary trend towards unhealthy diets of fried foods, or fast foods (cf. FAO, 2005a; Carmichael et al., 2009).

- Around 40% of **sugar** consumption derives from sweetened beverages (cf. Sharma et al., 2008). Consumption of sugar is twice as high as recommended levels, particularly high among young adults (< 30 years) (cf. Sharma et al., 2008; Carmichael et al., 2009).

Surprisingly fruit and vegetable consumption is lower than recommended, since agriculture production in the Caribbean concentrates mostly on fruit and vegetables and imports of vegetables make up for a larger part of the total food import basket (cf. Table 14, p. 160 and Figure 27, p. 193). Relatively high availability of fruits and vegetables and concomitant low consumption indicates consumption preferences of other foodstuff. High protein consumption mirrors the high proportion of meat imports. Since there is no detailed data on imports or domestic production of fats or the like and sugary beverages, evaluation relies on qualitative studies.

Despite data from nutrition profiles and consumption surveys, Food Balance Sheets (FBS) provide data on national food supply of different macronutrients. FBS can be instructive to disclose changes in food consumption patterns, when assuming that supply is mainly driven by demand. However, this data must be interpreted with caution, since FBS do

---

40   Fruit consumption recommendation is 400g or 5 servings per person per day (cf. FAO, 2004a)
41   Nutrient intake goals for the Caribbean are 10% to 15% of energy supply should be composed of proteins and 15% to 20% of total fat (cf. FAO, 2005a).

not present the actual food intake of the population or individuals (cf. chapter 4.1.2). Table 20 displays the most recent average supply values of energy, fat and protein in the Caribbean countries. The average energy supply compared with the ADER discloses that the available average energy supply levels in some countries are considerably above the country-specific ADER; especially in Barbados, Belize, Dominica, Guyana, and St. Vincent and the Grenadines. Average energy supply in addition, is notably lower in countries of Cluster I. The highest energy supply values are found in Cluster III, the most food and nutrition secure countries in the sample. The Caribbean Food and Nutrition Institute (CFNI) found that figures of high energy supply persist on high levels since the 1970s (cf. Henry, 2007). Average fat and protein supply seem to be high in all sample countries; however, there is no data on the Recommended Dietary Allowance (RDA) for the Caribbean countries, which would allow a meaningful comparison and interpretation of these indicators.

Table 20:   **National supply of selected macronutrients, Caribbean countries, most recent years**

		Average energy supply (kcal/p.c./day) (2009-2011)	Average dietary energy requirements (kcal/p.c./day) (2011-2013)	Average fat supply (g/p.c./day) (2008-2011)	Average protein supply (g/p.c./day) (2008-2010*)
Cluster I	Antigua and Barbuda	2450	2420	86	85
	Grenada	2540	2420	90	75
	St. Kitts and Nevis	2560	2420	81	73
	Suriname	2580	2380	67	56
Cluster II	The Bahamas	2770	2470	97	88
	Barbados	3020	2520	99	90
	Jamaica	2740	2410	87	77
	St. Lucia	2660	2430	78	88
	St. Vincent and the Grenadines	2940	2440	84	86
	Trinidad and Tobago	2820	2430	76	68
Cluster III	Belize	2700	2240	66	67
	Dominica	3160	2420	84	95
	Guyana	2970	2390	52	75

Note: * preliminary data
Source: own compilation. FAO (2013b)

Despite the fact that FBS do not represent any information about actual dietary intake of food or in particular, nutrients, they do not disclose any information about the distribution of food within a population on a national level. In the sample countries, income disparities, poverty or food poverty, and prevalence of undernourishment exist on relatively high levels (cf. Table 3, p. 96 and Figure 15, p. 125). Hence, high levels of energy supply suggest that access to food is either unequally distributed, or that high levels of calories, fats and sugars are consumed through affordable or cheaper food items, particularly among the poor population groups.

Moreover, food consumption may be a personal decision driven by various motives. Caribbean consumption patterns are influenced by cultural and religious factors, due to the countries multicultural characteristics and the different ethnicities within the population (cf. Richards-Greaves, 2012). This ethnic diversity is also mirrored in the variety of local foods and cuisines. Despite cultural and religious factors, food tastes, family members, health condition, prices and availability of foodstuff influence personal food selection (cf. Benjamin et al., 2004). Nevertheless, traditional diets, which consist of a variety of indigenous staples (e.g. starchy roots), fruits, vegetables, and a smaller amount of meat, changed rapidly over time. Now, diets consist of higher consumption of ready available processed foods and imported foodstuffs (cf. Carmichael et al., 2009; Henry, 2007). In the context of momentous social and economic changes, in the past century, the Caribbean countries experienced a *nutrition transition*. According to Popkin (2003) societies are subject to this transition, since they have adopted 'western diets', rich in fats, sugar, and processed foods, and modern sedentary lifestyles. These changes, particularly noticeable in the past decades, in the developing countries, led to a diet shift and low physical activity (cf. Popkin, 2003). In the Caribbean, the nutrition transition is driven by related and specific crucial socio-economic factors.

- **Urbanization**: approximately 43% (2011) of the total population in the Caribbean lives in urban areas, where food availability and food supply variety is high due to the high concentration of supermarkets, restaurants and street vendors (cf. The World Bank, 2013d). However, modern urban lifestyles, which are predominantly sedentary and related time issues, lead to unhealthy food choices.
- The consumption of **fast foods**, snacks, and in general processed foods is mostly common among young adults; concurrently, this is being observed with increased frequency of eating outside of home (cf. Carmichael et al., 2009).
- Higher **incomes and inequality**: on the one hand, increased incomes can lead to higher consumption of processed foodstuffs purchased in supermarkets or eaten outside, where availability and variety of mostly imported food is abundant. On the other hand, lower incomes and poverty can limit access to affordable and nutritious foods.
- **Supply-side factors**: the phenomenal spread of supermarkets and retail grocery stores in major urban areas, in the Caribbean is linked to

changes of consumption patterns towards 'western diets' (cf. Carmichael et al., 2009). Additionally, mass media, marketing and advertising mould consumer tastes (cf. IICA, 2010). The previous analysis of food imports in chapter 5.1 showed that domestic food supply in some Caribbean countries is mainly composed of imported food – up to 80% (cf. Table 16, p. 173). This demand of imported foodstuff is primarily driven by supermarkets, restaurants, and travel and tourism facilities. Consequently, food imports increased not only the variety and the availability of processed foods, but also triggered lower prices for energy-dense foods (cf. Silva et al., 2011).

- CFNI studies show that there is a lack of **knowledge** about the relationship between food and health, or mismatch of knowledge and food choices behaviour (cf. Benjamin et al., 2004). Therefore, food choices are based on availability of food and taste, rather than on knowledge about nutritional values of food.

Based on the findings of the relationship between nutrition and health in chapter 2.1.2, the nutrition transition, which the Caribbean is currently experiencing, has severe negative effects on the health status and ultimately on human development of the population. In the past decades, consumption patterns and unhealthy lifestyles have increased the prevalence of overweight and obesity and, therefore, the risk of nutrition related diseases in the Caribbean countries.

Box 3:   Dietary Guidelines in the Caribbean

A balanced diet and good nutrition are vital to a healthy life. Caribbean consumption patterns seem to be determined by unhealthy and unbalanced diets high in fat, sugar and salt. Nutritional education is a precondition for choosing healthy and nutritious food. One of the most important interventions to promote healthy lifestyles are *Food-Based Dietary Guidelines* (FBDGs). In comparison to common dietary guidelines, FBSGs include country-specific information on the availability of healthy traditional and modern foods, considering cultural acceptance of different foods and current public health problems (cf. Henry, 2007). The Ministries of Health (MoH), the Ministries of Agriculture (MoA) together with the Pan American Health Organization (PAHO), the Caribbean Food and Nutrition Institute (CFNI), and the FAO, compiled and promote such guidelines within the Caribbean countries (cf. FAO, 2012b). Based on the required levels of nutrients for a healthy diet, these guidelines serve to inform the population and guide their selection, utilization and consumption of healthy foods (cf. Henry, 2007). Ideally, the population adopts these guidelines for their daily food consumption. In the Caribbean countries, six food groups are identified according to their importance in the daily consumption: staples, legumes and nuts, vegetables, food from animals, fruits, fats and oils. Nine out of the 13 sample countries in the Caribbean already adopted country-specific FBDGs: The Bahamas, Barbados, Belize, Dominica, Grenada, Guyana, St. Kitts and Nevis, St. Lucia, St. Vincent and the Grenadines. Trinidad and Tobago is in preparation of these guidelines, whereas Antigua and Barbuda, Barbados and Jamaica currently are developing FBDGs (cf. FAO, 2012b).

FBDGs are particularly important for the population in the Caribbean countries because excessive or deficient food consumption is associated with a rise of nutrition related diseases, which may lead to disability and premature death (< 70 years) (cf. WHO, 2011a). Therefore, "sound and effective nutrition" guidelines are crucial to develop adequate food policies and programs, which can improve the nutritional status of a population (Henry, 2007: 187).

The overview of current consumption patterns and undergoing nutrition transition in the Caribbean countries reveals the lack of information and data on the household level, in order to fully assess the change in dietary patterns. Moreover, such information could be helpful to disclose the driving forces and determinants of consumption behaviour, and possibly monitor future changes in these patterns. Why is this information on consumption and lifestyles important? Research on nutrition and changes in dietary habits can provide significant information about the health status of the population and allows implementing and adjusting national public health policies and programs. However, intervention can be limited by social and individual factors that influence food choices.

6.1.2 Risk factors and nutrition related diseases in the Caribbean

Nutrition related diseases result from inadequate intake of macronutrients or micronutrients, or the combination of both. Macronutrients comprise proteins, carbohydrates, and fats, which are generally consumed in large amounts. Whereas micronutrients include a range of vitamins and minerals, of which the most important for health are iodine, iron, and Vitamin A, consumed in smaller quantities. Caribbean consumption patterns disclose an inadequate deficiency of micronutrients and an excessive intake of macronutrients, leading to the assumption that micronutrient deficiency and over-nutrition are the most prevalent forms of malnutrition in the Caribbean countries; both leading to health problems and to chronic diseases[42]. Malnutrition in form of under-nutrition is still prevalent and in several Caribbean countries a successful improvement has been observed, in the past 20 years (cf. Figure 15, p. 124). Micronutrient deficiencies, such as Vitamin A deficiency (VAD) and Iron Deficiency Anaemia (IDA), are also prevalent in the Caribbean countries, causing moderate to severe health problems, particularly for children and pregnant women (cf. chapter 4.1.2). However, the most recent and alarming concern, in the sample countries, is the rise of over-nutrition associated with overweight and obesity. Overweight and obesity refer to the excessive accumulation of fat in the human's body, measured by the Body Mass Index (BMI). The BMI is calculated by a person's weight in kilograms divided by the square of his height in meters (kg/m^2). The normal weight of a person ranges between a BMI of 18.5 and 24.99. A person is considered to be overweight with a

---

42   Chronic diseases refer to Non-Communicable Diseases (NCDs) and consequently will be used interchangeably in this thesis.

BMI equal to or more than 25; whereas a person with a BMI equal to or more than 30 is considered to be obese. (cf. WHO, 2013h).

Changes in consumption patterns that are associated with the nutrition transition refer to the shift from undernutrition to overnutrition. The latter is associated with excess body weight (BMI $\geq$ 25) due to excessive intake of fat, proteins and sugars, leading to overweight and obesity. In the Caribbean, obesity is considered to be the main risk factors for chronic diseases. Further risk factors for chronic diseases include excessive alcohol intake, high sodium intake, sedentary lifestyles and age. Stress, tobacco use and genetic factors are also considered as high risk factors for chronic diseases; however, the focus of this thesis lies on nutrition and lifestyle related risk factors. Table 21 presents the primary risk factors, which contribute to chronic diseases and intermediate risk factors such as obesity, hypertension, diabetes, and certain types of cancer. Obesity results from the risk of excess body weight, and occurs when energy intake is higher than energy expenditure determined by an excessive intake of calories – particularly of fat and sugars, increased by the risk of sedentary lifestyles (cf. CFNI/PAHO, 2004). Hypertension, caused by high or increased blood pressure, is a high risk factor for Cardiovascular Disease (CVD), heart attack, stroke, and kidney failure. Other risk factors such as excess energy intake, excessive alcohol intake, lack of physical activity, obesity and diabetes are also risk factors for the consequences of hypertension (cf. CFNI, 2004; WHO, 2013b). The risk factor for diabetes mellitus type 2[43] increases with overweight and obesity, and decreases with regular physical activities and a normal Body Mass Index (BMI) in adults (cf. Steyn et al., 2004). According to WHO estimates, 30% of all cancer are caused by an excess body weight, unhealthy consumption patterns, lack of physical activity and sedentary lifestyles, excessive alcohol intake, and tobacco use (cf. WHO, 2013a).

---

43   Diabetes type 1 results from the inability of the body to produce enough insulin; whereas diabetes type 2 occurs, when the body cannot use its own insulin effectively (cf. WHO, 2013c).

Table 21:   Selected risk factors to nutrition related diseases

	Obesity	Hypertension	Diabetes[a]	Cancer[b]
Excess Energy Intake	X	X	X	
Excessive Alcohol Intake		X		X
High Sodium Intake		X		
Sedentary Lifestyles	X	X	X	X
Excess Body Weight	X	X	X	X

Note: [a] diabetes mellitus type 2; [b] the risk increases only for certain types of cancer
Source: own compilation based on CFNI (2004)

Dimension of the major risk factor: Obesity

Due to unhealthy lifestyles and diets, high prevalence of overweight and
obesity became the major public health problem in the Caribbean, leading
to a rapid increase in the rise of nutrition related chronic diseases. According to WHO estimates, the prevalence of overweight and obesity among
adolescents and adults in the Caribbean will rise on average from 55% in
2002 to 64% in 2015 (own calculation based on WHO, 2011c). This
alarming high figure and the inexorable increase are particularly caused by
unhealthy consumption patterns among the younger age groups in the Caribbean, which increase the risk for obesity and subsequent nutrition related
diseases in their future as adolescents and adults. Even more alarming is
the rise of overweight and obesity among children (< 15 years). Although,
there is no recent comparable or reliable data for childhood obesity in the
Caribbean countries, various studies indicate an increasing tendency of the
prevalence of overweight and obesity among pre-school children, school
children, and adolescents (cf. CARPHA, 2013; Gaskin et al., 2012). For
instance, the Pan American Health Organization (PAHO) estimates that in
Antigua and Barbuda in 2010, 16% of children (<5 years) were overweight and 5 % obese. While the Ministry of Health (MoH) of Guyana
stated that the level of overweight among the same age group was over 2%
in 2009 (cf. MoH Guyana, 2009; PAHO, 2013). According to a
UNICEF/WHO/The World Bank joint study, the prevalence of children
affected by overweight in the greater Caribbean region[44] increased from

---

44   Here, the Caribbean region refers to the greater region.

4% in 1990 to 8% in 2010 – globally this level rose from 5% to 7% (cf. UNICEF et al., 2012). In Trinidad and Tobago higher rates of obesity of 23% were found in primary school children (cf. MoH Trinidad and Tobago, 2011). Among Caribbean scientists and policy makers, the epidemic of childhood overweight and obesity raises a growing concern. However, prevention programmes for childhood or effective public health policies in the Caribbean countries are scant or merely drafted (cf. CARPHA, 2013; CFNI, 2009). Since nutrition and health are directly interrelated, the current health situation of children will shape the future health situation of the whole Caribbean population; hence determining its social and economic development.

In addition to the high rates of obesity among children, obesity in adults (> 20 years) reaches the highest prevalence rates, while these rates are consistently higher among women than among men (cf. Figure 30). This gender difference results from several biological, social and cultural factors. Evidently, the female body is more likely to store dispensable energy in form of body fat, while women also tend to have a higher intake in fat (cf. Henry, 2004b). For instance, the Jamaican Lifestyle survey found that fat and oil utilization was higher among women than men (cf. Wilks et al., 2008).

According to WHO data, the Caribbean has one of the highest prevalence of obesity (BMI ≥ 30) among adults and adolescents in the world – although global data may not be directly comparable between different countries because of different data collection procedures (cf. WHO, 2011c). The WHO *Global Health Observatory* estimates are compiled by using standard measurement and estimation methods to make data comparable across countries and years (cf. WHO, 2013e). Figure 29 represents this data of the prevalence of overweight and obesity among the Caribbean countries for the most recent year 2008 available. Since there is no visible cluster result based on this data, countries are ranged according to their scale. The highest prevalence of overweight and obesity within both sexes of the population can be observed in St. Kitts and Nevis with a total of 76%, of which 41% is obese; followed by Belize and the Bahamas with overweight rates of 71% and 69%, respectively. All sample countries reach prevalence overweight plus obesity rates well above 50% in total, except for Guyana with 45% of the population being overweight and 17% being obese (cf. WHO, 2013e). In the sample countries, the average overweight rate is considerably high at 33%, whereas the average obesity rate as share of the overweight rate is only slightly lower at 28% (own calculation based on WHO, 2013e). This small difference between over-weight and obesity relative figures gives cause for concern, since high obesity rates indicate a higher risk of the population to be affected by NCDs, which will be discussed in the up-coming subchapter.

Figure 29: **Prevalence of overweight (BMI ≥ 25) and obesity (BMI ≥ 30) among adults (>20 years), both sexes, (in % of country's population), Caribbean countries, 2008**

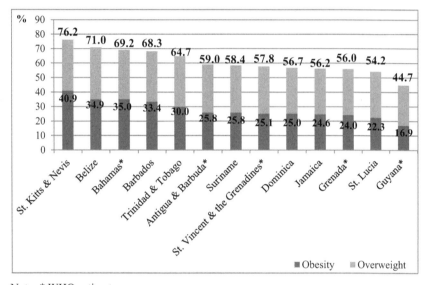

Note: * WHO estimates
Source: own compilation. WHO (2013e)

Obesity prevalence not only varies between, but within countries. While a higher obesity prevalence among the population with higher incomes is more apparent in low income countries, in high income countries, the population with lower incomes is rather affected by obesity (cf. Swinburn et al., 2004). Other studies found an inverse relationship between the edu-cational level within the population and their prevalence rates of obesity (cf. Brathwaite et al., 2011). In the Caribbean, there is no information about the distribution of obesity rates within different income groups with-in the population. Nevertheless, it can be observed that in countries where obesity rates are high, the Prevalence of Undernourishment (PoU) was significantly lower. This relationship was also observed between dif-ferent clusters. A high Dietary Energy Supply (DES) was more present in countries with lower PoU levels (cf. chapter 4.2). The highest PoU levels can be found in countries of Cluster I, consequently disclosing lower DES levels than in the rest of the countries (cf. Appendix C).

However, most recent data from 2008 on the PoU levels and obesity prevalence rates show that, in two countries, both were on a nearly equal high level. In Antigua and Barbuda obesity prevalence rates constituted 26% and were nearly equal to PoU levels of 25%; in Grenada, a PoU level of 25% and a prevalence of obesity rate of 24% were observed (cf. FAO, 2013b; WHO, 2013e). This is also one prevalent phenomenon in other countries and regions, such as in many poor countries in Latin America, which are afflicted by this 'double burden of malnutrition' (cf. FAO, 2012a). Whereas the PoU indicator showed further significant improvement through an increase in both countries between 2011 and 2013, obesity levels are constantly rising in both countries – in Antigua and Barbuda the PoU level decreased to 14%, and in Grenada to 19% (cf. FAO, 2013b; WHO, 2011c). However, these figures need to be interpreted with caution, since data from different sources are not unquestionably comparable due to different methods of measurement and different age groups of the population.

Regarding to the gender-specific rates of obesity, noticeable differences can be observed among women and men in the Caribbean. According to the WHO *Global Infobase* estimates, that by 2015, 75% of all women and 65% of men in the Caribbean will be overweight and obese (BMI ≥ 25) (cf. Appendix H). In 2008, the most recent year for which data is available, the prevalence of obesity for women was much higher than for men in individual Caribbean countries, presented in Figure 30. The highest and lowest obesity rates among females are found to be 50% in St. Kitts and Nevis from Cluster I, and 27% in Guyana from Cluster III, respectively. Obesity among men is most notably prevalent in The Bahamas with 27% and lowest in Guyana with 8%. The greatest differences between female and male obesity rates are found in Dominica and Jamaica. The CFNI notes that obesity rates in the Caribbean have increased between 1980 and 2000 by almost 400% and, therefore, accounts as one of the major causes of death in the Caribbean (cf. Henry, 2004a).

Figure 30:   **Prevalence of obesity (BMI ≥ 30) among adults (>20 years), women and men, (in % of country's population), Caribbean countries, 2008**

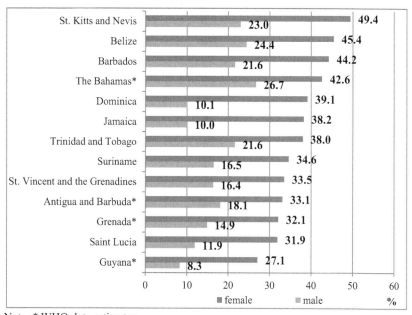

Note: * WHO data estimates
Source: own compilation. WHO (2013e)

These high figures show that women are at greater risk for diabetes and other chronic diseases than men. Higher prevalence of obesity among women not only triggers higher prevalence of chronic diseases, but additionally, this fact may increase the prevalence of obesity among the other household members. High obesity rates among women and increasing obesity rates among children suggest that female obesity may have also an impact on childhood obesity. For instance, overweight and obese mothers transmit nutrition and activity patterns to their children, who are more likely to become overweight or obese, themselves in adulthood (cf. Yach et al., 2006). Moreover, maternal overweight and obesity are associated with a range of serious health risks for children and mothers, such as maternal morbidity (cf. Black et al., 2013). Therefore, public health policies should aim obesity prevention and management programmes for the most affected groups of the population, which are women and children. This requires more research, for it is necessary in order to understand on the one hand, the relationship between obesity and education, and on the other hand, between obesity and socio-economic status in the Caribbean.

Public health programmes and policies can only be effective as long as adequate and reliable data and information on the distribution of obesity is available, on national and regional level. Since overweight and obesity result from a range of factors, such as lifestyle changes, nutrition related behaviour, and socio-economic changes, it is difficult to assess the attributive and country-specific factors in order to explain variations between the overweight and obesity prevalence in the Caribbean countries. Monitoring and analysing changes over time require micro data through household surveys and comprehensive information on these factors. Sufficient and reliable data on the obesity problem is crucial to implement policy programmes for prevention and public health management of emerging health risks and diseases. Obesity is associated with major health problems, including hypertension, diabetes and certain types of cancers. The following chapter examines the major causes of death from NCDs in the sample countries.

6.2   The growing concern of Non-communicable Diseases in the Caribbean

The nutrition transition, in the Caribbean countries, has resulted in unhealthy lifestyles and a rapid rise in overweight and obesity rates as intermediate risk factors for chronic diseases. This has led to a rapid *epidemiological transition* from communicable or infectious diseases to chronic diseases or NCDs. Communicable or infectious diseases are caused by bacteria, viruses, parasites or fungi, and can be directly or indirectly transmitted from one person to another. Non-communicable, or chronic diseases result from different risk factors and are one of the leading causes of death worldwide, in 2008 accounting for 63% of all deaths (cf. WHO, 2011a). The WHO identified four NCDs contributing to the largest death burden worldwide: cancer, Cardiovascular Diseases (CVDs), Chronic Respiratory Diseases (CRDs), and diabetes.[45]

---

45   Central to this study, are NCDs that are triggered by nutrition related risk factors, therefore CRD and other health disorders will not be addressed in further discussion.

Box 4:   Defining Non-communicable Diseases[46]

- Certain types of **cancers** result from primary and intermediate risk factors: Excessive alcohol intake increases the risk for cancers of the oral cavity, pharynx, oesophagus, and liver, and a smaller risk for breast cancer. High sodium intake can increase the risk for stomach cancer. Overweight and obesity increase the risk for cancers of the oesophagus, colorectum, breast, endometrium and kidney (cf. Key et al., 2004). Studies found that healthy lifestyles and consumption can prevent 30% to 40% of all cancers (cf. Donaldson, 2004; WHO, 2013a).
- **Cardiovascular Diseases (CVDs)** result from harmful conditions of the heart and blood vessels. Tobacco use, obesity and unhealthy dietary patterns, physical inactivity, and diabetes can increase the risk of heart diseases, such as Coronary Heart Disease (CHD), causing heart attacks, and cerebrovascular disease, including stroke (cf. Reddy and Katan, 2004; WHO, 2011a). CVDs also include raised blood pressure (hypertension), peripheral arterial disease, rheumatic heart disease, congenital heart disease, and heart failure count as CVDs. Studies found that the consumption of fruit and vegetables has a protective impact on CHD and stroke (Reddy and Katan, 2004).
- **Chronic Respiratory Disease (CRD)** is defined as disease of the airways and lung disease. CRDs include asthma and respiratory allergies, Chronic Obstructive Pulmonary Disease (COPD), occupational lung diseases, sleep apnea syndrome, and pulmonary hypertension. The risk factors range from tobacco use, air pollution, allergen exposure, early childhood respiratory infections, and the exposure to dusts and chemicals (WHO, 2009). Several studies have found a positive association between the consumption of fruit and vegetables, asthma and COPD (Smit et al., 1999).
- **Diabetes** has different forms, most commonly type 1 diabetes and type 2. Diabetes type 1 results from the inability of the body to produce enough insulin, a hormone that is responsible for regulating blood sugar; whereas type 2 diabetes occurs, when the body cannot effectively use the insulin it produces. A high level of blood sugar and the reduced blood flow can cause visual impairment and kidney

---

46 Mental illness is also discussed in the context of NCDs but is excluded from the definition of NCDs by the WHO.

failure. It further can damage the heart, blood vessels, and nerves. Diabetes also increases the risk for heart disease and stroke. 90% of the people diagnosed with diabetes suffer from diabetes type 2 (WHO, 2013b). The risk for diabetes type 2 increases with overweight and obesity, physical inactivity, and maternal obesity. Conversely, the risk of diabetes decreases with physical activity and a normal BMI (18.50-24.99).

As explained previously, socio-economic factors in the Caribbean underlie primary and intermediate risk factors for NCDs. Risk factors can be divided into primary risk factors and intermediate risk factors (cf. Figure 31). Common primary risk factors include modifiable factors, associated with unhealthy consumption patterns, and non-modifiable factors such as age and congenital factors. The array of primary factors increases the risk for intermediate factors such as hypertension, high blood sugar, high cholesterol levels, and obesity. Consequently, primary and intermediate risk factors can directly or indirectly cause chronic diseases. This sequence of causes of chronic diseases is presented in Figure 31 and shows that NCDs are preventable by primarily addressing modifiable and socio-economic factors.

Figure 31:   Causal factors of Non-communicable Diseases (NCDs) in the Caribbean

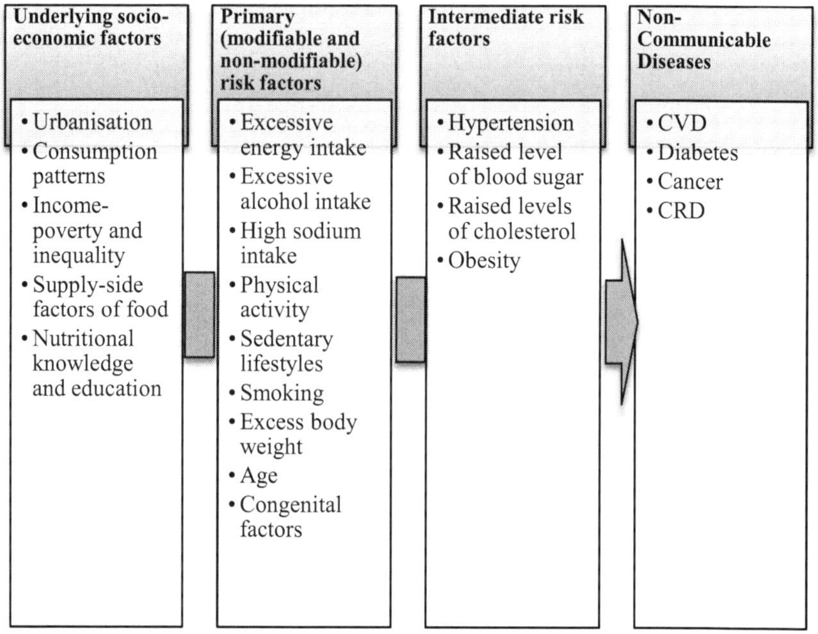

Underlying socio-economic factors	Primary (modifiable and non-modifiable) risk factors	Intermediate risk factors	Non-Communicable Diseases
• Urbanisation • Consumption patterns • Income-poverty and inequality • Supply-side factors of food • Nutritional knowledge and education	• Excessive energy intake • Excessive alcohol intake • High sodium intake • Physical activity • Sedentary lifestyles • Smoking • Excess body weight • Age • Congenital factors	• Hypertension • Raised level of blood sugar • Raised levels of cholesterol • Obesity	• CVD • Diabetes • Cancer • CRD

Source: own compilation based on CFNI (2004); WHO (2005)

In order to analyse the impact of NCDs in the Caribbean, the following sections assess the dimension of NCDs in these countries. Epidemiological data serves to examine changes of incidence, prevalence and mortality rates within the investigative period of time from 2000 to 2011. For this purpose, data and information are mainly drawn from the WHO and PAHO database, or if available from national data sources. It is important to notice, that data cannot always be compared due to broad estimates or different measurement methods.

Prevalence of NCDs in the Caribbean

From an epidemiological point of view, the *incidence rate* refers to the number of people becoming ill or being newly infected by a disease, among a certain population group and in a given period of time. The incidence rate provides information about the spread of a disease (cf. Shields and Twycross, 2003). The *prevalence proportion* represents the proportion of people in a population who are affected by a disease at a certain point of time. The prevalence rate rises with an increase in the incidence rate, and with the duration of a disease. It therefore declines, when people quickly recover from a disease or due to grave diseases that lead to rapid deaths. Prevalence rates for NCDs are usually higher because they have a longer duration and people affected by such diseases can live longer with them, albeit they do not recover (cf. Rothman, 2012). Moreover, rising incidence and prevalence rates may indicate insufficient or inadequate prevention measurements and increasing health risk factors.

In addition to the fact that data for major risk factors, such as overweight and obesity rates is not adequately reported, there is also little data on the incidence and prevalence rates of NCDs in the Caribbean countries. A quantitative and comparative analysis of NCD incidence and prevalence in the sample countries for the investigative period of time is not feasible. Much more data and information over time would be necessary to assess changes in NCD incidence and prevalence rates. It has to be noted, that prevalence rates might be underestimated, since some NCDs, such as diabetes might be left undiagnosed (cf. IDF, 2013). A selective examination of NCD registry data and information in some countries, for which data is available serve to reflect the magnitude of NCDs for the sample countries.

The National Registry Centres for diseases and Ministries of Health (MoH) collect and compile data, mainly based on hospital information on the incidence of the NCD epidemic within the population. According to studies and MoHs statistics for some sample countries, a rising incidence of NCDs has been noticed since the 1980s and 1990s, with high incidence rates of CVD and diabetes (cf. Boyne, 2009; MoH Guyana, 2009). Appendix G displays prevalence rates for hypertension and diabetes. Since overall data for the prevalence rates of CVDs is not available, the prevalence rate of raised blood sugar (hypertension) is used to represent CVD prevalence among the Caribbean countries. Although prevalence rates vary widely across countries, the prevalence rate for raised blood pressure is higher than for diabetes.[47] For instance, Antigua and Barbuda, which has the highest obesity rate among the sample countries, also reaches the highest level of hypertension with 42%, and respectively lower rates of diabetes with 13%. Trinidad and Tobago has the lowest rates of

---

47   No data available for Grenada and St. Vincent and the Grenadines.

hypertension and diabetes with 23% and 7%, respectively. However, the highest diabetes rate has been reported for Belize and Guyana with each 16% (cf. IDF, 2013; PAHO, 2012a).

This trend of high NCD prevalence rates correlates with an ageing population. The incidence rates for diabetes as well as for CVD increases drastically with the on-going *demographic transition.* The share of the population in the advanced age groups (> 45 years) is more susceptible to develop NCDs, especially for CVD and hypertension than younger age groups (cf. CARICOM, 2011d). The demographic transition refers to the transition from high fertility and mortality rates to low fertility and mortality rates (cf. Popkin, 2003). This demographic transition is also evident in the Caribbean countries, where life expectancy increased rapidly over the past decades.

> "A long Life correlates closely with adequate nutrition, good health and education [...]. Life expectancy is thus a proxy measure for several other important variables in human development" (UNDP, 1990: 11).

Further health indicators underscore the current demographic transition in the Caribbean. For instance, the infant mortality rate (< 1 year) decreased from 23 infants per 1,000 live births to 18 infants in the same period of time, whereas the fertility rate has decreased on average from 2.4 to 2.2 births per women (cf. The World Bank, 2013d). Progress, however, has been uneven within the Caribbean countries (Appendix I). In 2011, life expectancy at birth for the Caribbean countries was on average 72 years and increased approximately of three years between 2000 and 2011, due to better access to nutrition and improved health care (cf. The World Bank, 2013d; UN, 2010). The PAHO estimates that, in 2025, 17% of the Caribbean population will be over 60 years, which concomitantly increases the incidence and prevalence of NCDs (cf. CARICOM and PAHO, 2006). The 2010 Barbados National Registry (BRN) report showed for instance that, from the age of 45 years, Barbadians are more likely to get a Myocardial Infarction (MI) or heart attack (cf. BNR, 2010). Additionally, NCD prevalence in Jamaica was found to be approximately 24% in adults between 40 and 49 and significantly higher at approximately 68% in the elderly population (> 60 years) and (cf. The World Bank, 2012b).

Box 5:   The Barbados National Registry (BNR) for Chronic Non-communicable Diseases (NCDs)

Among the national registries for NCDs, the Barbados National Registry for Chronic Non-communicable Disease (BNR) is using a surveillance system covering BNR-Stroke, BNR-Heart, and BNR-Cancer data and information, providing a broad range of statistics on incidence, mortality and survival of these diseases. This surveillance system is unique and an exemplary institurion in the Caribbean countries. The BNR acts on behalf of the Ministry of Health and is conducted by the Chronic Disease Research Centre of The University of the West Indies (UWI) (cf. BNR, 2009). The BNR reports that, in 2010, half of the patients with Myocardial Infarction (MI) cases (heart attack) were obese or had diabetes, which are the major risk factors for CVD. The findings in the 2010 report show a drastic increase in the incidence rate of MI cases from the age of 65-74 years within the population, which i.a. supports the increasing incidence rate of NCDs with age. In comparison with the previous 2009 report, the incidence rate of stroke increased from approximately 46 strokes per month in 2009 to 49 in 2010. CVDs as one of the leading incidence of NCDs in Barbados rise with the major risk factors age, hypertension, diabetes and obesity (cf. BNR, 2010). These contributively factors to CVDs may as well be observed in and also be transposed for the other Caribbean countries. The incidence rates of NCDs and growing rates of obesity show a rising trend in all Caribbean countries due to increasing risk factors, such as obesity.

Mortality and morbidity rates of Non-communicable Diseases in the Caribbean

In comparison to other countries or world regions, the Caribbean countries are one of the worst affected by the NCD epidemic, mirrored by its high NCD *morbidity* and *mortality* rates (cf. WHO, 2011c). Mortality rates refer to the actual death rates within the population, whereas morbidity rates refer to the number of people afflicted by a disease within a healthy population group and, therefore, reflect disease statistics also used by the prevalence rate. While data on the incidence and prevalence of NCDs is nearly absent, WHO data on NCD mortality rates is available for 2002 and 2004 and serves to examine the most prevalent cause of death in the Caribbean countries. Additional MoH statistics or more precisely hospital statistics on morbidity reveal that NCDs account for the highest frequency of cases (cf. MoH Guyana, 2009; MoH Trinidad and Tobago, 2005). In 2004, NCDs constituted 76% of all deaths in the Caribbean (cf. Figure 32). This figure was even higher than the global average of 58%. Communicable diseases in the Caribbean were the second leading cause of death and contributed only 17% to total deaths. This figure was headed by infectious and parasitic diseases. Injuries account for the lowest share of total deaths, with 7% (own calculation based on WHO, 2011c). Among the sample countries, Guyana has the highest NCD death rates with 827 deaths per 100,000 populations (age-standardized) and also the highest mortality rates of communicable diseases were observed with 294 deaths per 100,000, in 2004. The lowest mortality rates of NCDs have been observed in The Bahamas (509 deaths per 100,000); and the lowest communicable disease death rate has been observed in St. Lucia with 69 deaths per 100,000 (cf. WHO, 2011c). Half of the NCD deaths (49%) occurred alone due to cardiovascular diseases, which correspond to the high prevalence rates of hypertension (cf. Appendix G). Grenada had the highest number of CVD deaths, 423 deaths per 100,000 of the population. Cancer has the second highest death rate and constituted 21% of all NCD deaths, and most cancer deaths occurred also in Grenada, where 13 people out of 100,000 died because of cancer in 2004. Diabetes death rates which made up 11% of all NCD deaths were highest in Trinidad and Tobago (128 people out of 100,000). Respiratory diseases account for the largest number of deaths in Jamaica with 63 deaths, and constitute for only a low share of all NCDs of 4% (cf. WHO, 2011c)

Figure 32:   Main causes of death (age-standardized), (in % of total deaths), in the Caribbean, 2004

Cause of death

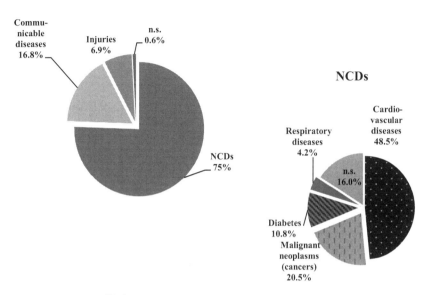

Note: n.s. = not specified
Source: own compilation. Own calculations based on WHO (2011c)

Since there is not sufficient and up-to-date surveillance data on the incidence, prevalence and mortality of NCDs, it is difficult to conclude whether high death rates are due to high prevalence rates or due to weak public health systems and the lack of sufficient and adequate medical care. However, such a conclusion would require a detailed examination on the efficiency of the public health systems and surveillance data.

6.3   *Economic, social and health burden of Non-communicable Diseases in the Caribbean*

The Caribbean Commission on Health and Development (CCHD) recognises: "a healthy population is an essential prerequisite for the economic growth and stability of the Caribbean" (CARICOM and PAHO, 2006: xiii). According to the previous analysis, socio-economic, primary and

225

intermediate risk factors, high overweight and obesity rates, and high NCD death rates indicate that another major issue may contribute to the overall burden of NCDs. This issue concerns the capacity of effectively responding to the needs of the unhealthy population groups. Access to affordable, quality health care services is essential for prevention and treatment of major risk factors associated with NCDs. The alarming health situation of the Caribbean population requires special treatment and corresponding health care services for the patients. Adequate treatment and public health care services have to be covered through appropriate financial expenditures, either public or private. The question is whether the public health system in the Caribbean can respond to these needs and how the individual countries are affected by the burden of NCDs. The following chapter addresses these questions, using most recent and available data to assess differences between countries.

6.3.1 Public health situation in the Caribbean

Public health has the function to improve the health status of the population through providing health care services, which can respond effectively to the needs of the individuals and prevention of disease. The government's spending on health care reflects its commitment to invest in human development and to adapt to new health challenges, such as the rising concern of NCDs in the Caribbean. Higher costs of NCD treatments and an increasing number of the population affected by these diseases, in general requires high healthcare expenditures. Access to adequate health care and health financing is challenging in several Caribbean countries due to limited resources. Thus, the availability and access to high specialized medical services and treatment for NCDs, for instance radiotherapy or chemotherapy for cancers is problematic (cf. HECORA, 2008; PAHO, 2012a). On a regional level, there has been a discussion about cost efficient regional medical centres and shared clinical services, but its realization lacks commitment and action (cf. CARICOM and PAHO, 2006; HECORA, 2008).

The national capacity and the actual situation of the public health system can be examined by comparing public health expenditure with private health expenditure, which in sum is the Total Health Expenditure (THE). Private health expenditure (PvtHE) comprises expenditure on health from private health insurances or other corporations and households. Direct health expenditures of households are termed Out-of-Pocket (OOP) expenditure. OOP expenditure can be expressed in percentage of PvtHE, or as a percentage of THE. The General Government Health Expenditure (GGHE) refers to the government budgets destined to health services, parastatal entities, and to compulsory health insurance payments (cf. WHO, 2011b). An overview of these indicators in the Caribbean countries for 2011 is presented in Appendix J. According to this data, GGHE is overall higher than private expenditure on health in all sample countries, except for The Bahamas, Grenada and St. Lucia. OOP expenditure is a crucial indicator, since high OOP expenditures have impoverishing effects on households and individuals. OOP expenditure on health as percentage of THE varies among the countries and ranges from 11% in Suriname to 53% in St. Lucia (cf. WHO, 2013d). National health insurances can decrease the costs for OOP expenditure by providing a "universal coverage and [...] a stable source of financing", although the size of the risk pool depends on the population size of a country (CARICOM and PAHO, 2006: 9). However, solely Antigua and Barbuda, Suriname and Belize have implemented a National Health Insurance (NHI) in their framework of social security. Out-of-Pocket (OOP) expenditure as a percentage of PvtHE, therefore, is pretty high and ranges from 24% in Suriname to 100% in St. Vincent and the Grenadines (cf. WHO, 2013d). Several studies on health expenditure found that serious financial burden for households and the risk for impoverishment is 'catastrophic', where OOP expenditure of THE is high and exceeds 40% (cf. Xu et al., 2010). This is the case for Grenada (51%), and St. Lucia (53%); whereas Trinidad and Tobago is at the limit with 40% (cf. Appendix J) (cf. WHO, 2013d).

On a national level, the public health sector has a critical role to finance and manage national health services, and to provide adequate access to quality services (cf. CARICOM and PAHO, 2006). While THE as share of the total GDP reveals the magnitude of health investments into the overall health system, GGHE per capita values[48] are useful to assess investments into the public health system for individuals, making expenditure data comparable across the sample countries. Figure 33 presents data on the per capita government expenditures on health and the THE as percentage of GDP. In 2011, per capita public health expenditures varied widely from

---

48   To compare expenditure in different currencies, the WHO converts values in International Dollars (Int$).

Int\$ 1157.01 in The Bahamas and Int\$ 182.27 in Guyana. GGHE per capita expenditure was highest in The Bahamas and Barbados, where constituting Int\$ 1024.60. These figures correspond with high levels of THE as percentage of GDP in both countries reaching a level of 8% (cf. WHO, 2013d, 2013e). High levels of THE and GGHE per capita represent in both countries good quality of health care services, which Barbados additionally provides for free to its citizens (cf. PAHO, 2012b). Antigua and Barbuda, and Trinidad and Tobago, rank at high levels of per capita public health spending, with Int\$ 787.17 and Int\$ 652.55 respectively; and relatively high levels of THE as percentage of GDP. These high expenditures reflect the governmental provision of free access to public health care services and facilities in Trinidad and Tobago, whereas Antigua and Barbuda provides health funds and additional assistance for its population. Lower levels of THE in percentage of GDP are reported in Jamaica (5%), St. Kitts and Nevis (4%), and St. Vincent and the Grenadines (5%). Although St. Lucia reports a high THE as percentage of GDP at 7%, GGHE per capita, however, is ranked at the lower range with 325.95 (cf. WHO, 2013d). Since PvtHE as share of THE and OOP expenditure as share of THE in St. Lucia are one of the highest (cf. Appendix J), public health investment may not adequately cover the health care needs for the population.

Figure 33:   Government expenditure on health p.c. (in Int$) and total expenditure on health (in % of country's GDP), Caribbean countries, 2011

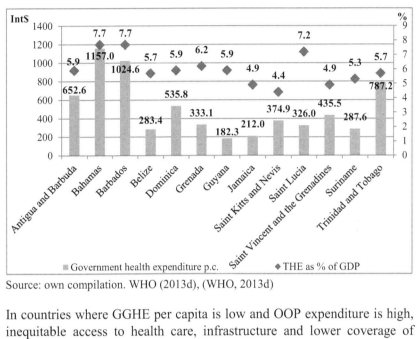

Source: own compilation. WHO (2013d), (WHO, 2013d)

In countries where GGHE per capita is low and OOP expenditure is high, inequitable access to health care, infrastructure and lower coverage of even primary and secondary *care* have been identified as main issues (cf. PAHO, 2012b). *Primary health care* includes promotive, preventive, curative, and rehabilitative services, whereas *secondary health care* provides services for patients from specialist in the respective field of disease. Health care in specialised facilities, where advanced and diagnostic technology is used for treatment of diseases, is thereby called *tertiary health care* (cf. NYU, 2013; WHO, 1978). A comprehensive PAHO report on the general health situation and on the public health care system found, that except for The Bahamas and Barbados, in some countries such as Guyana and Belize there is room of improvement for the quality of health care services at all levels of health care, primary, secondary and tertiary. Inequitable access to health care is the result of lack of resources such as skilled and trained personnel, sufficient equipment, facilities and infrastructure. While in most countries infrastructure, poor information system and data collection have been identified as additional problems (cf. PAHO, 2012b, 2012a).

Moreover, the Caribbean countries have to respond to the ever increasing need for special tertiary health care for treating NCDs, which is limited in most of the countries, due to the lack of resources. An efficient response to the increasing risk of NCDs will require even more finances channelled through public as well as private expenditures, and ideally without increasingly burden the affected population. Furthermore, health care expenditure should effectively and efficiently be spent, in order to achieve better health outcomes of the population. This increasing challenge for the public health systems requires a twofold approach of prevention measurements and appropriate response through medical care and treatment. Furthermore, inequity due to relatively high levels of poverty in some Caribbean countries impedes adequate access to health care. High NCD death rates may reflect these inequalities and the underinvestment at all levels of the health care system.

6.3.2   The economic and social burden of Non-communicable Diseases in the Caribbean

Observing the high incidence and prevalence of NCDs, the burden of these diseases can be understood as the economic burden. It includes high public and private expenditures on the provision of special healthcare treatment. From a socio-economic view, diseases such as NCDs reduce the quality of life of the affected individuals due to disability. Therefore, NCDs have a far-reaching impact on the social life of individuals and the national economies. Both, social and economic impacts can be defined as the total burden of NCDs. The *economic burden* and *social burden* of NCDs can be assessed on the macro level, meaning the society or economy as a whole (national level), and on the micro level (individual and household level). Both, the social and economic burden are mutually dependent and do not necessarily require individual examination.

The *economic burden* includes *direct costs* and *indirect costs* on the macro and micro level. The approach for classification of different costs of diseases derives from the Cost-of-Illness (COI) method, which is used to calculate the total costs of a disease. The COI method requires a broad set of data on personal and non-personal NCD costs (cf. Bloom et al., 2011).

Figure 34 displays the composition of the economic burden on these levels. Direct costs on the **macro level** refer to monetary costs for the economy as a whole, including governmental and private expenditure for the provision of public healthcare services and special treatment on a national level. Therefore, private and public health expenditure enables the provision of adequate facilities and quality healthcare services. As the previous subchapter showed, public health expenditure is unevenly distributed across the Caribbean countries and higher per capita public health expenditures correlate with better assistance and quality of healthcare. Indirect costs on the macro level are associated with the economy's loss of productivity due to fluctuant shortages of productive labour forces or due to premature death (cf. Bloom et al., 2011).

Direct costs on the **micro level** cover all costs that households and individuals have to dedicate directly to patient visits, inpatient and outpatient care, and medications equalling the OOP expenditures; additionally, nonmedical costs such as costs for transportation may also count to these costs. The amount of direct costs that burden households and individual can vary significantly according to the NCD. The higher the direct costs for individuals are, the lower the coverage of PvtHE through insurances. Indirect costs on an individual level can be defined as the loss of income, due to disability[49] or premature death. These costs can be measured by the human capital approach[50] (cf. Bloom et al., 2011; Glied, 1996).

Figure 34:   The economic burden of NCDs on the micro and macro level

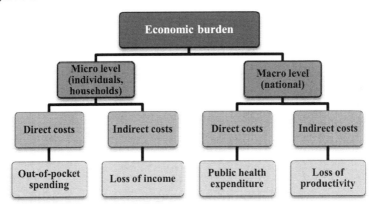

Source: own compilation

---

49   Disability is defined as the loss of health
50   Here, the human capital approach is defined as total time of absence multiplied with the wage rate of the person (cf. Glied, 1996).

On the one hand, the assessment of direct costs of NCDs on the micro level and macro level in the Caribbean depends on comprehensive microeconomic data of OOP expenditures on health from household surveys and national health account macroeconomic data. On the other hand, indirect costs on both levels are difficult to assess, thus determining the loss of income and loss of productivity due to disability or premature death is mainly based on broad estimations. Although necessary and specific NCD cost data on the micro and macro level in the Caribbean is limited, some studies have been conducted to assess the economic burden of NCDs in selected sample countries, which help to reflect the current situation.

Based on the 2007 *Jamaican Survey of Living Conditions*, a study of The World Bank (2102) on the prevention of NCDs in Jamaica found that 71% of the economic burden of NCDs for individuals (micro level), were caused by direct costs in form of individual OOP expenditures. Data has been collected for a two-year period of time from 2006 to 2007; these direct costs amounted US$ 742 per capita and per year. Consequently, indirect costs due to income losses constituted 29% of the individual economic burden of NCDs and in absolute terms US$ 307 per person per year. Under poor living conditions, individuals affected by NCDs spend up to one-third of their income on healthcare and pharmaceuticals (direct costs) (cf. The World Bank, 2012b). Nevertheless, in absolute terms, the poor spent less on health care for treatment and medications due to the lack of resources for direct spending, for health insurance, and the preferred use of public healthcare services. Wealthy household and individuals can afford better services and medication and, therefore, spend more on healthcare services than the poor. The inequality of access to health care needs to be addressed through social protection programmes for the poor (cf. The World Bank, 2011, 2012b). In 2009, the economic burden of NCDs on the micro level was estimated to account for 3% of GDP in Jamaica, and 3% of GDP in St. Lucia (cf. The World Bank, 2011). In an earlier study, Barcelo et al (2003) even found that the indirect costs of diabetes exceeded the direct cost on the micro level in selected countries[51] of the study. In Trinidad and Tobago the indirect costs on the micro level were six-times higher than the direct costs, whereas in Guyana direct costs were slightly higher (cf. Barcelo et al., 2003).

---

51   In this study The Bahamas, Barbados, Guyana, Jamaica and Trinidad and Tobago were included.

Moreover, the costs and burden differ according to the NCD. Based on the COI approach, studies showed that the largest total economic burden of NCDs, the sum of direct and indirect costs, in The Bahamas, Barbados and Jamaica is due to hypertension. Whereas costs per person show that diabetes accounted for the largest burden in these countries (cf. Abdulkadri et al., 2009; CARICOM and PAHO, 2006; The World Bank, 2012b). In Trinidad and Tobago diabetes is the most costly NCD, in absolute and per capita terms (cf. Abdulkadri et al., 2009). There are no studies that calculate the economic burden of cancer.

However, these estimated high costs contributing to the economic burden of NCDs may be underestimated, because they often merely present the economic burden on the micro level; including the costs of the macro level to the overall economic burden would show that the costs exceed unsustainable levels. These current and future "astronomical costs [...] sharpen the region's awareness of the need for primary prevention programmes" (cf. CARICOM and PAHO, 2006). Health care expenditure will have to increase in the future, in order to increase equitable access to efficient and good quality healthcare services for treatment of NCDs – since the burden of NCDs is unequally distributed within the population. Evidence from the different studies showed that health inequity is a concern in Caribbean countries, where high poverty rates are most prevalent and the poor lack adequate access to healthcare. Prevalence and mortality rates may be higher in the poorer segments of a country and emphasize the need for social safety nets and health funds for the poor (cf. CARICOM and PAHO, 2006; The World Bank, 2011, 2012b).

While the economic burden of NCDs is associated with monetary costs, the *social burden* primary refers to the loss of healthy life years due to disability or premature death. Further, economic consequences of NCDs induced by the loss of incomes due to high NCD related costs, can lead to a higher risk of impoverishment of vulnerable population groups. The 2010 WHO report on NCDs found that NCDs and poverty are closely interrelated, by stating that:

> "NCDs and poverty create a vicious cycle whereby poverty exposes people to behavioural risk factors for NCDs and, in turn, the resulting NCDs may become an important driver to the downward spiral that leads families towards poverty" (WHO, 2011a).

Since poverty is understood as a multidimensional concept, this may also include the paucity of access to education, food and health services. Poverty and the loss of healthy life increase the risk of social exclusion and the loss of opportunities thereby impairing quality of life. In particular, the pain and suffering from the NCDs directly contribute to the social burden of NCDs, resulting from disability and premature death (cf. WHO, 2011a). The total social burden on the national level is the sum of the aggregated burden of the NCD affected individuals on the micro level. The social burden consequently comprises the loss of healthy life years and poverty on the micro and the macro level (cf. Figure 35).

Figure 35:   The composition of the social burden of Non-communicable Diseases (NCDs)

Source: own compilation

Disability and premature death, contributing significantly to the economic and social burden of NCDs, can be measured by the Disability-Adjusted Life Years (DALYs), a method that is widely adopted in studies that measure the burden of disease by calculating the lifespan of an individual living with any disease. With the DALYs method, lost years of a healthy life can be calculated by adding up two components, the Years of Life Lost (YLLs)[52] due to premature death and the Years Lived with Disability (YLDs)[53](cf. WHO, 2013f). In the same way as high mortality rates, DALYs due to NCDs may indicate a 'health gap' on national level, since "they measure the state of a population's health compared to a normative goal. The goal is [...] to live the standard life expectancy in full health" (cf. Murray et al., 2012: 2199). Consequently, the loss of healthy years of

---

52   "The YLL [...] correspond to the number of deaths multiplied by the standard life expectancy at the age at which death occurs" (WHO, 2013f).

53   "[...] the number of incident cases in that period is multiplied by the average du-ration of the disease and a weight factor that reflects the severity of the disease on a scale from 0 (perfect health) to 1 (dead)" (WHO, 2013f).

life may be the greatest social burden for the individuals living with NCDs and for the society as a whole. In the Caribbean countries, up to 79 % of DALYs are due to NCDs, globally one of the highest percentage next to Australia, the European countries, and North America (cf. IHME, 2013b). In general, the increase in DALYs is driven by an increasing population. The 2010 *Global Burden of Disease* (GBD) study revealed that in the Caribbean region, the rate of DALYs increased over the past 20 years as a proportion of the population (cf. Murray et al., 2012). Recent 2010 data from the GBD shows that DALYs due to NCDs vary widely across the sample countries from the highest number in Jamaica with 499,591 DALYs in both sexes and all ages, to the lowest in Dominica 15,248 DALYs (cf. IHME, 2013a). According to the PAHO, between 1990 and 2010, DALYs in the Caribbean countries have increased mainly due to an increase of YLL. In 1999/2000, 1092 premature deaths from CVD were recorded in Jamaica, approximately resulting in 92,023 YLL (cf. CARICOM and PAHO, 2006; IHME, 2013a). This figure increased to 96,893, in 2010. Whereas in Trinidad and Tobago, 71,235 YLL were recorded due to CVD, in 1995, which slightly decreased in 2010 to 70,166 YLL (cf. IHME, 2013a). DALYs representing both the economic and social burden of NCDs, show the growing concern and severe impacts of NCDs on the economies and societies in the Caribbean.

The previous chapter of this thesis found that poverty and inequality in the Caribbean countries are widely spread (cf. chapter 3.3.1). Ideally, data on poverty would be comparable between the countries and data on inequality would be adequate, to examine the linkages between income-poverty and the social burden of NCDs. Increasing impoverishment and lower incomes can also lead to less spending on nutritious or specific foods needed for recovery or for supporting the function of the human body, such as diabetic food. Otherwise, in some cases, an inadequate nutrition can increase the risk of NCD mortality, due to comorbidity – the coexisting of two NCD cases, for instance hypertension and diabetes. Those who live in poverty affected by NCDs, rely on social safety and health-supporting and -prevention programs, which can reduce the social burden for individuals and on the national level. Moreover, "for nutrition security the preventive and promotional aspects are as important as the curative ones" (Oshaug et al., 1994: 501).

This examination on the economic and social burden of NCDs shows that cost-efficient measures should be taken to effectively reduce modifiable risk factors for NCDs in the Caribbean, requiring a multidimensional approach from different sectors and policy purviews. Consequently, risk factors such as overweight and obesity should be addressed in the framework of FNS, in order to understand the underlying causes and to implement appropriate actions for better controlling of NCDs and primary prevention. Reducing the economic and social burden of NCDs in the Caribbean countries reduces also direct and indirect costs. Investments in health systems is one important step to reduce this burden, particularly in the Caribbean where the provision of adequate healthcare services for the NCD-affected population or access to health care is inadequate (cf. CARICOM and PAHO, 2006; Jamison et al., 2013).

6.4   Conclusion: Health investments are crucial to address Non-communicable Diseases in the Caribbean

From this comprehensive analysis of causes and consequences of NCDs in the Caribbean countries ensues that overweight and obesity are the most crucial primary and intermediate factors, influencing the emergence of NCDs in the Caribbean. This corresponds with the fact that "prevailing social and economic conditions influence people's exposure and vulnerability to NCDs" (cf. WHO, 2011a). Rapid changes in lifestyles have occurred due to socio-economic factors in the Caribbean, driving unhealthy consumption patterns apparently in all income groups. Based on existing data, approximately 76% of all deaths are attributable to NCDs, and 49% of these deaths occur due to CVDs in the Caribbean (cf. WHO, 2011c).

These high NCD mortality rates and high NCD prevalence rates indicate a high economic and social burden for the population and the society as a whole, impeding human development and possibly holding back economic development in these countries. Health, education and productivity are strongly inter-related and can influence well-being and economic growth in a country (cf. chapter 2.1.2). Maintaining a healthy and active life depends on a healthy environment, but also on adequate access to disease prevention and good quality of healthcare services. In this context, prevention measures of primary and intermediate risk factors are more cost-effective than treating NCDs (cf. Bloom et al., 2011). Sometimes life-long treatment for NCDs is expensive, consequently affecting the population in the Caribbean countries through high OOP expenditures. Public and personal health expenditures will rise inexorably if prevention measures fail or cost-effective intervention on intermediate risk factors is absent. A summary of different indicators from this analysis of the economic and social burden is displayed in Table 22.

Therefore, two-fold health investments and public health policies to ensure appropriate prevention and treatment measures are essential, in order to foster economic development and health (cf. Jamison et al., 2013). Health investments in the Caribbean are necessary to mobilise resources for improved infrastructure, access and care for the rapidly increasing numbers of people affected by NCDs. In addition, special attention must be drawn to the poor population groups affected by NCDs.

In the ongoing post-2015 MDG debate, and the alarming concern of NCDs worldwide, particularly in low-income and middle-income countries, there is a great necessity for better data collection and surveillance on the incidence, prevalence and mortality of NCDs on the global level. Public health research, information and data collection is indispensable for policy decision making, which are based on information and data. Data and information on NCDs in the Caribbean countries are based on regional estimates, few patient hospital data and information provided by the MoH. The question is: how can policy makers effectively respond to an urgent health problem, whose causes or consequences they can barely define? Health related institutes and institutions such as the CFNI, the Caribbean Public Health Agency (CARPHA) the PAHO, the CARICOM, and the MoH together could take a leading role in this concern, collecting and providing reliable data and information for all member countries.

Table 22:   Summary of cluster results from the economic and social burden of Non-communicable Diseases analysis, Caribbean countries

		Obesity ate	FBDG	Surveillance	OOP as % of THE	Primary cause of NCD-YLL
Cluster I	Antigua and Barbuda	< 30%	No	No	20%-40%	Ischemic heart disease
	Grenada	< 30%	Yes	In process	> 40%	Ischemic heart disease
	St. Kitts and Nevis	≥ 30%	Yes	Yes	> 40%	n.a.
	Suriname	< 30%	No	In process	< 20%	Stroke
Cluster II	The Bahamas	≥ 30%	Yes	Yes	20%-40%	Ischemic heart disease
	Barbados	≥ 30%	Yes	Yes	20%-40%	Ischemic heart disease
	Jamaica	< 30%	No	Yes	20%-40%	Stroke
	St. Lucia	< 30%	Yes	In process	>40%	Diabetes
	St. Vincent and the Grenadines	< 30%	Yes	No	20%-40%	Ischemic heart disease
	Trinidad and Tobago	≥ 30%	No	In process	>40%	Ischemic heart disease
Cluster III	Belize	≥ 30%	Yes	Yes	20%-40%	Ischemic heart disease
	Dominica	< 30%	Yes	Yes	20%-40%	Ischemic heart disease
	Guyana	< 30%	Yes	In process	20%-40%	Ischemic heart disease

Note: n.a. = not available
Source: own compilation based on study findings. Obesity rates: WHO (2013e); Surveillance: CARICOM (2011d); OOP expenditure: WHO (2013d); NCD-YLL: IHME (2013a)

7.   Final conclusion: The double burden creates a twin challenge in the Caribbean

This last chapter outlines the main study findings based on the key re-search question: What the main implications of food and nutrition insecu-rity in the Caribbean? This thesis aimed to identify, to examine and to as-sess the socio-economic implications of food and nutrition insecurity in the Caribbean, by means of a comprehensive analysis of the Food and Nu-trition Security (FNS) situation in 13 selected Caribbean countries. In ad-dition, recommendations for further research and approaches towards FNS in the Caribbean are based on the evaluation of current target-orientated policies.

Summary of study findings

The FNS concept, in this study, has been used to detect issues beyond the prevailing understanding of food and nutrition insecurity in the sense of undernutrition and poverty. The FNS concept is not rigid, but dynamic and, therefore, it can adjust to the complexity of issues on different dimen-sions. Based on a holistic understanding and the definition of the FNS concept, given in chapter 2.2, an analysis of all four dimensions – availa-bility, access, utilization, and stability – and the overall FNS situation was conducted for a set of 13 Caribbean countries. Due to their particular char-acteristics as Small Island Developing States (SIDS), the selected Carib-bean countries were identified and clustered according to three FNS groups: least vulnerable to food and nutrition insecurity (Cluster I), mod-erately vulnerable to food and nutrition insecurity (Cluster II), and most vulnerable to food and nutrition insecurity (Cluster III). Figure 36 displays a short overview of the main findings from this analysis on each dimen-sion of the FNS concept.

Figure 36:   Food and Nutrition Security in the Caribbean – study findings on each dimension

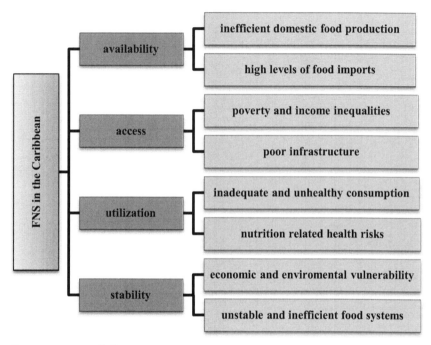

Source: own compilation

Significant differences between food and nutrition insecure groups of countries indicated two specific problems, one on the supply side of food availability, and the other on the demand side of food utilization and consumption. An in-depth analysis on the causes and consequences of these issues, in the sample countries and clusters, has been defined as scope of this thesis:

1. High world food prices and limited agricultural output determine the **burden of high dependency on food imports** and the unsustainable high levels of food import bills. High levels of food imports have induced a market shift and influence consumer decisions primary through prices and the diversity of food supply.
2. Unhealthy consumption patterns and the lack of appropriate prevention and health care measurements lead to the **burden of the major health**

risk factor obesity. High obesity rates induce the risk of being affected by Non-communicable Diseases (NCDs), impeding human development and challenging the public health systems.

The first burden of food and nutrition insecurity in the Caribbean is concerned with insufficient food availability and inadequate access to food in the Caribbean. Insufficient food availability is characterized by low agricultural output, especially in Net Agricultural Import (NAEIM) countries, such as the majority of the sample countries (Cluster I and II). Alongside the structural constraints and agricultural liberalization policies, food imports have become the main source of food supply. High dependence on food imports aggravated the precarious economic and financial situation, particularly in countries, which have less capacity to import foods, such as Antigua and Barbuda, Grenada, and St. Kitts and Nevis. High food imports adversely affect the domestic food production sector through impeding investments and crowding-out small-scale farmers in all the Caribbean countries. Moreover, the escalating costs of food imports, triggered through high global food prices, are reflected in the countries' Food Import Bill (FIB). A high FIB does not necessarily correlate with a high food import dependency ratio, but with a higher food import capacity and higher national demand for imported foodstuff. Therefore, countries in Cluster II have overall higher FIB levels than the other clusters. Nevertheless, the economic and financial burden of the FIB hits all sample countries. High FIB levels, unsustainable debt levels and structural constraints collectively increase the risk of a macroeconomic crisis in the Caribbean economies. Ultimately, price volatility on global markets triggering domestic consumer prices inflation for food, together with high poverty and inequality rates determine the inadequate access to food. The combination of these factors leads to a spiral effect, where one problem causes the other.

The second burden in the context of food and nutrition insecurity in the Caribbean concerning the dimension utilization is determined by a range of factors from poverty, changing consumption patterns, access to healthcare services to the availability and access to healthy and nutritious foods. Food consumption, nutrition and health are closely interrelated and ultimately influence human development. Given the information on food consumption patterns, nutrition intake and health outcomes, two trends have been observed for all the Caribbean sample countries: a nutrition transition and an epidemiological transition. The former, is the result of a range of socio-economic factors that influenced the shift from traditional and nutritious food consumption to an overconsumption of energy-dense, high sodium and high sugary foodstuff, beverages, and imported processed foodstuff. Obesity rates are overall above 20%, except for Guyana. The epidemiological transition refers to the shift from infectious diseases to NCDs. Mortality rates of total death rates due to NCDs are substantially high at 76% for all the Caribbean countries. Prevention and treatment for these diseases in the Caribbean is lacking adequate public and private financing. In addition, access to healthcare services is unequally distributed among the sample countries and within countries, due to high poverty and inequality rates. This increases the personal and social costs for affected individuals in form of high out-of-pocket expenditures for healthcare services and in form of loss of healthy life years. Out-of-pocket expenditures indicating an inadequate access to healthcare services are particularly alarming in Grenada, St. Kitts and Nevis, St. Lucia, and Trinidad and Tobago. Two important implications of this burden were found in this study:

1. The overall economic and social burden of nutrition related health risks and diseases is marked by the loss of productivity, the loss of healthy life years, and high financial costs on the national and individual level.
2. The poor and low-income groups within a population are mostly affected. They lack adequate access to healthcare services and additionally depend heavily on public health support and social safety programs. Ultimately, there is little reliable data collection and surveillance on the utilization and consumption of food, on the incidence and prevalence of NCDs, and on mortality rates due to NCDs in the Caribbean countries.

Due to the lack of reliable and adequate data and information, it was not possible or feasible to prove a direct relation between high food imports and nutrition related health risks. However, the main scope of this thesis revealed that food consumption and nutrition are partially a problem of the Caribbean food system and, therefore, one that also results from the burden of high food imports. This is not only an enduring and challenging task in the selected Caribbean countries, but one that even prevails on a global level.

> "The interstices between this process of globalization and changes in diet are [...] multiple. It remains a challenge to link changes in consumption patterns to those in production, distribution, retailing and advertising" (WHO, 2002: 6).

However, the findings of this comprehensive FNS analysis in the sample countries shows that the identified double burden of high food imports and endemic health risks in the Caribbean countries are in fact two sides of the same coin. The double burden of food and nutrition insecurity therefore results in a twin challenge for the Caribbean countries.

Managing Food and Nutrition Insecurity in the Caribbean countries

The common basis of the detected issues on all four dimensions and particularly the concerns of food imports and health risks is that they root in the underlying structural socio-economic constraints in the investigated Caribbean countries, which have been analysed in chapter 3 in detail. These structural constraints are also comprised under the emergence of vulnerability, which has been identified in the context of FNS (cf. chapter 4.1). Consequently, the problem of food and nutrition insecurity in the Caribbean roots in social, cultural and economic structures, in the legacy of history, in the geographical and natural conditions, and in economic structures. This array of issues put serious obstacles in the way to FNS, health and sustainable economic development, leading to a two-fold question: What could possibly be done in order to improve the situation of food and nutrition insecurity in the Caribbean? What approach is the best fit for the 13 countries?

Various compelling reasons encourage a national and country specific approach for addressing food and nutrition insecurity in the Caribbean countries. First and foremost, this thesis showed that the degree of FNS and the magnitude of the identified issues vary significantly across countries and groups of countries – based on their degree of vulnerability to food and nutrition insecurity. Consequently, countries or groups of countries, facing similar problems, require similar approaches. However, a one-size-fits-it-all approach would only scratch on a rough surface of the profound and diverse food and nutrition insecurity problem in the Caribbean. For this purpose, an in-depth analysis of the potentials and constraints of national food systems and production structures, as well as micro studies on the health and nutritional status of the Caribbean population, are per-quisites to collect essential information and data. Thereby relevant sectors and target groups within the population can be identified. Reliable, substantial and consistent data and information on the micro and on the macro level is a stumbling block in the Caribbean countries, but one that must be removed immediately, in order to implement sound and effective policies.

Given the small size of the region and the limited economic, financial and natural resources, some issues of food and nutrition insecurity could be addressed at a regional level by the Caribbean Community (CARICOM) (cf. ECLAC, 2008). National, as well as regional initiatives need to formulate a clear and sound framework for actions. Several programmes and regional strategies such as the 2007 *Regional Transformation Program in Agriculture*, the *Regional Special Program for Food Security* and the *Jagdeo Initiative*, have attempted to address food insecurity by enhancing agricultural development and production. In general, these programmes aimed to improve the development of the agricultural sector, which faces various constraints (cf. Table 14, p. 160), but failed to consider land use issues, water resources use and infrastructural constraints. Hence, success of improving food and nutrition insecurity in the Caribbean countries on a regional level, has been limited, thus far (cf. CARICOM, 2010).

In 2010, the Caribbean countries as Member States of the CARICOM adopted a common *Regional Food and Nutrition Security Policy* (RFNSP) under the *Revised Treaty of Chaguaramas* Article 56 the *Community Agricultural Policy* (CAP). This project is supported by the Food and Agriculture Organization (FAO) under the *Hunger Free Latin America and the Caribbean Initiative* (HFLAC), promoting the integration of the Human Right to Food into national and regional policies and actions. Recently, the *Regional Food and Nutrition Security Action Plan* (RFNSAP) has been approved for a fifteen-year period of time from 2012 to 2026. The nature of the RFNSAP, which understands the multidimensional character of FNS, focuses on addressing multi-sectoral and interlinked issues of food and nutrition insecurity. The "development goal" of the RFNSAP is "to contribute to ensuring long-term food security and the enjoyment by all of the right to food" (CARICOM, 2011c: 16). The RFNSAP comprises four policy objectives, corresponding to the four dimensions of FNS: sustainable food production, increasing access through investments in agro-based industries, ensuring nutritional well-being, prevention of NCDs, and strengthening the capacity to respond efficiently to natural disasters (cf. CARICOM, 2011c). According to FAO's *twin-track* approach, immediate and medium-long-term actions are defined, and each responds to the six Programme Components of the Action Plan. Ultimately, through its multi-sectoral approach to FNS and the inclusion of different national and regional institutions, the civil society, and the private sector, the Action Plan avoids overloading the CARICOM with the whole policy implementation process. Most importantly, the RFNSAP provides a comprehensive framework, under which regional and national actions and strategies can only be successfully implemented by joining common resources and capacities. This thesis has shown that the precise assessment of national constraints and issues of food and nutrition insecurity are perquisites to implementing country-tailored policies and strategies on a national level. Nevertheless, different approaches have to be fitted into a common regional framework to strengthen and benefit from synergetic effects. Figure 37 describes such a process between the national and the regional level.

Figure 37:   Interaction of national and regional Food and Nutrition Security policies and strategies

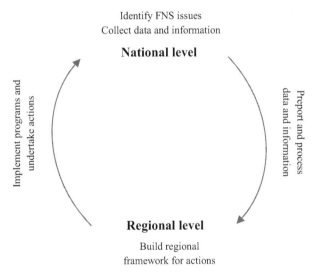

Source: own compilation

Outlook

The challenge of responding to food and nutrition insecurity in the Caribbean has become increasingly difficult under the global conditions of rising food price volatility, rising competition on the world markets for agricultural exports, external economic shocks, and the susceptibility to natural disasters. Consequently, this puts increased pressure on policy-makers and governments to 'manage' the twin challenge of food and nutrition insecurity in the Caribbean countries. Whether a regional or a country specific approach is aimed, resources have to be mobilized within countries or joined together within the region, primary to increase data and information collection – based on the rational that policies can only act on what is known. Additionally, participation and leadership are perquisites to any successful policy or strategy. The conclusion drawn from this thesis is that FNS requires the activation of capacities and potentials that may disengage the Caribbean countries from the persistent dependency on food imports. Moreover, in order to solve the twin challenge in the Caribbean, it requires the will of governments and civil societies to achieve the basic Human Right to Food and to provide access to affordable and nutritious food for a healthy life.

The Caribbean may not occupy an important seat in terms of the current global economy or politics; nonetheless, this study discloses that it can be a representative example for the complex global issue of FNS. These issues are not exclusively a problem in the Caribbean countries, but an emerging concern in different facets in other countries around the world; particularly in other SIDS. Moreover, the Caribbean can learn from its experiences and become a precursor and a good example for other SIDS. Further issues remain to be a great challenge in the context of vulnerability and FNS issues to these countries, such as climate change and extreme weather events that increasingly threaten the livelihoods of the population living in small to large, but vulnerable areas of land. The use of vital resources such as water and energy pose another question of environmental sustainability and sustainable food production, not only in the Caribbean countries, but even more urgently on a global level.

The global challenge of FNS persists in the unprecedented impotence of global leadership, which that allows people to suffer from poverty, and malnutrition, while rather exploiting natural resources for the pursuit of prosperity. In the late 18th century Helvetius explained these circumstances:

> "As the physical world is ruled by the laws of movement, so is the moral universe ruled by the laws of interest" (Helvetius).

Global leaders, therefore, ignore that human health and well-being are indispensable assets to achieve their consistent goal of economic growth and productivity, by concomitantly disregarding the essential Human Right to Food, and thus impeding individual freedom.

Bibliography

Abdulkadri, Abdullahi O.; Cunningham-Myrie, Colette; Forrester, Terrence (2009): Economic Burden of Diabetes and Hypertension in the CARICOM States. *Social and Economic Studies,* Vol. 58 (3/4), p. 175-197.

Alleyne, Dillon; Amonde, Tom; Hendrickson, Michael; Yoshida, Kohei; Dookie, Michele (2013): Economic Survey of the Caribbean 2011-2012: Positive growth amidst lingering downside risks. Studies and Perspectives. Economic Commission for Latin America and the Caribbean (ECLAC) Subregional Headquaters for the Caribbean. Nations.

Alleyne, Dillon; Lugay, Beverly (2011): Inflation and the variability of relative prices in the Caribbean: Evidence from panel threshold models. Economic Commission for Latin America and the Caribbean (ECLAC) Subregional headquarters for the Caribbean

Barcelo, Alberto; Aedo, Cristian; Rajpathak, Swapnil; Robles, Sylvia (2003): The cost of diabetes in Latin America and the Caribbean. *Bulletin of the World Health Organization,* Vol. 81 (1), p. 19-27.

Barrett, Christopher B. (2006): Food Aid's Intended and Unintended Consequences. *Background Paper for FAO State of Food and Agriculture 2006.* Cornell University.

Barrett, Christopher B.; Lentz, Erin C.; Mathys, Cynthia; Upton, Joanna B.; Villa, Kira M. (2011): Misconceptions about food assistance. Global Public Policy Institute. Policy Brief No. 2.

Beckford, Clinton L. (2012): Issues in Caribbean Food Security: Building Capacity in Local Food Production Systems. *In:* Aladjadjiyan (ed.) *Food Production - Approaches, Challenges and Tasks.* Rijeka: InTech.

Beckford, Clinton L.; Campbell, Donovan R. (2013): Domestic Food Production and Food Security in the Caribbean: Building Capacity and Strengthening Local Food Production Systems. New York: Palgrave Macmillan.

Beckford, George L. (1972): Persistent Poverty: Underdevelopment in Plantation Economies of the Third World. New York: Oxford University Press.

Behrman, Jere R. (1996): The Impact of Health and Nutrition on Education. *The World Bank Research Observer,* Vol. 11 (1), p. 23-37.

Benjamin, Cynthia; Jackson, Valdrina; Isaac, Elaine; Scotland, Joanne; Samuel-Christian, Valerie; Gordor, Emanuel; James, Juanita; Barnesa, Casey; Samudab, Pauline (2004): Food Consumption in Antigua and Barbuda: Qualitative Analysis of Dietary Patterns in Adolescents. *Caribbean Food and Nutrition Institute (CFNI) Cajanus,* Vol. 37 (2), p. 82-100.

Best, Lloyd A. (1968): A Model of Pure Plantation Economy. *Social and Economic Studies* Vol. 17 (3), p. 283-326.

Bhargava, Alok (2008): Food, economics, and health. Oxford: Oxford Univ. Press.

Black, Robert E.; Allen, Lindsay H.; Bhutta, Zulfiqar A.; Caulfield, Laura E.; Onis, Mercedes de; Ezzati, Majid; Mathers, Colin; Rivera, Juan (2008): Maternal and child undernutrition: global and regional exposures and health consequences. *The Lancet,* Vol. 371 (9608), p. 243-260.

Black, Robert E.; Victora, Cesar G.; Walker, Susan P.; Bhutta, Zulfiqar A.; Christian, Parul, et al. (2013): Maternal and child undernutrition and overweight in low-income and middle-income countries. *The Lancet,* Vol. 382 (9890), p. 427-451.

Bloom, David E.; Cafiero, Elizabeth T.; Jané-Llopis, Eva; Abrahams-Gessel, Shafika; Bloom, L.R., et al. (2011): The Global Economic Burden on Non-communicable Diseases. World Economic Forum. Geneva.

Bloom, David E.; Canning, David; Sevilla, Jaypee (2004): The Effect of Health on Economic Growth: A Production Function Approach. *World Development,* Vol. 32 (1), p. 1-13.

BNR [Barbados National Registry for Chronic Non-Communicable Disease] (2009): The Barbados National Registry for Chronic Non-Communicable Disease [Online]. Available: http://www.bnr.org.bb/cms/ [Accessed 14.12.2013].

BNR [Barbados National Registry for Chronic Non-Communicable Disease] (2010): 2010 Annual Report. Bridgetown: BNR.

Bokeloh, Georg (2009): Actions/Interventions to Improve Food and Nutrition Security at Macro Level. *In:* Klennert (ed.) *Achieving Food and Nutrition Security. Actions to Meet the Global Challenge. A Training Course Reader.* Feldafing: Internationale Weiterbildung gGmbH.

Bongaarts, John (1996): Population Pressure and the Food Supply System in the Developing World. *Population and Development Review,* Vol. 22 (3), p. 483-503.

Boswell, Thomas D. (2009): The Caribbean: Geographic Preface. *In:* Richard S. Hillman (ed.) *Understanding the Contemporary Caribbean.* 2nd ed. Kingston: Ian Randle.

Bouis, Howarth; Raney, Terri; McDermott, John (2013): Priorities for Public Sector Research on Food Security and Nutrition. *Food Security Futures.* 11-12 April 2013, Dublin, Ireland.

Boyne, Michael S. (2009): Diabetes in the Caribbean: Trouble in paradise. *Insulin,* Vol. 4 (2), p. 94-105.

Brathwaite, Chelston W. D. (2009): True Impact of Agriculture in the Economy. *In:* Agriculture, ed. *IICA-OAS Food Security Conference "Agriculture for Development and Food Security in the Americas".* 01 October 2009, Washington, D.C.

Brathwaite, N; Brathwaite, A; Taylor, M. (2011): The Socio-economic Determinants of Obesity in Adults in the Bahamas. *West Indian Medical Journal,* Vol. 60 (4), p. 434.

Braun, Joachim von; Bouis, Howarth; Kumar, Shubh; Pandya-Lorch, Rajul (1992): Imrpoving Food Security of the Poor: Concept, Policy and Programs. Washington, D.C.: International Food Polica Research Institute (IFPRI).

Braveboy-Wagner, Jaqueline Anne (2009): International Relations. *In:* Hillman; D'Agostino (eds.) *Understanding the Contemporary Caribbean.* 2nd ed. Kingston: Ian Randle.

Briguglio, Lino; Cordina, Gordon; Farrugia, Nadia; Vella, Stephanie (2009): Economic Vulnerability and Resilience: Concepts and Measurements. *Oxford Development Studies,* Vol. 37 (3), p. 229-247.

Britannica, Encyclopædia (2013). Encyclopædia Britannica Inc. Available: http://www.britannica.com/EBchecked/topic/463409/plantation [Accessed 30.01.2014].

Bühl, Achim (2012): SPSS 20: Einführung in die moderne Datenanalyse. München: Pearson.

Burchi, Francesco; De Muro, Pasquale (2012): A Human Development and Capability Approach To Food Security: Conceptual Framework and Informational Basis. United Nations Development Programme (UNDP). WP 2012-009.

Canuto, Otaviano (2011): Fiscal Consequences of Food and Agricultural Commodities Inflation. *Remarks for the GAIM/GMA, Geopolitical Risk, Macroeconomics and Alternative Investment* 11-12 October 2011, New York. World Bank.

CARDI [Caribbean Agricultural Research and Development Institute] (2011): Improving lives through agricultural research [Online]. Available: http:// www.cardi.org/ [Accessed 31.01.2014].

CARICOM [Caribbean Community] (2010): Regional Food and Nutrition Security Policy (RFNSP).

CARICOM [Caribbean Community] (2011a): Establishing the CARICOM Single Market and Economy (CSME) [Online]. Available: http://www.caricom.org/jsp/single_market/free_movement.jsp?menu=csme [Accessed 16.01.2014].

CARICOM [Caribbean Community] (2011b): History of the Caribbean Community (CARICOM) [Online]. Available: http://www.caricom.org/jsp/community/history.jsp?menu=community [Accessed 16.01.2014].

CARICOM [Caribbean Community] (2011c): Regional Food and Nutrition Security Action Plan (RFNSAP).

CARICOM [Caribbean Community] (2011d): Strategic Plan of Action for the Prevention and Control of Chronic Non-Communicable Diseases (NCDs) for countries of the Caribbean Community (CARICOM) 2011-2015. Pan American Health Organisation (PAHO), World Health Organisation (WHO).

CARICOM [Caribbean Community] (2012): CARICOM's selected economic indicators 2001,2004-2008. *In:* REGIONAL STATISTICS PROGRAMME (ed.) The CARICOM Secretariat.

CARICOM [Caribbean Community] (2013a): Caribbean Community Secretariat [Online]. Available: http://www.caricom.org/

CARICOM [Caribbean Community Secretariat] (2013b): CARICOM's selected economic indicators. 2002, 2006-2010. A Statistical Profile of the CARICOM Single Market and Economy.

CARICOM [Caribbean Community] (2013c): CARICOM Regional Statistics [Online]. Available: http://caricomstats.org/databases.html [Accessed 16.09.2013].

CARICOM [Caribbean Community] (2013d): CARICOM Single Market and Economy (CSME) [Online]. Available: http://www.csmeonline.org/index.php [Accessed 22.11.2013].

CARICOM; PAHO [Caribbean Community; Pan American Health Organization] (2006): Report of the Caribbean Commission on Health and Development. Caribbean Commision on Health and Development, Caribbean Community (CARICOM), Pan American Health Organization (PAHO). Kingston: Ian Randle.

Cariolle, Joël (2011): The Economic Vulnerability Index: 2010 Update. Fondation pour les Études et Recherches sur les Développement International (FERDI). Clermont-Ferrand.

Carmichael, Charles; Jacque, Andrew; Francis, Diana (2009): Investing in Food and Nutrition Security - Identifying Potential Investment Opportunities in the Agriculture and Food Industries in CARICOM. *In:* Francis (ed.) Inter-American Institute for Cooperation on Agriculture (IICA). Port of Spain.

CARPHA. (2013): Obesity in Children in the Caribbean Doubles in the last 10 years. *Media Release*, 4 May 2013, Port of Spain, Trinidad and Tobago.

CDB [Caribbean Development Bank] (2006): Trade Adjustment and Poverty in St. Lucia 2005/06. Bridgetown.

CDB [Caribbean Development Bank] (2007): Living Conditions in Antigua and Barbuda: Poverty in a Services Economy in Transition. Bridgetown.

CDB [Caribbean Development Bank] (2008): Country Poverty Assessment St. Kitts and Nevis 2007/08. Barbados.

CDB [Caribbean Development Bank] (2009a): Country Poverty Assessment Belize 2009. Bridgetown.

CDB [Caribbean Development Bank] (2009b): Country Poverty Assessment Dominica 2009. Bridgetown.

CDB [Caribbean Development Bank] (2012): Barbados Country Assessment of Living Conditions 2010. Bridgetown: Sir Arthur Lewis Institute of Social and Economic Studies (SALISES).

CEPAL [Comisión Económica para América Latina y el Caribe] (2012): Statistical Yearbook for Latin Ameica and the Caribbean 2012. Santiago de Chile.

CEPALSTAT [Comisión Económica para América Latina y el Caribe Statistics] (2013): Databases and Statistical Publications [Online]. Economic Commission for Latin America and the Caribbean (ECLAC) Available: http://estadisticas.cepal.org/ [Accessed: 18.09.2013]

CFNI [Caribbean Food and Nutrition Institue] (2004): Protocol for the Nutritional Management of Obesity, Diabetes and Hypertension in the Caribbean. Caribbean Food and Nutrition Institute (CFNI), Pan American Health Organization (PAHO) Office of Caribbean Program Coordination. Jamaica/Barbados.

CFNI [Caribbean Food and Nutrition Institute] (2007): Vulnerability and Food and Nutrition Security in the Caribbean. Food and Agriculture Organization (FAO), Caribbean Food and Nutrition Institute (CFNI), Pan American Health Organization (PAHO). Government of Italy.

CFNI [Caribbean Food and Nutrition Institute] (2009): Food and Nutrition Priorities in the Caribbean 2010-2015. *Cajanus,* Vol. 42 (4), p. 185-208.

CFNI/PAHO (2004): Protocol for the Nutritional Management of Obesity, Diabetes and Hypertension in the Caribbean. Caribbean Food and Nutrition Institute (CFNI), PAHO/WHO Office of Caribbean Program Coordination.

CFS [Committee on World Food Security] (2012): Coming to Terms with Terminology. Thirty-ninth Session. 15-20 October 2012, Rome, Italy. Food and Agriculture Organization (FAO).

Chambers, Robert (1988): Sustainable Livelihoods, Environment and Development: Putting Poor Rural People First. Instittute of Development Studies. IDS Discussion Papers No. 240.

Chambers, Robert (1995): Poverty and livelihoods: whose reality counts? *Environment and Urbanization,* Vol. 7 (173), p. 173-204.

Chambers, Robert; Conway, Gordon R. (1991): Sustainable rural livelihoods: practical concepts for the 21st century. Institute of Development Studies. IDS Discussion Papers No. 296.

Chesney, H. Arlington D.; Francis, Diana (2004): Issues, Options and Prospects for Caribbean Agriculture. *34th Annual Meeting of the Board of Directors of the Caribbean Development Bank Seminar "Agriculture and Rural Development".* May 11, 2004, Tobago. Inter-American Institute for Cooperation on Agriculture (IICA).

Conforti, Piero; Ford, J.R. Deep (2007): Addressing trade preferences and their erosion in the Caribbean. *In:* Ford, Dell'Aquila, et al. (eds.) *Agricultural trade policy and food security in the Caribbean. Structural issues, multilateral negotiations and competitiveness.* Rome: Food and Agriculture Organization (FAO).

CSO Trinidad and Tobago [Central Statistical Office of Trinidad and Tobago] (2012): Trinidad and Tobago Human Development Atlas 2012. United Nations Development Program (UNDP), Central Statistical Office (CSO) Trinidad and Tobago. Port of Spain.

Currie, Janet (2009): Healthy, Wealthy, and Wise: Socioeconomic Status, Poor Health in Childhood, and Human Capital Development. *Journal of Economic Literature,* Vol. 47 (1), p. 87-122.

Currie, Janet; Madrian, Brigitte C. (1999): Chapter 50 Health, health insurance and the labor market. *In:* Orley; David (eds.) *Handbook of Labor Economics.* 3rd ed. Amsterdam: Elsevier.

D'Agostino, J. Thomas (2009): Caribbean Politics. *In:* Richard S. Hillman (ed.) *Understanding the Contemporary Caribbean.* 2nd ed. Kingston: Ian Randle.

DFID [Department for International Development] (1999): Sustainable Livelihood Guidance Sheets. Department for International Development.

Dilley, Maxx; Boudreau, Tanya E. (2001): Coming to terms with vulnerability: a critique of the food security definition. *Food Policy,* Vol. 26 (3), p. 229-247.

Donaldson, Michael S. (2004): Nutrition and cancer: A review of the evidence for an anti-cancer diet. *Nutrition Journal,* Vol. 3 (1), p. 1-21.

Drèze, Jean; Sen, Amartya Kumar (1989): Hunger and public action. Oxford: Clarendon Press.

ECCB [Eastern Caribbean Central Bank] (2013): Monetary and Capital Markets [Online]. Available: http://www.eccb-centralbank.org/Money/index.asp [Accessed 30.01.2014].

Ecker, Olivier; Breisinger, Clemens (2012): The food security system: A new conceptual framework. International Food Policy Research Institute (IFPRI). Discussion Paper No. 01166.

ECLAC [Economic Commission for Latin America and the Caribbean] (2008): The escalation in world food prices and its implications for the Caribbean. Santiago de Chile.

ECLAC [Economic Commission for Latin America and the Caribbean] (2009): Caribbean Development Report, Volume II. Santiago de Chile.

ECLAC [Economic Commission for Latin America and the Caribbean] (2011): Price volatility in agricultural markets (2000-2010): implications for Latin America and policy options. Newsletter ECLAC/FAO/IICA. Economic Commission for Latin America and the Caribbean (ECLAC), Food and Agriculture Organization (FAO), Inter-American Institute for Cooperation on Agriculture (IICA). No. 1/2011.

ECLAC [Economic Commission for Latin America and the Caribbean] (2013a): The Caribbean Regional Synthesis Report, Final Draft. Third International Conference on Small Island Developing States. Economic Commission for Latin America and the Caribbean (ECLAC) Subregional Headquarters for the Caribbean. Port of Spain.

ECLAC [Economic Commission for Latin America and the Caribbean] (2013b): Preliminary overview of the economies of the Caribbean 2012-2013. Studies and Perspectives. Economic Commission for Latin America and the Caribbean (ECLAC) Subregional Headquarters for the Caribbean. Port of Spain.

ECLAC [Economic Commission of Latin America and the Caribbean] (2013c): Shaping Sustainable Development Agenda to address the Caribbean Reality in the Twenty-First Century. *Conference on Sustainable Development in Latin America and the Caribbean: Caribbean Forum.* 5-6 March 2013, Bogotá.

Edward, Linda N.; Grossman, Michael (1980): The Relationship Between Children's Health and Intellectual Development. *National Bureau of Economic Research Working Paper Series,* Vol. No. 213 (1980), p. 915–930.

EIU [Economist Intelligence Unit] (2012): Global Food Security Index. Methodology. [Online]. Available: http://foodsecurityindex.eiu.com/Home/Methodology [Accessed 31.01.2014].

EIU [Economist Intelligence Unit] (2013): Global food security index 2013: An annual measure of the state of global food security. Available: http:// foodsecurityindex.eiu.com/Home/Sources [Accessed 30.01.2014].

EM-DAT [Emergency Events Database] (2009): The OFDA/CRED International Disaster Database [Online]. Brussels Centre for Research on the Epidemiology of Disasters (CRED), Université catholique de Louvain. Available: www.emdat.be [Accessed: 14.10.2013]

Encyclopædia Britannica Online (2014): "West Indies" Map [Online] http://www.britannica.com/EBchecked/media/61990 [Accessed: 14.07.2014]

Eugenio Diaz-Bonilla, Marcelle Thomas, Sherman Robinson, Andrea Cattaneo (2000): Food security and trade negotiations in the World Trade Organization: A Cluster Analysis of Country Groups. International Food Policy Research Institute (IFPRI). Washington, D.C.

FAO [Food and Agriculture Organization] (1974): International Undertaking on World Food Security. *Sixty-Fourth Session*. Rome: The Council of the Food and Agriculture Organization (FAO).

FAO [Food and Agriculture Organization] (1992): World Declaration and Plan of Action for Nutrition. Food and Agriculture Organization (FAO), World Health Organization (WHO). Rome.

FAO [Food and Agriculture Organization] (1996): Rome Declaration on World Food Security and World Food Summit Plan of Action. *World Food Summit*. 13-17 November 1996, Rome.

FAO [Food and Agriculture Organization] (2001): Food Balance Sheets. A Handbook. Rome.

FAO [Food and Agriculture Organization] (2003): Trade Reforms and Food Security. Conceptualizing the linkages. Rome.

FAO [Food and Agriculture Organization] (2004a): Fruit and Vegetables for Health. *Joint FAO/WHO Workshop*. 1–3 September 2004, Kobe, Japan. Food and Agriculture Organization (FAO), World Health Organization (WHO).

FAO [Food and Agriculture Organization] (2004b): Incorporating Nutrition Considerations into Development Policies and Programmes. Rome.

FAO [Food and Agriculture Organization] (2005a): The Barbados Food Consumption and Anthropometric Surveys 2000. Rome.

FAO [Food and Agriculture Organization] (2005b): A Historical Background on Food Aid and Key Milestones. Committee on Commodity Problems.

FAO [Food and Agriculture Organization] (2008): An Introduction to the Basic Concept of Food Security. Available: www.foodsec.org/docs/concepts_guide.pdf [Accessed 30.01.2014].

FAO [Food and Agriculture Organization] (2009): Declaration of the World Summit on Food Security. *World Summit on Food Security (WSFS)*. 16-18 November 2009, Rome.

FAO [Food and Agriculture Organization] (2011a): Evaluation of FAO's Role and Work in Nutrition. Food and Agriculture Organization (FAO) Office of Evaluation Rome.

FAO [Food and Agriculture Organization] (2011b): Summary of Proceedings. *Regional Consultation on Policy and Programmatic Actions to address High Food Prices in the Caribbean.* 13-14 June 2011, Port of Spain, Trinidad and Tobago. Food and Agriculture Organization (FAO) Sub-Regional Office for the Caribbean.

FAO [Food and Agriculture Organization] (2012a): PANORAMA de la Seguridad Alimentaria y Nutricional en América Latina y el Caribe. Rome.

FAO [Food and Agriculture Organization] (2012b): Report of the FAO/PAHO/WHO Sub-Regional Meeting on preparations for the International Conference on Nutrition Twenty-one years later (ICN+21). 2-4 October 2012, Bridgetown, Barbados. Food and Agriculture Organization (FAO), Pan American Health Organization (PAHO).

FAO [Food and Agriculture Organizatio] (2012c): The State of Food Insecurity in the World 2012. Technical Note. Food and Agriculture Organization (FAO), International Fund for Agricultural Development (IFAD), World Food Programme (WFP). Rome.

FAO [Food and Agriculture Organization] (2013a): FAO Food Price Index [Online]. Available: http://www.fao.org/worldfoodsituation/foodpricesindex/en/ [Accessed 26.11.2013].

FAO [Food and Agriculture Organization] (2013b): Food Seurity Indicators [Online]. Available: http://www.fao.org/economic/ess/ess-fs/ess-fadata/en/ [Accessed: 30.11.2013]

FAO [Food and Agriculture Organization] (2013c): The State of Food Insecurity in the World 2013. The multiple dimensions of food security. Food and Agriculture Organization (FAO), International Fund for Agricultural Development (IFAD), World Food Programme (WFP). Rome.

FAO [Food and Agriculture Organization] (2013d): The State of Food Insecurity in the World 2013. The multiple dimensions of food security. Food and Agriculture Organization (FAO), International Fund for Agricultural Development (IFAD), World Food Programme (WFP). Rome.

FAO [Food and Agriculture Organization] (2013e): World Food Situation: FAO Food Price Index [Online]. Available: http://www.fao.org/worldfoodsituation/ foodpricesindex/en/ [Accessed 05.11.2013].

FAO [Food and Agriculture Organization] (2014a): Economic and Social Development Department [Online]. Available: http://www.fao.org/economic/ en/#.UscbDrTJISp [Accessed 03.01.2013].

FAO [Food and Agriculture Organization] (2014b): Hunger Portal [Online]. Available: http://www.fao.org/hunger/en/ [Accessed 12.12.2013].

FAO [Food and Agriculture Organization] (2014c): A short history of FAO [Online]. Available: http://www.fao.org/about/en/ [Accessed 02.01.2014].

FAO; WHO; UNU [Food and Agriculture Organization; World Health Organization; United Nations University] (1985): Energy and protein requirements. Food and Agriculture Organization (FAO), World Health Organization (WHO), United Nations University (UNU). Geneva: Organization.

FAOSTAT [Food and Agriculture Organization Statistics] (2013a): Consumer Price Indices.

FAOSTAT [Food and Agriculture Organization Statistics] (2013b): FAO Statistics Database [Online]. Available: http://faostat.fao.org/ [Accessed 30.01.2014].

Ford, J. R. Deep; Rawlins, Gregg (2007): Trade policy, trade and food security in the Caribbean. *In:* Ford, Dell'Aquila, et al. (eds.) *Agricultural trade policy and food security in the Caribbean. Structural issues, multilateral negotiations and competitiveness.* Rome: Food and Agriculture Organization (FAO) of the United Nations.

Gaskin, Pamela S.; Lai, Pamela; Guy, Devon; Knight, JaDon; Jackson, Maria; Nielsen, Anders L. (2012): Diet, Physical Activity, Weight Status, and Culture in a Sample of Children from the Developing World. *Journal of Nutrition and Metabolism,* Vol. 2012 (Article ID 242875), p. 1-8.

Gaztambide-Géigel, Antonio (2004): The Invention of the Caribbean in the 20th Century. The Definitions of the Caribbean as a Historical and Methodological Problem. *Social and Economic Studies,* Vol. 53 (3), p. 127-157.

Girvan, Norman (2001): Reinterpreting the Caribbean. *In:* Meeks; Lindahl (eds.) *New Caribbean Thought.* Kingston: University of West Indies Press.

Girvan, Norman (2005): W.A. Lewis, The Plantaion School and Dependency: An Interpretation. *Social and Economic Studies,* Vol. 54 (3), p. 198-221.

GIZ [Gesellschaft für Internationale Zusammenarbeit] (2013): Nahrungsmittelreserven als Instrument der Ernährungssicherung. Eschborn: Gesellschaft für Internationale Zusammenarbeit.

Glied, Sheny (1996): Estimating the Indirect Cost of Illness: An Assessment of the Forgone Earnings Approach. *American Journal of Public Health,* Vol. 86 (12), p. 1723-1728.

Goble, Frank G. (2004): The Third Force: The Psychology of Abraham Maslow. Chapel Hill: Maurice Bassett.

Government of Guyana (2011): Poverty Reduction Strategy Paper 2011-2015.

Government of The Bahamas (2004): Bahamas Living Conditions Survey 2001. Department of Statistics. Nassau, The Bahamas.

Graham, Barbara (2012): Profile of the Small-Scale Farming in the Caribbean. Workshop on Small-Scale Farming in the Caribbean. Food and Agriculture Organization (FAO).

Grantham-McGregor, Sally; Cheung, Yin Bun; Cueto, Santiago; Glewwe, Paul; Richter, Linda; Strupp, Barbara (2007): Developmental potential in the first 5 years for children in developing countries. *The Lancet,* Vol. 369 (9555), p. 60-70.

Grossman, Michael (1973): The Correlation Between Health and Schooling. *National Bureau of Economic Research Working Paper Series,* Vol. No. 22 (December 1973), p.

Haddad, Lawrence (1994): Intrahousehold resource allocation : an overview / Lawrence Haddad, John Hoddinott, Harold Alderman. Washington, DC (1818 H St., NW, Washington 20433) : World Bank.

Hair, Joseph F.; Black, William C.; Babin, Barry J.; Anderson, Rolph E. (ed.) (2010): Multivariate data analysis : a global perspective, Upper Saddle River, NJ ; Munich: Pearson.

Harvey, Paul; Proudlock, Karen; Clay, Edward; Riley, Barry; Jaspars, Susanne (2010): Food aid and food assistance in emergency and transitional contexts. *In:* group (ed.) Overseas Development Institute.

Headey, Derek; Fan, Shenggen (2010): Reflections on the Global Food Crisis: How Did It Happen? How Has It Hurt? And How Can We Prevent the Next One? International Food Policy Research Institute. Washington, D.C.

HECORA [Health Care Organizers and Advisors] (2008): Strategic Plan on Health and Related Social Services in the CARICOM. Draft Report

Henry, Fitzroy (2007): Food-Based Dietary Guidelines: A Vital Tool to Improve Health in the Caribbean. *Caribbean Food and Nutrition Institute (CFNI), Cajanus,* Vol. 40 (4), p.

Henry, Fritzroy J. (2004a): New Strategies Needed to Fight Obesity in the Caribbean. *Cajuns,* Vol. 37 (1), p.

Henry, Fritzroy J. (2004b): The Obesity Epidemic – A Major Threat To Caribbean Development: The Case For Public Policies. *Cajuns,* Vol. 37 (1), p.

IAASTD [International Assessment of Agricultural knowledge, Science and Technology for Development] (2009): Agriculture at a crossroads. Global Report. *In:* McIntyre, Herren, et al. (eds.). Washington, DC: Press.

IADB [Inter-American Development Bank] (2005): Caricom Report. No. 2, Buenos Aires.

IDF [International Diabetes Federation] (2013): IDF Diabetes Atlas. 6th edition, Brussels.

IFPRI [International Food Policy Research Institute] (2013): Global Hunger Index The Challenge of hunger: Ensuring Sustainable Food Security under Land, Water, and Energy Stresses. International Food Policy Research Institute (IFPRI), Concern Worldwide, Welthungerhilfe, Institute of Development Studies (IDS). Bonn/ Washington, D.C./Dublin.

IHME [Institute for Health Metrics and Evaluation] (2013a): GBD data [Online]. University of Washington. Available: http://www.healthmetricsandevaluation.org/ search-gbd-data [Accessed: 15.01.2014]

IHME [Institute for Health Metrics and Evaluation] (2013b): The Global Burden of Disease: Generating evidence, Guiding Policy. Latin America and Caribbean Regional Edition. Institute for Health Metrics and Evaluation (IHME), Human Development Network, The World Bank. Seattle: IHME.

IICA [Inter-American Institue for Cooperation on Agriculture] (2010): The Agriculture, Food and Health Challenge: Critical Issues, Perspectives and Options.

IICA [Inter-American Institute for Cooperation on Agriculture] (2012): Farming Change: growing more food with a changing resource base: critical issues, perspectives and options. Inter-American Institute for Cooperation on Agriculture (IICA), Caribbean Agricultural Research and Development Institute (CARDI), Centre for Agricultural and Rural Cooperation (CTA). Port of Spain.

IICA [Inter-American Institute for Cooperation on Agriculture] (2013). Available: http://www.iica.int/ [Accessed 31.01.2014].

ILO [International Labour Office] (1976): Employment, Growth and Basic Needs: A One-World Problem. New York.

Jamaican MoAF [Ministry of Agriculture and Fisheries] (2013): Minister's Speech at the 2012 Denbigh Agricultural and Industrial Food Show [Online]. Available: http://www.moa.gov.jm/Speeches/2012/2012080004_Minister%27s_speech_%20at _the_Denbigh_Agricultural_and_Industrial_Food-Show.php [Accessed 25.11.2013].

Jamison, Dean T.; Summers, Lawrence H.; Alleyne, George; Arrow, Kenneth J.; Berkley, Seth, et al. (2013): Global health 2035: a world converging within a generation. *The Lancet,* Vol. 382 (9908), p. 1898-1955.

Kendall, Patrick; Petracco, Marco (2003): The Current State and Future of Caribbean Agriculture. *23rd Annual Review Seminar, Research Department,* Vol.), p.

Key, Timothy J; Schatzkin, Arthur; Willett, Walter C; Allen, Naomi E; Spencer, Elizabeth A; Travis, Ruth C (2004): Diet, nutrition and the prevention of cancer. *Public Health Nutrition,* Vol. 7 (1a), p. 187-200.

Konandreas, Panos (2012): Trade Policy Responses to Food Price Volatility in Poor Net Food-Importing Countries. ICTSD Programme on Agricultural Trade and Sustainable Development. Issue Paper No. 42, Geneva: (ICTSD).

La Via Campensina (2013): International Peasant's Movement [Online]. Available: http://viacampesina.org/en/ [Accessed 30.12.2013].

Lappé, Frances Moore; Collins, Joseph (1977): Food first : the myth of scarcity. Boston, Mass.: Houghton Mifflin.

Lewis, W. Arthur (1954): Economic Development with Unlimited Supplies of Labour. *The Manchester School,* Vol. 22 (2), p. 139-191.

Lora, Eduardo; Powell, Andrew; Tavella, Pilar (2011): How Will the Food Price Shock Affect Inflation in Latin America and the Caribbean? POLICY BRIEF. Inter-American Development Bank.

Løvendal, Christian Romer; Jakobsen, Kristian Thor; Jacque, Andrew (2007): Food Prices and Food Security in Trinidad and Tobago. Food and Agriculture Organization.

Malthus, Thomas (1798): An Essay on the Principle of Population London: Electronic Scholarly Publishing Project.

Masset, Edoardo (2011): A Review of Hunger Indices and Methods to Monitor Country Commitment to Fighting Hunger. *Food Policy,* Vol. 36), p. S102-S108.

Maxwell, Simon ; Smith, Marisol (1992): Household food security: a conceptual review. *In:* Simon Maxwell (ed.) *Household food security: concepts, indicators, and measurements: a technical review.* New York and Rome: UNICEF and IFAD.

McGregor, Duncan (2011): Contemporary Caribbean Ecologies. The Weight of History. *In:* Stephan Palmié (ed.) *The Caribbean: a history of the region and its peoples.* Chicago: The University of Chicago.

Meadows, Donella H. (ed.) (1972): The limits to growth : a report for The Club of Rome's project on the predicament of mankind, New York, NY: Universe Books.

Mintz, Sidney W.; Du Bois, Christine M. (2002): The Anthropology of Food and Eating *Annual Review of Anthropology,* Vol. 31 (1), p. 99-119.

MoH Guyana [Ministry of Health] (2009): Statistical Bulletin 2009.

MoH Trinidad and Tobago [Ministry of Health] (2005): Annual Statistical Report 2004-2005.

MoH Trinidad and Tobago [Ministry of Health] (2011): Health Report Card for Trinidad and Tobago, 2011. Port of Spain.

Monge-Roffarello, Luca; Swidinsky, Michael; Vanzetti, David (2003): Diagnostic Study *In:* UNCTAD (ed.) *Turning Losses into Gains: SIDS and Multilateral Trade Liebralization in Agriculture.*

Mousseau, Frederic (2005): Food AID or Food Sovereignty? Ending World Hunger in our time. The Oakland Institute. Oakland.

Moya Pons, Frank (2007): History of the Caribbean : plantations, trade, and war in the Atlantic world. Princeton, NJ: Wiener.

Murphy, Arthur (1832): The Works of Samuel Johnson. New York: George Dearborn.

Murray, Christopher J. L.; Vos, Theo; Lozano, Rafael; Naghavi, Mohsen; Flaxman, Abraham D., et al. (2012): Disability-adjusted life years (DALYs) for 291 diseases and injuries in 21 regions, 1990?2010: a systematic analysis for the Global Burden of Disease Study 2010. *The Lancet,* Vol. 380 (9859), p. 2197-2223.

National Hurricane Center (2013). Available: http://www.nhc.noaa.gov/ [Accessed 23.09.2013].

Nielsen, Lynge (2011): Classifications of Countries Based on Their Level of Development: How it is Done and How it Could be Done. International Monetary Fund (IMF). IMF.

Nita Thaker, Sebastian Acevedo, Roberto Perrelli (2012): Caribbean Growth in an International Perspective: The Role of Tourism and Size. IMF Working Paper [Online].

NYU [New York University] (2013): Knowledge Development [Online]. New York. Available: http://www.nyu.edu/mph/discover/knowledge_development.html [Accessed 11.12.2013].

ODI [Overseas Development Institute] (1978): Basic Needs. No. 5, London.

OECS [Organisation of Eastern Caribbean States] (2007): Grenada: Macro-Socio-Economic Assessment of the damages caused by Hurricane Ivan

Oshaug, Arne; Eide, Wenche Barth; Eide, Asbjørn (1994): Human rights: a normative basis for food and nutrition-relevant policies. *Food Policy,* Vol. 19 (6), p. 491-516.

PAHO [Pan American Health Organization] (2007): Barbados STEPS Survey 2007. Fact Sheet. Vol.), p.

PAHO [Pan American Health Organization] (2008a): Dominica STEPS Survey 2008. Fact Sheet.

PAHO [Pan American Health Organization] (2008b): St. Kitts STEPS Survey 2008. Fact Sheet.

PAHO [Pan American Health Organization] (2012a): Country Profiles on NonCommunicable Diseases. Washington, D.C.

PAHO [Pan American Health Organization] (2012b): Health in the Americas. Regional Outlook and Country Profiles. Washington, D.C.

PAHO [Pan American Health Organization] (2013): Health in the Americas, 2012 Edition - country profiles [Online]. Available: http://www.paho.org/ saludenlasamericas/index.php?lang=en [Accessed 01.12.2013].

Pangaribowo, Evita Hanie; Gerber, Nicolas; Torero, Maximo (2013): Food and Nutrition Security Indicators: A Review. ZEF Working Paper [Online], 108. [Accessed Februrary 2013].

Payne, Philip R. (1985): The nature of malnutrition. *In:* Biswas; Pinstrup-Andersen (eds.) *Nutrition and development.* Oxford: Oxford University Press.

Perez, Esteban (2007): Debt accumulation in the Caribbean: origins, consequences and strategies. Studies and Perspectives. ECLAC Subregional Headquarters for the Caribbean. Port of Spain.

Pinnock, Fritz H.; Ajagunna, Ibrahim A. (2012): The Caribbean Maritime Transportation Sector: Achieving Sustainability through Efficiency The Centre for International Governance Innovation. 13.

PIOJ [Planning Institute of Jamaica] (2012): Jamaica Country Assessment. Preliminary Draft. Kingston.

Popkin, Barry M. (2003): The Nutrition Transition in the Developing World. *Development Policy Review,* Vol. 21 (5/6), p. 581-597.

Randall, Stephen J. (2009): The Historical Context. *In:* Richard S. Hillman (ed.) *Understanding the Contemporary Caribbean.* 2nd ed. Kingston: Ian Randle.

Reddy, Srinath K.; Katan, Martijn B. (2004): Diet, nutrition and the prevention of hypertension and cardiovascular diseases. *Public Health Nutrition,* Vol. 7 (1A), p. 167-186.

Richards-Greaves, Gillian (2012): The Intersections of "Guyanese Food" and Constructions of Gender, Race, and Nationhood. *In:* Garth (ed.) *Food and Identity in the Caribbean.* London: Berg.

Richardson, Bonham C. (1992): The Caribbean in the wider world.A regional geography. 1492 - 1992 Cambridge: Cambridge University Press.

Riely, Frank; Mock, Nancy; Cogill, Bruce; Bailey, Laura; Kenefick, Eric (1999): Food Security Indicators and Framework for Use in the Monitoring and Evaluation of Food Aid Programs. U.S. Agency for International Development. Washington, D.C.

Rothman, Kenneth J. (2012): Epidemiology: an introduction. Oxford: Oxford University Press.

Scanlan, Stephen J. (2001): Food Availability and Access in Lesser-Industrialized Societies: A Test and Interpretation of Neo-Malthusian and Technoecological Theories. *Sociological Forum,* Vol. 16 (2), p. 231-262.

Scanlan, Stephen J. (2003): Food Security and Comparative Sociology: Research, Theories, and Concepts. *International Journal of Sociology,* Vol. 33 (3), p. 88-111.

Sen, Amartya Kumar (1981): Poverty and famines: an essay on entitlement and deprivation. Oxford: Clarendon Press.

Sen, Jean Drèze and Amartya (1989): Hunger and Public Action. New York: Oxford University Press.

Sharma, Ramesh P. (1992): Monitoring access to food and household food security. *Food, nutrition and agriculture (FAO),* Vol. 2 (4), p. 2-9.

Sharma, Sangita ; Cao, Xia; Harris, Rachel; Hennis, Anselm J. M.; Wu, Suh-Yuh; Leske, M. Cristina (2008): Assessing dietary patterns in Barbados highlights the need for nutritional intervention to reduce risk of chronic disease. *Journal of Human Nutrition and Dietetics,* Vol. 21 (2), p. 150-158.

Shaw, John D. (2007): World Food Security: a history since 1945. New York: Palgrave Macmillan.

Shields, Linda; Twycross, Alison (2003): The difference between incidence and prevalence. *Paediatric Nursing,* Vol. 15 (7), p. 50.

SIDSnet [Small Island Developing States Network] (2013): Country Profiles: Caibbean Region [Online]. Available: http://www.sidsnet.org/regions/18/Caribbean [Accessed 30.01.2014].

Silva, Sacha; Best, Robert; Tefft, James (2011): Reducing the CARICOM Food Import Bill and the Real Cost of Food: Policy and Investment Options. Port of Spain: Food and Agriculture Organization (FAO).

Smit, Henriette A.; Grievink, Linda; Tabak, Cora (1999): Dietary influences on chronic obstructive lung disease and asthma: a review of the epidemiological evidence. *Proceedings of the Nutrition Society,* Vol. 58 (02), p. 309-319.

Solesbury, William (2003): Sustainable Livelihoods: A Case Study of the Evolution of DFID Policy. Overseas Development Institute. London.

Steyn, NP; Mann, Jim; Bennett, Peter H.; Temple, Norman; Zimmet, Paul; Tuomilehto, Jaako; Lindström, Jaana; Louheranta, Anne (2004): Diet, nutrition and the prevention of type 2 diabetes. *Public Health Nutrition,* Vol. 7 (1a), p. 147-165.

Stoneman, Richard; Pollard, Justice Duke; Inniss, Hugo (2012): Turning Around CARICOM: Proposals to Restructure the Secretariat. Landell Mills Ltd. Wiltshire.

Strauss, John; Thomas, Duncan (1998): Health, Nutrition, and Economic Development. *Journal of Economic Literature,* Vol. 36 (2), p. 766-817.

Stuart, Sheila (2006): Nutrition, Gender and Poverty in the Caribbean Subregion. Studies and Perspectives. Economic Commission for Latin America and the Caribbean (ECLAC) Subregional Headquarters for the Caribbean. Port of Spain.

Svedberg, Peter (2000): Poverty and undernutrition: theory, measurement, and policy. Oxford: Oxford University Press.

Swinburn, Boyd A.; Caterson, Ian; Seidell, Jaap C. ; James, W. Philip T. (2004): Diet, nutrition and the prevention of excess weight gain and obesity. *Public Health Nutrition,* Vol. 7 (1a), p. 123-146.

The World Bank (2006): Repositioning Nutrition as Central to Development. A Strategy for Large-Scale Action. The International Bank for Reconstruction and Development (IBRD). Washington, D.C.

The World Bank (2008): World Development Report 2008. Agriculture for Development. Washington, D.C.

The World Bank (2011): The Growing Burden of Non-Communicable Diseases in the Eastern Caribbean. Washington, D.C.

The World Bank (2012a): Food Prices, Nutrition, and the Millennium Development Goals. Washington, D.C.

The World Bank (2012b): Non-communicable diseases in Jamaica: moving from prescription to prevention. Washington, D.C.

The World Bank (2013a): Bilateral Remittances Matrix 2011 [Online]. Available: http://econ.worldbank.org/WBSITE/EXTERNAL/EXTDEC/EXTDECPROSPECT S/0,,contentMDK:22759429~pagePK:64165401~piPK:64165026~theSitePK:47688 3,00.html [Accessed 15.01.2014].

The World Bank (2013b): Country and Lending Groups [Online]. Available: http:// data.worldbank.org/about/country-classifications/country-and-lending-groups [Accessed 30.01.2014].

The World Bank (2013c): How we classify countries [Online]. Available: http:// data.worldbank.org/about/country-classifications [Accessed 12.08.2013].

The World Bank (2013d): World Development Indicators (WDI) [Online]. Available: http://databank.worldbank.org/data/views/variableSelection/selectvariables.aspx?so urce=world-development-indicators [Accessed: 31.01.2014]

Thomson, Anne; Metz, Manfred (1998): Implications of Economic Policy for Food Security: A Training Manual. Rome: Food and Agriculture Organization (FAO).

Timms, Benjamin F. (2008): Development Theory and Domestic Agriculture in the Caribbean: Recurring Crises and Missed Opportunities. *Caribbean Geography,* Vol. 15 (2), p. 101-117.

UN [United Nations] (1948): Universal Declaration of Human Rights (UDHR).

UN [United Nations] (1966): International Covenant on Economic, Social and Cultural Rights. *In:* United Nations General Assembly (ed.) *Resolution 2200A (XXI).*

UN [United Nations] (1974): Universal Declaration on the Eradication of Hunger and Malnutrition. *In:* General Assembly of the United Nations (ed.) *Resolution 3348 (XXIX).*

UN [United Nations] (1992): Agenda 21. *United Nations Conference on Environment and Development (UNCED).* 3-14 June 1992, Rio de Janeiro, Brazil. United Nations Division for Sustainable Development.

UN [United Nations] (2010): Achieving the Millennium Development Goals with equality in Latin America and the Caribbean: Progress and Challenges. Santiago de Chile.

UN [United Nations] (2013): World Population Prospects: The 2012 Revision. Key Findings and Advance Tables. United Nations Population Division. New York.

UN COMTRADE [United Nations Commodity Trade Statistics Database] (2010): United Nations Commodity Trade Statistics Database [Online]. Available: http:// comtrade.un.org/pb/CountryPagesNew.aspx?y=2012 [Accessed: 31.01.2014]

UN COMTRADE [United Nations Commodity Trade Statistics Database] (2011): International Trade Statistics Yearbook 2011. Country Trade Profiles.

UN DESA [United Nations Department of Economic and Social Affairs] (2013): LDC data retrieval [Online]. Available: http://www.un.org/en/development/desa/ policy/cdp/ldc/ldc_data.shtml [Accessed: 30.01.2014]

UN SCN [United Nations System Standing Committee on Nutrition] (2004): 5th Report on the World Nutrition Situation: Nutrition for Improved Development Outcomes. SCN Secretariat. Geneva.

UNAIDS [Joint United Nations Programme on HIV/AIDS] (2013): AIDSinfo [Online]. Available: http://www.unaids.org/en/dataanalysis/datatools/aidsinfo/ [Accessed: 13.12.2013]

UNCSD [United Nations Commission on Sustainable Development] (2013): Sustainable Development Knowledge Platform [Online]. Available: http:// sustainabledevelopment.un.org/csd.html [Accessed 19.12.2013].

UNCTAD [United Nations Conference on Trade and Development] (2013): Classification. Standard International Trade Classification (SITC) Revision 3. United Nations Statistics Division. New York.

UNCTADSTAT [United Nations Conference on Trade and Development Statistics] (2013): Population and Labour Force [Online]. Available: http:// unctadstat.unctad.org/ReportFolders/reportFolders.aspx?sRF_ActivePath=p,7&sRF_Expanded=,p,7 [Accessed: 31.01.2014]

UNDP [United Nations Development Programme] (1990): Human Development Report 1990. Concept and Measurement of Human Development. New York.

UNDP [United Nations Development Programme] (2013a): Human Development Atlas Suriname. Paramaribo.

UNDP [United Nations Development Programme] (2013b): Human Development Report 2013. The Rise of the South: Human Progress in a Diverse World. New York.

UNEP [United Nations Environment Programme] (2008): Climate Change in the Caribbean and the Challenge of Adaptation. UNEP Regional Office for Latin America and the Caribbean. Panama City.

UNICEF [United Nations Children's Fund] (1990): Strategy for improved nutrition of children and women in developing countries. New York.

UNICEF [United Nations Children's Fund] (2013a): Improving Child Nutrition. The achievable imperative for global progress. New York.

UNICEF [United Nations Children's Fund] (2013b): Nutrition in Emergencies.

UNICEF; WHO; The World Bank [United Nations Children's Fund; World Health Organization; The World Bank] (2012): UNICEF-WHO-The World Bank Joint Child Malnutrition Estimates. New York, Geneva, Washington, D.C.

UNSD [United Nations Statistics Division] (2012): UNSD Annual Totals Table (ATT) for Imports and Exports

UNSD [United Nations Statistics Division] (2013a): Millennium Development Goal Indicators [Online]. Available: http://mdgs.un.org/unsd/mdg/Default.aspx [Accessed 12.10.2013].

UNSD [United Nations Statistics Division] (2013b): Millennium Development Goals Indicators [Online]. Available: http://mdgs.un.org/unsd/mdg/Data.aspx [Accessed: 04.10.2013]

USAID [U.S. Agency of International Development] (1992): Definition of Food Security. PD-19, Washington, D.C.

USDA [United States Department of Agriculture] (2013): International Food Security Assessment, 2013-2023. U.S. Department of Agriculture, Economic Research Service. Washington, D.C.

Valdés, Alberto; McCalla, Alex F. (1999): Issues, Interests and Options of Developing Countries. *Conference on Agriculture and The New Trade Agenda in the WTO 2000 Negotiations.* 1-2 October 1999, Geneva, Switzerland. The World Bank, World Trade Organization (WTO).

Victora, Cesar G.; Adair, Linda; Fall, Caroline; Hallal, Pedro C.; Martorell, Reynaldo; Richter, Linda; Sachdev, Harshpal Singh (2008): Maternal and child undernutrition: consequences for adult health and human capital. *The Lancet,* Vol. 371 (9609), p. 340-357.

Washington Post. (1985): Higher Quotas Would Ease Severe Economic Crisis, Nations Say: Caribbean Sugar Growers Plead for U.S. Help. *Los Angeles Times,* August 26, 1985,

Weingärtner, Lioba (2009): The Concept of Food and Nutrition Security. *In:* Klennert (ed.) *Achieving Food and Nutrition Security.* Feldafing: Internationale Weiterbildung gGmbH (InWent).

Welthungerhilfe (2013): Hunger und Ernährungssicherung [Online]. Available: http://www.welthungerhilfe.de/hunger.html

WFP [World Food Programme] (2012): 2011 Food Aid Flows. International Food Aid Information System. Rome.

WHO [World Health Organization] (1978): Declaration of Alma-Ata. *International Conference on Primary Health Care.* 6-12 September 1978, Alma-Ata, USSR.

WHO [World Health Organization] (2002): Globalization, Diets and Noncommunicable Diseases. Geneva.

WHO [World Health Organization] (2005): Preventing chronic diseases: a vital investment. Geneva.

WHO [World Health Organization] (2008): Worldwide prevalence of anaemia 1993–2005: WHO Global Database on Anaemia. *In:* de Benoist, McLean, et al. (eds.). Geneva.

WHO [World Health Organization] (2009): Chronic Respiratory Disease. NMH Fact Sheet. Available: http://www.who.int/nmh/publications/fact_sheet_respiratory_en.pdf [Accessed 31.01.2014].

WHO [World Health Organization] (2011a): Global status report on Non-Communicable Diseases 2010. Geneva.

WHO [World Health Organization] (2011b): Indicator and Measurement Registry version 1.7.0 [Online]. Available: http://apps.who.int/gho/indicatorregistry/App_Main/browse_indicators.aspx

WHO [World Health Organization] (2011c): WHO Global Infobase [Online]. Available: https://apps.who.int/infobase/Index.aspx [Accessed: 31.01.2014]

WHO [World Health Organization] (2013a): Cancer Fact Sheet N°297 [Online]. Available: http://www.who.int/mediacentre/factsheets/fs297/en/ [Accessed 31.01.2014].

WHO [World Health Organization] (2013b): Cardiovascular diseases (CVDs) Fact sheet N°317 [Online]. Available: http://www.who.int/mediacentre/factsheets/fs317/en/index.html [Accessed 31.01.2014].

WHO [World Health Organization] (2013c): Diabetes Fact Sheet N°312 [Online]. Available: http://www.who.int/mediacentre/factsheets/fs312/en/index.html [Accessed 31.01.2014].

WHO [World Health Organization] (2013d): Global Health Expenditure Database [Online]. Available: http://apps.who.int/nha/database/DataExplorerRegime.aspx [Accessed: 31.01.2014]

WHO [World Health Organization] (2013e): Global Health Observatory Data Repository [Online]. Available: http://apps.who.int/gho/data/node.main [Accessed: 31.01.2014]

WHO [World Health Organization] (2013f): Metrics: Disability-Adjusted Life Year (DALY) [Online]. Available: http://www.who.int/healthinfo/global_burden_disease/metrics_daly/en/ [Accessed 31.01.2014].

WHO [World Health Organization] (2013g): Nutrition health topics [Online]. Available: http://www.who.int/nutrition/topics/en/ [Accessed 31.01.2014].

WHO [World Health Organization] (2013h): Obesity and overweight Fact Sheet N°311 [Online]. Available: http://www.who.int/mediacentre/factsheets/fs311/en/index.html [Accessed 31.01.2014].

Wilks, Rainford; Younger, Novie; Tulloch-Reid, Marshall; Francis, Shelly McFarlane & Damian (2008): Jamaica Health and Lifestyle Survey 2007-8. Epidemiology Research Unit Tropical Medicine Research Institute, University of the West Indies (UWI). Kingston: University of the West Indies.

Wilson, Marisa (2012): From Colonial Dependency to Finger-lickin' Values: Food, Commoditization, and Identity in Trinidad. *In:* Garth (ed.) *Food and Identity in the Caribbean.* London: Berg.

Windfuhr, Michael; Jonsén, Jennie (2005): Food Sovereignty. Towards democracy in localized food systems. FIAN-International. Warwickshire, UK: ITDG.

WTO [World Trade Organization] (2005): Work Programme on Small Economies. *Small Economies Report to the Committee on Trade and Development in Dedicated Session.* 17 November 2005, Geneva.

WTO [World Trade Organization] (2013): Understanding the WTO: The Organization. Members and Observers [Online]. Available: http://www.wto.org/english/thewto_e/whatis_e/tif_e/org6_e.htm [Accessed 31.01.2014].

WTTC [World Travel and Tourism Council] (2013): Travel & Tourism. Economic Impact 2013. Antigua and Barbuda, The Bahamas, Barbados, Belize, Dominica, Grenada, Guyana, Jamaica, St. Kitts and Nevis, St. Lucia, St. Vincent and the Grenadines, Suriname, Trinidad and Tobago Travel & Tourism. Economic Impact 2013. World Travel and Tourism Council. London

Xu, Ke; Saksena, Priyanka; Jowett, Matthew; Indikadahena, Chandika; Kutzin, Joe; Evans, David B. (2010): Exploring the thresholds of health expenditure for protection against financial risk. World Health Report (2010) Background Paper, No 19. World Health Organization (WHO). Geneva.

Yach, Derek; Stuckler, David; Brownell, Kelly D. (2006): Epidemiologic and economic consequences of the global epidemics of obesity and diabetes. *Nat Med,* Vol. 12 (1), p. 62-66

APPENDICES

Appendix A: *FAO's suite of Food Security Indicators*

Food Security Indicators	Dimension	
Average dietary energy supply adequacy	Availability	Static and Dynamic Determinants
Average value of food production		
Share of dietary energy supply derived from cereals, roots and tubers		
Average protein supply		
Average supply of protein of animal origin		
Percentage of paved roads over total roads	Physical Access	
Road density		
Rail lines density		
Domestic food price index	Economic Access	
Access to improved water sources	Utilization	
Access to improved sanitation facilities		
Cereal import dependency ratio	Vulnerability	
Percentage of arable land equipped for irrigation		
Value of food imports over total merchandise exports		
Prevalence of undernourishment	Access	Outcomes
Share of food expenditure of the poor		
Depth of the food deficit		
Prevalence of food inadequacy		
Percentage of children under 5 years of age affected by wasting	Utilization	
Percentage of children under 5 years of age who are stunted		
Percentage of children under 5 years of age who are underweight		
Percentage of adults who are underweight		
Prevalence of anaemia among pregnant women		
Prevalence of anaemia among children under 5 years of age		

Source: own compilation based on FAO (2013c): 16

Appendix B: Net per capita production index (2004-2006=100), Caribbean countries, 1990-2011

	1990	1991	1992	1993	1994	1995	1996	1997	1998	1999	2000	2001	2002	2003	2004	2005	2006	2007	2008	2009	2010	2011
AB	128.8	129.6	145.9	151.1	146.4	125.6	127.2	115.1	106.5	111.7	111.9	114.5	111.4	109.2	109.4	94.5	96.1	102.6	103.6	105.1	104.6	106.8
BHS	n.a.	n.a.	95.2	77.6	69.6	64.9	69.7	62.8	68.6	74.9	80.6	87.5	91.6	95.0	91.0	103.5	105.5	103.7	109.4	119.8	115.0	119.9
BB	114.6	112.7	100.5	93.3	95.4	99.9	114.5	108.2	100.0	106.5	103.3	96.2	92.8	96.5	96.8	105.7	97.5	100.8	94.6	98.5	91.5	92.2
BLZ	74.5	69.1	81.5	88.9	78.5	82.2	88.9	90.0	84.6	88.8	95.2	94.3	86.7	88.9	102.4	96.3	101.4	91.0	85.9	81.5	81.4	76.5
DOM	155.0	148.8	143.7	147.3	128.3	117.0	138.1	134.7	128.3	122.4	121.7	113.5	108.7	101.5	103.2	95.1	101.7	107.4	101.0	114.1	115.2	110.7
GRD	150.9	146.2	143.1	146.2	148.1	136.6	132.4	126.8	119.7	126.4	124.2	117.0	137.4	129.5	134.2	77.4	88.4	88.1	85.1	82.5	86.1	88.3
GUY	50.9	62.0	74.1	80.3	87.1	101.2	105.6	109.4	97.4	109.3	100.1	104.3	103.4	110.2	108.0	94.3	97.8	97.9	94.8	97.1	105.0	107.0
JAM	102.8	104.7	110.2	110.6	113.1	114.8	120.5	111.0	108.4	116.6	102.8	106.4	103.8	108.6	104.0	95.5	100.4	99.7	94.8	97.1	94.7	98.6
SKN	151.8	175.3	226.8	182.9	158.2	158.4	170.3	229.6	188.8	160.0	150.3	147.6	146.4	145.6	178.1	90.9	30.9	33.4	35.5	33.4	31.8	33.6
SLC	361.0	301.1	343.4	345.1	276.8	306.3	288.8	245.7	203.6	170.7	137.2	114.0	139.2	117.8	113.2	89.0	97.8	97.8	114.0	107.1	86.0	65.9
SVG	169.4	144.5	168.7	150.3	97.2	125.5	117.7	94.5	103.9	102.2	104.8	96.0	110.5	97.7	97.0	102.0	101.0	104.5	99.7	97.6	107.2	99.3
SUR	149.2	157.5	165.1	146.3	142.5	149.4	129.0	129.8	109.1	111.9	104.2	111.4	88.7	93.7	96.8	98.4	104.8	112.0	105.9	118.8	125.1	101.5
TT	92.6	92.0	91.0	91.9	91.9	91.3	94.4	88.6	78.1	84.6	96.5	95.8	115.6	101.6	97.9	95.7	106.4	106.7	89.7	93.1	97.2	102.5

Note: AB=Antigua and Barbuda; BHS=The Bahamas, BB=Barbados, BLZ=Belize, DOM=Dominica, GRD=Grenada, GUY=Guyana, JAM=Jamaica, SKN= St. Kitts and Nevis, SLC=St. Lucia, SVG=St. Vincent and the Grenadines, SUR=Suriname, TT=Trinidad and Tobago
Source: own compilation. FAOSTAT (2013b)

Appendix C: *Final data of the three selected indicators for the cluster analysis,*
                  mean value, 2000-2011

	Value of food Production (in Int$)	Dietary energy supply (kcal/p.c./day)	Prevalence of undernourish-ment (in % of total population)
Cluster I			
Antigua and Barbuda	107	2223	31.3
Grenada	147	2376	25.6
St. Kitts and Nevis	117	2478	19.5
Suriname	182	2473	15.8
Cluster II			
The Bahamas	84	2738	7.3
Barbados	176	2896	5.1
Jamaica	200	2791	7.2
St. Lucia	147	2696	12.1
St. Vincent and the Grenadines	194	2788	7.5
Trinidad and Tobago	117	2701	12.8
Cluster III			
Belize	574	2689	7.0
Dominica	368	3086	5.0
Guyana	430	2774	8.2

Source: own compilation. Own calculations based on FAO (2013b)

Appendix D: *Cluster membership of Caribbean countries*

Case	Countries	3 Clusters
Case 1	Antigua and Barbuda	1
Case 2	The Bahamas	2
Case 3	Barbados	2
Case 4	Belize	3
Case 5	Dominica	3
Case 6	Grenada	1
Case 7	Guyana	3
Case 8	Jamaica	2
Case 9	St. Kitts and Nevis	1
Case 10	St. Lucia	2
Case 11	St. Vincent and the Grenadines	2
Case 12	Suriname	1
Case 13	Trinidad and Tobago	2

Source: calculated and generated with SPSS based on FAOSTAT (2013b)

Appendix E: *Standard International Trade Classification (SITC) Revision 3,*
                   UNCTAD, 12 June 2013

Code	Label
TOTAL	Total all products
0	**Food and live animals**
00	Live animals and other than animals of division 03
001	Live animals and other than animals of division 03
01	Meat and meat preparations
011	Meat of bovine animals, fresh, chilled or frozen
012	Other meat and edible meat offal, fresh, chilled or frozen (except meat and meat offal unfit or unsuitable for human consumption)
016	Meat and edible meat offal, salted, in brine, dried or smoked; edible flours and meals of meat or meat offal
017	Meat and edible meat offal, prepared or preserved, n.e.s.
02	Dairy products and birds' eggs
022	Milk and cream and milk products other than butter or cheese
023	Butter and other fats and oils derived from milk
024	Cheese and curd
025	Eggs, birds', and egg yolks, fresh, dried or otherwise preserved, sweetened or not; egg albumin
03	Fish (not marine mammals), crustaceans, molluscs and aquatic invertebrates, and preparations thereof
034	Fish, fresh (live or dead), chilled or frozen
035	Fish, dried, salted or in brine; smoked fish (whether or not cooked before or during the smoking process); flours, meals and pellets of fish, fit for human consumption
036	Crustaceans, molluscs and aquatic invertebrates, whether in shell or not, fresh (live or dead), chilled, frozen, dried, salted or in brine; crustaceans, in shell, cooked by steaming or boiling in water, whether or not chilled, frozen, dried, salted or in brine; flours, meals and pellets of crustaceans or of aquatic invertebrates, fit for human consumption
037	Fish, crustaceans, molluscs and other aquatic invertebrates, prepared or preserved, n.e.s.
04	Cereals and cereal preparations
041	Wheat (including spelt) and meslin, unmilled
042	Rice
043	Barley, unmilled
044	Maize (not including sweet corn), unmilled

045	Cereals, unmilled (other than wheat, rice, barley and maize)
046	Meal and flour of wheat and flour of meslin
047	Other cereal meals and flours
048	Cereal preparations and preparations of flour or starch of fruits or vegetables
05	**Vegetables and fruit**
054	Vegetables, fresh, chilled, frozen or simply preserved (including dried leguminous vegetables); roots, tubers and other edible vegetable products, n.e.s., fresh or dried
056	Vegetables, roots and tubers, prepared or preserved, n.e.s.
057	Fruit and nuts (not including oil nuts), fresh or dried
058	Fruit, preserved, and fruit preparations (excluding fruit juices)
059	Fruit juices (including grape must) and vegetable juices, unfermented and not containing added spirit, whether or not containing added sugar or other sweetening matter
06	**Sugars, sugar preparations and honey**
061	Sugars, molasses and honey
062	Sugar confectionery
07	**Coffee, tea, cocoa, spices, and manufactures thereof**
071	Coffee and coffee substitutes
072	Cocoa
073	Chocolate and other food preparations containing cocoa, n.e.s.
074	Tea and maté
075	Spices
08	**Feeding stuff for animals (not including unmilled cereals)**
081	Feeding stuff for animals (not including unmilled cereals)
09	**Miscellaneous edible products and preparations**
091	Margarine and shortening
098	Edible products and preparations, n.e.s.
1	**Beverages and tobacco**
11	**Beverages**
111	Non-alcoholic beverages, n.e.s.
112	Alcoholic beverages
12	**Tobacco and tobacco manufactures**
121	Tobacco, unmanufactured; tobacco refuse
122	Tobacco, manufactured (whether or not containing tobacco substitutes)
2	**Crude materials, inedible, except fuels**
21	**Hides, skins and furskins, raw**
211	Hides and skins (except furskins), raw

212	Furskins, raw (including heads, tails, paws and other pieces or cuttings, suitable for furriers' use), other than hides and skins of group 211
22	**Oil-seeds and oleaginous fruits**
222	Oil-seeds and oleaginous fruits of a kind used for the extraction of "soft" fixed vegetable oils (excluding flours and meals)
223	Oil-seeds and oleaginous fruits, whole or broken, of a kind used for the extraction of other fixed vegetable oils (including flours and meals of oil-seeds or oleaginous fruit, n.e.s.)
23	**Crude rubber (including synthetic and reclaimed)**
231	Natural rubber, balata, gutta-percha, guayule, chicle and similar natural gums, in primary forms (including latex) or in plates, sheets or strip
232	Synthetic rubber; reclaimed rubber; waste, parings and scrap of unhardened rubber

Note: n.e.s = not elsewhere specified
Source: UNCTAD (2013)

Appendix F: *Gross National Savings (GNS), (in % of country's GDP), Caribbean countries, 2002, 2006, 2008, 2010*

	2002	2006	2008	2010
Antigua and Barbuda	14.7	11.2	3.6	9.4
The Bahamas	24.2	18.6	18.2	13.7
Barbados	8.2	n.a.	n.a.	n.a.
Dominica	-1.6	6.5	-7.3	4.2
Grenada	4.4	3.2	0.6	-4.3
Guyana	22.5	n.a.	n.a.	n.a.
Jamaica	15.8	17.4	6.1	13.4
St. Kitts and Nevis	27.2	24.1	7.2	8.9
Saint Lucia	7.3	7.4	1.5	17.4
St. Vincent and the Grenadines	14.2	8.9	-3.7	-5.4
Suriname	n.a.	n.a.	n.a.	n.a.
Trinidad and Tobago	23.5	55.0	35.1	n.a.

Note: n.a. = not available
Source: own compilation. CARICOM (2012): 29

Appendix G: *Prevalence of hypertension and diabetes rates, (in % of total popu-lation), Caribbean countries, 2011/2013*

	Hypertension (2011)	Diabetes (2013)	Disease specific registries (2011)
Antigua and Barbuda	42.4%	13.3%	No
The Bahamas	37.5%	14.2%	Yes
Barbados	29.1%	12.4%	Yes
Belize	28.7%	15.9%	No
Dominica	32.1%	10.9%	Yes
Grenada	n.a.	9.4%	Yes
Guyana	40.5%	15.9%	Yes
Jamaica	35.3%	10.4%	Yes
St. Kitts and Nevis	35.0%	13.0%	No
St. Lucia	41.8%	8.2 %	n.s.
St. Vincent and the Grenadines	n.a.	10.0%	No
Suriname	33.1%	11.1%	Yes
Trinidad and Tobago	23.0%	13.0%	Yes

Note: n.a.= not available; n.s. = not specified
Source: own compilation. Hypertension, disease specific registries: PAHO (2012a);
Diabetes: IDF (2013)

Appendix H: *Prevalence of overweight and obesity (BMI ≥ 25), (in % of popula-*
tion), adults (>30 years) females and males, Caribbean countries,
2002-2015*

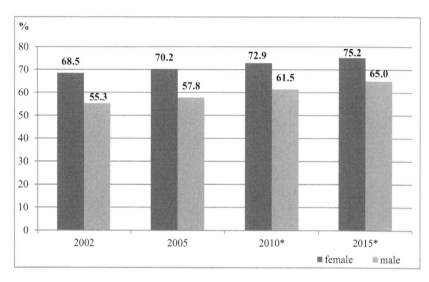

Note: Total prevalence rates for the Caribbean countries are calculated as simple (mean) average; * 2010 and 2015 are WHO estimates
Source: own compilation. Own calculations based on WHO (2011c)

Appendix I: *Selected health indicators, Caribbean countries, 2000 and 2011*

	Life expectancy at birth, total (years)		Fertility rate, total (births per woman)		Mortality rate, infant (per 1,000 live births)	
	2000	**2011**	**2000**	**2011**	**2000**	**2011**
Antigua and Barbuda	73.4	75.5	2.3	2.1	14.3	9.5
The Bahamas	72.3	74.8	2.1	1.9	14.3	14.1
Barbados	73.0	75.0	1.8	1.8	16.0	17.3
Belize	70.5	73.5	3.6	2.8	21.1	16.1
Dominica	n.a.	n.a.	n.a.	n.a.	13.6	11.8
Grenada	70.3	72.5	2.6	2.2	13.4	11.7
Guyana	63.5	65.9	2.6	2.6	37.0	29.7
Jamaica	70.5	73.1	2.6	2.3	19.9	14.9
St. Kitts and Nevis	n.a.	n.a.	n.a.	n.a.	13.6	7.2
St. Lucia	71.4	74.6	2.3	2.0	15.0	15.2
St. Vincent and the Grenadines	70.6	72.3	2.4	2.1	19.1	21.3
Suriname	67.9	70.6	2.7	2.3	28.9	19.1
Trinidad and Tobago	68.6	69.7	1.8	1.8	24.6	19.0

Note: n.a = not available
Source: own compilation. The World Bank (2013d)

Appendix J: *Public health expenditure, private health expenditure, and out-of-pocket expenditure, Caribbean countries, 2011*

	General government expenditure as % of total health expenditure	Private health expenditure on health as % of total health expenditure	Out-of-pocket expenditure as a % of total health expenditure
Antigua and Barbuda	68.2	31.8	28.2
The Bahamas	46.4	53.6	28.9
Barbados	64.0	36.0	29.0
Belize	66.5	33.5	23.4
Dominica	73.6	26.4	21.8
Grenada	48.2	51.8	50.7
Guyana	79.1	20.9	18.0
Jamaica	53.6	46.4	32.9
St. Kitts and Nevis	56.3	43.7	41.4
St. Lucia	46.6	53.4	52.9
St. Vincent and the Grenadines	81.7	18.3	18.3
Suriname	53.2	46.8	11.0
Trinidad and Tobago	51.8	48.2	39.2

Source: own compilation. WHO (2013d)